CASEBOOK
ON AGENCY

E. R. Hardy Ivamy, LL.B., Ph.D., LL.D.

Of the Middle Temple, Barrister
Emeritus Professor of Law in the University of London

Lloyd's of London Press Ltd
Legal Publishing and Conferences Division
26–30 Artillery Lane, London E1 7LX

USA AND CANADA
Lloyd's of London Press Inc
817 Broadway
New York, NY 10003, USA

GERMANY
Lloyd's of London Press
PO Box 11 23 47
Deichstrasse 41, 2000 Hamburg 11
West Germany

SOUTH EAST ASIA
Lloyd's of London Press (Far East) Ltd
903 Chung Nam Building
1 Lockhart Road, Wanchai
Hong Kong

© E. R. Hardy Ivamy 1987

First published 1971
Second Edition 1980
Third Edition 1987

British Library Cataloguing in Publication Data
Ivamy, E. R. Hardy
Casebook on agency.——3rd ed.
1. Agency (Law)——England——Cases
I. Title
344.206'29   KD2020.A7
ISBN 1 85044 112 X

Text set in 9/11 pt Linotron 202 Times by
Columns, Reading
Printed in Great Britain by
WBC Print Ltd, Bristol

PREFACE

The purpose of this new edition remains the same as that of earlier ones, i.e., to set out in a convenient form the leading and important cases relating to the law of Agency. At the head of each case there is a short statement of the principle involved. This is followed by a summary of the facts, the decision given, and extracts from one or more of the judgments delivered.

In Part I ("Relation between Principal and Agent") *R.* v. *Braithwaite* [1983] 2 All E.R. 87 establishes that the word "consideration" in the Prevention of Corruption Act 1916, s. 2 is used in its legal sense and connotes the existence of something in the nature of a contract or bargain between the parties. In *Alpha Trading Ltd.* v. *Dunnshaw-Patten Ltd.* [1981] 1 All E.R. 483 the Court implied a term that once the principal had entered into a contract with a third party he would not break it and thereby deprive the agent of the commission to which, if the contract had been performed, the agent would have been entitled.

In Part II ("Relation between Principal and Third Party") *Waugh* v. *H. B. Clifford & Sons Ltd.* [1982] 1 All E.R. 1095, C.A. shows that a solicitor's ostensible authority *vis-à-vis* an opposing litigant to compromise an action is wider than his implied authority *vis-à-vis* his own client to do so. In *UBAF Ltd.* v. *European American Banking Corp.* [1984] 2 All E.R. 226, C.A. it was decided that a representation signed on behalf of a limited company by a properly authorised officer acting in the course of his duties constitutes the company's signature for the purpose of the Statute of Frauds Amendment Act 1828, s. 6. In *Armagas Ltd.* v. *Mundogas S.A.: The "Ocean Frost"* [1986] 2 Lloyd's Rep. 385, H.L. the extent to which a principal is vicariously liable for the fraudulent misrepresentation of his agent was considered.

In Part III ("Relation between Agent and Third Party") *Resolute Maritime Inc. and another* v. *Nippon Kaiji Kyokai and others: The "Skopas"* [1983] 2 All E.R. 1 lays down the rule that an agent, acting under his express or ostensible authority, who makes a statement that is untrue in circumstances in which he did not have reasonable ground to believe that it was true, cannot be held liable under the Misrepresentation Act 1967, s. 2(1).

I am grateful to the Incorporated Council of Law Reporting for England and Wales, Butterworth & Co. (Publishers) Ltd. and Lloyd's Law Reports for giving me permission to use extracts from the judgments in the cases summarised in this work.

I should like to thank Mr E. Martin and Miss Catherine Anderson, both of the

Legal Publishing & Conferences Division of Lloyd's of London Press Ltd., for seeing the book through the press.

December 1986   E. R. HARDY IVAMY

TABLE OF CONTENTS

	PAGE
Preface	iii
Table of Cases	x
Table of Statutes	xviii

PART I—RELATION BETWEEN PRINCIPAL AND AGENT

(A) DUTIES OF AGENT

(1) *Duty to obey instructions* — 1
The "Hermione" — 1
Wragg *v.* Lovett — 2
Ireland *v.* Livingston — 4

(2) *Duty to show proper skill and care* — 4
Keppel *v.* Wheeler — 4
Sarginson Brothers *v.* Keith Moulton & Co. Ltd. — 5

(3) *Duty to carry out instructions personally* — 7
De Bussche *v.* Alt — 7
John McCann & Co. *v.* Pow — 8
Calico Printers' Association *v.* Barclays Bank — 9
Thomas Cheshire & Co. *v.* Vaughan Bros. & Co. — 10

(4) *Duty not to take advantage of principal or make secret profit* — 11
Armstrong *v.* Jackson — 11
Boston Deep Sea Fishing and Ice Co. *v.* Ansell — 12
R. *v.* Manners — 13
R. *v.* Carr-Briant — 15
R. *v.* Braithwaite — 16

(5) *Duty not to disclose confidential information* — 19
Lamb *v.* Evans — 19

(B) PRINCIPAL'S REMEDIES
Christoforides *v.* Terry — 21

(C) AGENCY OF NECESSITY
Prager *v.* Blatspiel, Stamp & Heacock Ltd. — 21

Jebara *v.* Ottoman Bank   23

(D) RIGHTS OF AGENT

(1) *Commission*   23
  (a) General Rules applicable to all Agents   23
    G. T. Hodges & Sons *v.* Hackbridge Park Residential Hotel Ltd.   23
    Alpha Trading Ltd. *v.* Dunnshaw-Patten Ltd.   25
    Fullwood *v.* Hurley   27
    Andrew *v.* Ramsay & Co.   27
    Hippisley *v.* Knee Brothers   28
    Harrods Ltd. *v.* Lemon   29
    Wilson *v.* Harper Sons & Co.   31
    Crocker Horlock Ltd. *v.* B. Lang & Co. Ltd.   32
    Les Affréteurs Réunis Société Anonyme *v.* Leopold
      Walford (London) Ltd.   34
  (b) Estate Agents' Commission   35
    Luxor (Eastbourne) Ltd. *v.* Cooper   35
    Bentall, Horsley & Baldry *v.* Vicary   36
    Murdoch Lownie Ltd. *v.* Newman   37
    Bennett, Walden & Co. *v.* Wood   38
    Graham & Scott (Southgate) Ltd. *v.* Oxlade   39
    Christie Owen & Davies Ltd. *v.* Rapacioli   40
    Peter Long & Partners *v.* Burns   41
    Drewery & Another *v.* Ware-Lane   43
    Jaques *v.* Lloyd D. George & Partners Ltd.   44
    Blake & Co. *v.* Sohn and Another   46

(2) *Indemnity*   48
  Anglo Overseas Transport Ltd. *v.* Titan Industrial
    Corporation (United Kingdom) Ltd.   48
  Lage *v.* Siemens Brothers & Co. Ltd.   49
  Barron *v.* Fitzgerald   49
(3) *Lien*   50
  Near-East Relief *v.* King, Chasseur & Co.   50

(E) TERMINATION OF AGENCY

(1) *Modes of termination*   52
  Gillow & Co. *v.* Lord Aberdare   52
  Marshall *v.* Glanville   53
  Campanari *v.* Woodburn   54

(2) *Authority coupled with interest*   54
  Re Hannan's Empress Gold Mining and Development
    Co. Ltd.: Ex parte Carmichael   54
  Frith *v.* Frith   56

(3) *Effect of termination on agent's right to commission*   57
    Reigate *v.* Union Manufacturing Co. (Ramsbottom) Ltd.   57
    L. French & Co. Ltd. *v.* Leeston Shipping Co. Ltd.   58
    Rhodes *v.* Forwood   59
    Turner *v.* Goldsmith   60

(4) *Effect of termination on agent's right to indemnity*   61
    Chappell *v.* Bray   61
    Rhodes *v.* Fielder, Jones & Harrison   62

(5) *Period of notice of termination*   63
    Levy *v.* Goldhill & Co.   63
    Martin-Baker Aircraft Co. Ltd. *v.* Murison   64

PART II—RELATION BETWEEN PRINCIPAL AND THIRD PARTY

(1) *Rights and liabilities of undisclosed principals*   67
    Watteau *v.* Fenwick   67
    Archer *v.* Stone   68
    Said *v.* Butt   69
    Dyster *v.* Randall & Sons   69
    Fred. Drughorn Ltd. *v.* Rederiakt. Transatlantic   71

(2) *Ratification*   72
    Kelner *v.* Baxter   72
    Ashbury Railway Carriage & Iron Co. Ltd. *v.* Riche   73
    Keighley, Maxsted & Co. *v.* Durant   74
    Bolton & Partners Ltd. *v.* Lambert   76
    Watson *v.* Davies   77
    Managers of the Metropolitan Asylums Board *v.* Kingham & Sons   78
    Grover and Grover Ltd. *v.* Mathews   79
    Forman & Co. Pty. Ltd. *v.* The Ship "Liddesdale"   80

(3) *Apparent authority of agent*   81
    Farquharson Brothers & Co. *v.* King & Co.   81
    Waugh *v.* H. B. Clifford & Sons Ltd.   82

(4) *Dispositions under the Factors Act 1889*   85
    Lowther *v.* Harris   85
    Staffs Motor Guarantee Ltd. *v.* British Wagon Co. Ltd.   86
    Oppenheimer *v.* Attenborough & Son   88
    Pearson *v.* Rose & Young Ltd.   91
    Newtons of Wembley Ltd. *v.* Williams   92

(5) *Effect of judgment against agent*   96
    Kendall *v.* Hamilton   96

(6) *Third party's right of set-off*   97
    Cooke & Sons *v.* Eshelby   97

Greer *v*. Downs Supply Co.   98

(7) *Effect of principal settling with agent*   99
    Armstrong *v*. Stokes and Others   99
    Irvine & Co. *v*. Watson & Sons   101

(8) *Effect of third party settling with agent*   103
    Butwick *v*. Grant   103
    Bradford & Sons Ltd. *v*. Price Brothers   103
    Sorrell *v*. Finch   104

(9) *Bribery of agent*   105
    Shipway *v*. Broadwood   105
    Mahesan *v*. Malaysia Government Officers' Co-operative
        Housing Society Ltd.   107
    Industries & General Mortgage Co. Ltd. *v*. Lewis   109

(10) *Knowledge of Agent*   110
    Newsholme Brothers *v*. Road Transport and General
        Insurance Co. Ltd.   110
    Vacuum Oil Co. *v*. Union Insurance Society of Canton Ltd.   111
    Wilkinson *v*. General Accident Fire and Life Assurance
        Corporation Ltd.   112

(11) *Principal's liability for agent's misrepresentation*   113
    Armstrong *v*. Strain and Others   113
    Ludgater *v*. Love   114
    Armagas Ltd. *v*. Mundogas S.A.: The "Ocean Frost"   115
    Overbrooke Estates Ltd. *v*. Glencombe Properties Ltd.   116
    UBAF Ltd. *v*. European American Banking Corp.   117

(12) *Effect of termination of agency*   118
    Blades *v*. Free   118
    Drew *v*. Nunn   119
    Willis Faber & Co. Ltd. *v*. Joyce   121

PART III—RELATION BETWEEN AGENT AND THIRD PARTY

(1) *Personal liability of agent in respect of contract*   123
    Universal Steam Navigation Co. Ltd. *v*. James McKelvie   123
    Gadd *v*. Houghton & Co.   124
    Benton *v*. Campbell, Parker & Co. Ltd.   125
    Vlassopulos Ltd. (N. & J.) *v*. Ney Shipping Ltd.: The "Santa Carina"   126
    J. S. Holt & Moseley (London) Ltd. *v*. Sir Charles Cunningham
        & Partners   129
    Hersom *v*. Bernett   130

(2) *Personal liability of agent on bill of exchange*   131
    Elliott *v*. Bax-Ironside and Another   131

(3) *Effect of judgment against principal*   133
    London General Omnibus Co. *v.* Pope   133

(4) *Third party's right of election*   134
    Clarkson, Booker Ltd. *v.* Andjel   134

(5) *Breach of warranty of authority*   135
    Yonge *v.* Toynbee   135
    Halbot *v.* Lens   137
    Lilly, Wilson & Co. *v.* Smales, Eeles & Co.   138
    Starkey *v.* Governor & Co. of the Bank of England   139

(6) *Personal liability of agent under Misrepresentation Act 1967*   140
    Resolute Maritime Inc. and Another *v.* Nippon Kaiji Kyokai and
    Others: The "Skopas"   140

INDEX   143

TABLE OF CASES

Page numbers printed in heavy type indicate where an extract from the case is set out

Alexander *v*. Davis & Co. (1885) 2 T.L.R. 142; 1 Digest (Repl.) 637 64
Alpha Trading Ltd. *v*. Dunnshaw-Patten Ltd. [1981] 1 All E.R. 483, C.A. 25
Andrew *v*. Ramsay & Co. [1903] 2 K.B. 635; 72 L.J.K.B. 865; 89 L.T. 450; 52
  W.R. 126; 19 T.L.R. 620; 47 Sol. Jo. 728; 1 Digest (Repl.) 613 .... 11, **27**, 29
Anglo Overseas Transport Ltd. *v*. Titan Industrial Corporation (United Kingdom)
  Ltd. [1959] 2 Lloyd's Rep. 152 .... **48**
Anglo-Scottish Beet Sugar Corpn. Ltd. *v*. Spalding Urban District Council (1937] 2
  K.B. 607; [1937] 3 All E.R. 335; 106 L.J.K.B. 885; 157 L.T. 450; 53 T.L.R.
  822; 81 Sol. Jo. 734; 35 Digest (Repl.) 164 114
Archer *v*. Stone (1898) 78 L.T. 34; 35 Digest (Repl.) 42 .... **68**, 70
Armagas Ltd. *v*. Mundogas S.A.: The "Ocean Frost" [1986] 2 Lloyd's Rep. 385,
  H.L. 115
Armstrong *v*. Jackson [1917] 2 K.B. 822; [1916-17] All E.R. Rep. 1117; 86
  L.J.K.B. 1375; 117 L.T. 479; 33 T.L.R. 444; 61 Sol. Jo. 631; 44 Digest (Repl.)
  413 11
Armstrong *v*. Stokes (1872) L.R. 7 Q.B. 598; 41 L.J.Q.B. 253; 26 L.T. 872; 21
  W.R. 52; 1 Digest (Repl.) 677 ....**99**, 102
Armstrong *v*. Strain [1952] 1 K.B. 232; [1952] 1 All E.R. 139; [1952] 1 T.L.R. 82,
  C.A.; 35 Digest (Repl.) 28 113
Ashbury Railway Carriage and Iron Co. Ltd. *v*. Riche (1875) L.R. 7 H.L. 653; 44
  L.J. Ex. 185; 33 L.T. 450; 24 W.R. 794, H.L.; 13 Digest (Repl.) 269 73
Aspin *v*. Wilkinson (1879) 23 S.J. 388 84
Astley Industrial Trust Ltd. *v*. Miller (Oakes, Third Party) [1968] 2 All E.R. 36;
  Digest Supp. 86

Bagnall *v*. Carlton (1877) 6 Ch.D. 371, C.A. 107, 108
Barron *v*. Fitzgerald (1840) 6 Bing. N.C. 201; 8 Scott, 460; 9 L.J.C.P. 153; 4 Jur.
  88; 1 Digest (Repl.) 628 49
Barwick *v*. English Joint Stock Bank (1867) L.R. 2 Exch. 259; [1861-73] All E.R.
  Rep. 194, Ex. Ch. 118
Beattie *v*. Lord Ebury (1872) L.R. 7 Ch. App. 777; 41 J. Ch. 804; 27 L.T. 398; 20
  W.R. 994; affirmed (1874) L.R. 7 H.L. 102, H.L.; 1 Digest (Repl.) 762 137
Bennett, Walden & Co. *v*. Wood [1950] 2 All E.R. 134; 66 (pt. 2) T.L.R. 3, C.A.; 1
  Digest (Repl.) 589 38
Bentall, Horsley and Baldry *v*. Vicary [1931] 1 K.B. 253; 100 L.J.K.B. 201; 144
  L.T. 365; 47 T.L.R. 99; 74 Sol. Jo. 862; 1 Digest (Repl.) 606 36
Bentley *v*. Craven (1853) 17 Beav. 204; 47 Digest (Repl.) 108 11
Benton *v*. Campbell, Parker & Co. Ltd. [1925] 2 K.B. 410; [1925] All E.R. Rep.
  187; 94 L.J.K.B. 881; 134 L.T. 60; 89 J.P. 187; 41 T.L.R. 662; 69 Sol. Jo. 842;
  1 Digest (Repl.) 759 .... **125**, 128
Blades *v*. Free (1829) 9 B. & C. 167; 4 Man. & Ry. K.B. 282; 7 L.J.O.S.K.B.
  211; 1 Digset (Repl.) 795 ....81, **118**
Blake & Co. *v*. Sohn and another [1969] 3 All E.R. 123; [1969] 1 W.L.R. 1412; 113
  Sol. Jo. 690; Digest Supp. 46

x

Bolton & Partners Ltd. *v.* Lambert (1889) 41 Ch.D. 295; 58 L.J. Ch. 425; 60 L.T.
687; 37 W.R. 434; 5 T.L.R. 357, C.A.; 1 Digest (Repl.) 460 .... **76**, 77, 78, 79
Boston Deep Sea Fishing and Ice Co. *v.* Ansell (1888) 39 Ch.D. 339; 59 L.T.
345, C.A.; 1 Digest (Repl.) 551 12
Bradford & Sons Ltd. *v.* Price Bros. (1923) 92 L.J.K.B. 871; 129 L.T. 408; 39
T.L.R. 272; 1 Digest (Repl.) 422 103
Brandt (H.O.) & Co. *v.* H. N. Morris & Co. Ltd. [1917] 2 K.B. 784, C.A. 127
Burial Board of the Parish of St. Margaret, Rochester *v.* Thompson (1871) L.R. 6
C.P. 445 9
Butwick *v.* Grant [1924] 2 K.B. 483; [1924] All E.R. Rep. 274; 93 L.J.K.B. 972;
131 L.T. 476; 1 Digest (Repl.) 418 103

Calico Printers' Association *v.* Barclays Bank (1931) 145 L.T. 51; Com. Cas. 197,
C.A.; 1 Digest (Repl.) 448 9
Campanari *v.* Woodburn (1854) 15 C.B. 400; 3 C.L.R. 140; 24 L.J.C.P. 13; 24
L.T.O.S. 95; 1 Jur. N.S. 17; 3 W.R. 59; 1 Digest (Repl.) 463 54
Chappell *v.* Bray (1860) 6 H. & N. 145; 30 L.J. Ex. 24; 3 L.T. 278; 9 W.R. 17;
1 Digest (Repl.) 621 61
Cheshire (Thomas) & Co. *v.* Vaughan Bros. & Co. [1920] 3 K.B. 240; 89 L.J.K.B.
1168; 123 L.T. 487; 84 J.P. 233; 15 Asp. M.L.C. 69; 25 Com. Cas. 242; 3
Ll.L.Rep. 213, C.A.; 29 Digest (Repl.) 101 10
Christie Owen & Davies Ltd. *v.* Rapacioli [1974] Q.B. 81; [1974] 2 All E.R. 311,
C.A. 40
Christoforides *v.* Terry [1924] A.C. 566; [1924] All E.R. Rep. 815; 93 L.J.K.B.
481; 131 L.T. 84; 40 T.L.R. 485, H.L.; 1 Digest (Repl.) 535 21
Clarkson, Booker Ltd. *v.* Andjel [1964] 2 Q.B. 775; [1964] 3 All E.R. 260; [1964] 3
W.L.R. 466; 108 Sol. Jo. 580, C.A.; Digest Cont. Vol. B 11 134
Clerk *v.* Laurie (1857) 2 H. & N. 199; 26 L.J. Ex. 317; 29 L.T.O.S. 203; 3 Jur. N.S.
647; 5 W.R. 629; 1 Digest (Repl.) 792 .... 55, 56, 57
Cole *v.* North Western Bank (1875) L.R. 10 C.P. 354; [1874-80] All E.R. Rep.
486; 44 L.J.C.P. 233; 32 L.T. 733; 1 Digest (Repl.) 385 86
Cooke & Sons *v.* Eshelby (1887) 12 App. Cas. 271; [1886-90] All E.R. Rep. 791; 56
L.J.Q.B. 505; 56 L.T. 673; 35 W.R. 629; 3 T.L.R. 481, H.L.; 1 Digest (Repl.)
665 97
Crocker Horlock Ltd. *v.* B. Lang & Co. Ltd. [1949] 1 All E.R. 526 .... 31, 32
Currie *v.* Misa (1875) L.R. 10 Exch. 153, Ex. Ch.; affd. Misa *v.* Currie (1876) 1
App. Cas. 554; [1874-80] All E.R. Rep. 686, H.L. 18

De Bussche *v.* Alt (1878) 8 Ch.D. 286; 47 L.J. Ch. 381; 38 L.T. 370; 3 Asp. M.L.C.
584, C.A.; 45 Digest (Repl.) 315 7
Debtor, *Re* a [1914] 2 K.B. 758 84
Dennis Reed Ltd. *v.* Goody [1950] 2 K.b. 277; [1950] 1 All E.R. 919, C.A.: 41, 46
Derry *v.* Peek (1889) 14 App. Cas. 337; [1886-90] All E.R. Rep. 1; 58 L.J. Ch. 864;
61 L.T. 265; 54 J.P. 148; 38 W.R. 33; 5 T.L.R. 625; 1 Meg. 292, H.L.; 35
Digest (Repl.) 27 113
Drakeford *v.* Piercy (1866) 7 B. & S. 515; 14 L.T. 403; 1 Digest (Repl.) 418 103
Drew *v.* Nunn (1879) 4 Q.B.D. 661; [1874-80] All E.R. Rep. 1144; 48 L.J.Q.B.
591; 40 L.T. 671; 43 J.P. 541; 27 W.R. 810, C.A.; 1 Digest (Repl.) 798 .. 81, **119**, 122
Drewery and another *v.* Ware-Lane [1960] 3 All E.R. 529; [1960] 1 W.L.R.
1204; 104 Sol. Jo. 933, C.A.; 1 Digest (Repl.) 595 43
Drughorn (F.) Ltd. *v.* Rederiaktiebolaget Transatlantic [1919] A.C. 203;
[1911-18] All E.R. Rep. 1122; 88 L.J.K.B. 233; 120 L.T. 70; 35 T.L.R. 73; 63
Sol. Jo. 99; 14 Asp. M.L.C. 400; 24 Com. Cas. 45, H.L.; 1 Digest (Repl.) 739 . 71
Dutton *v.* Marsh (1871) L.R. 6 Q.B. 361; 40 L.J.Q.B. 175; 24 L.T. 470; 19 W.R.
754; 1 Digest (Repl.) 746 132
Dyster *v.* Randall & Sons [1926] Ch. 932; [1926] All E.R. Rep. 151; 95 L.J. Ch.
504; 135 L.T. 596; 70 Sol. Jo. 797; [1926] B. & C.R. 113; 1 Digest (Repl.) 659 . 69

Elliott v. Bax-Ironside and another [1925] 2 K.B. 301; [1925] All E.R. Rep. 209; 94 L.J.K.B. 807; 133 L.T. 624; 41 T.L.R. 631, C.A.; 6 Digest (Repl.) 106 ...... **131**

Farquharson Bros. & Co. v. King & Co. [1902] A.C. 325; [1900-3] All E.R. Rep. 120; 71 L.J.K.B. 667; 86 L.T. 810; 51 W.R. 94; 18 T.L.R. 665; 46 Sol. Jo. 584, H.L.; 1 Digest (Repl.) 432 .... **81**

Fleet v. Murton (1871) L.R. 7 Q.B. 126 .... **128**

Folkes v. King [1923] 1 K.B. 282; [1922] All E.R. Rep. 658; 92 L.J.K.B. 125; 128 L.T. 405; 39 T.L.R. 77; 67 Sol. Jo. 227; 28 Com. Cas. 110, C.A.; 1 Digest (Repl.) 390 .... **92**

Forman & Co. Pty. Ltd. v. The "Liddesdale" [1900] A.C. 190; 69 L.J.P.C. 44; 82 L.T. 331; 9 Asp. M.L.C. 45, P.C.; 1 Digest (Repl.) 473 .... **80**

Formby Bros. v. Formby (1910) 102 L.T. 116; 54 Sol. Jo. 269, C.A.; 1 Digest (Repl.) 737 .... **71**

French (L.) & Co. Ltd. v. Leeston Shipping Co. Ltd. [1922] A.C. 451; [1922] All E.R. Rep. 314; 91 L.J.K.B. 655; 127 L.T. 169; 38 T.L.R. 459; 15 Asp. M.L.C. 544; 27 Com. Cas. 257, H.L.; 1 Digest (Repl.) 591 .... **58**

Frith v. Frith [1906] A.C. 254; 75 L.J.P.C. 50; 94 L.T. 383; 54 W.R. 618; 22 T.L.R. 388, P.C.; 1 Digest (Repl.) 799 .... **56**

Fuentes v. Montis (1868) L.R. 3 C.P. 268; 37 L.J.C.P. 137; 18 L.T. 21; 16 W.R. 900; affirmed, L.R. 4 C.P. 93; 38 L.J.C.P. 95; 19 L.T. 364; 17 W.R. 208; 1 Digest (Repl.) 391 .... **94**

Fullwood v. Hurley [1928] 1 K.B. 498; [1927] All E.R. Rep. 610; 96 L.J.K.B. 976; 138 L.T. 49; 43 T.L.R. 745, C.A.; 1 Digest (Repl.) 546 .... **27**

Gadd v. Houghton & Co. (1876) 1 Ex. D. 357; 46 L.J.Q.B. 71; 35 L.T. 222; 24 W.R. 975, C.A.; 1 Digest (Repl.) 730 .... **124**

Gaussen v. Morton (1830) 10 B. & C. 731; 5 Man. & Ry. K.B. 613; 8 L.J.O.S. K.B. 313; 1 Digest (Repl.) 799 .... **55**

Gillett v. Peppercorne (1840) 3 Beav. 78; 1 Digest (Repl.) 531 .... **12**

Gillow & Co. v. Lord Aberdare (1892) 9 T.L.R. 12, C.A.; 1 Digest (Repl.) 581 .... **52**

Graham & Scott (Southgate) Ltd. v. Oxlade [1950] 2 K.B. 257; [1950] 1 All E.R. 856; 66 (pt. 1) T.L.R. 808; 93 Sol. Jo. 209, C.A.; 1 Digest (Repl.) 588 .... **39, 41**

Greer v. Downs Supply Co. [1927] 2 K.B. 28; [1926] All E.R. Rep. 675; 96 L.J.K.B. 534; 137 L.T. 174, C.A.; 1 Digest (Repl.) 659 .... **98**

Griffiths v. Smith [1941] A.C. 170; [1941] 1 All E.R. 66, H.L. **14**

Grover and Grover Ltd. v. Mathews [1910] 2 K.B. 401; 79 L.J.K.B. 1025; 102 L.T. 650; 26 T.L.R. 411; 15 Com. Cas. 249; 29 Digest (Repl.) 70 .... **79**

Halbot v. Lens [1901] 1 Ch. 344; 70 L.J. Ch. 125; 83 L.T. 702; 49 W.R. 214; 45 Sol. Jo. 150; 1 Digest (Repl.) 761 .... **137**

Hannan's Empress Gold Mining and Development Co. Ltd., Re, Ex parte Carmichael [1896] 2 Ch. 643; 65 L.J. Ch. 902; 75 L.T. 45, C.A.; 1 Digest (Repl.) 799 .... **54, 57**

Harrods Ltd. v. Lemon [1931] 2 K.B. 157; [1931] All E.R. Rep. 285; 100 L.J.K.B. 219; 144 L.T. 657; 47 T.L.R. 248; 75 Sol. Jo. 119, C.A.; 1 Digest (Repl.) 528 .. **29**

Hastings Ltd. v. Pearson [1893] 1 Q.B. 62; 62 L.J.Q.B. 75; 67 L.T. 533; 57 J.P. 70; 41 W.R. 127; 9 T.L.R. 18; 36 Sol. Jo. 866; 5 R. 26, C.A.; 1 Digest (Repl.) 387 .... **86**

"Hayle", The [1929] P. 275; 99 L.J.P. 145; 141 L.T. 429; T.L.R. 560; 18 Asp. M.L.C. 50; 42 Digest (Repl.) 1132 .... **113**

Hayman v. Flewker (1863) 13 C.B.N.S. 519; 1 New Rep. 479; 32 L.J.C.P. 132; 9 Jur. N.S. 895; 1 Digest (Repl.) 384 .... **86**

Heald v. Kenworthy (1855) 10 Exch. 739; 24 L.J. Ex. 76; 24 L.T.O.S. 260; 1 Jur. N.S. 70; 3 W.R. 176; 3 C.L.R. 612; 1 Digest (Repl.) 677 .... **99, 102**

Hedley Byrne & Co. Ltd. v. Heller & Partners Ltd. [1963] 2 All E.R. 575;
  [1964] A.C. 465, H.L. 141
Henry v. Lowson (1885) 2 T.L.R. 199; 1 Digest (Repl.) 637 64
"Hermione", The [1922] P. 162; [1922] All E.R. Rep. 570; 91 L.J.P. 136; 126 L.T.
  701; 15 Asp. M.L.C. 493; 38 T.L.R. 381; 42 Digest (Repl.) 1030 1
Hersom v. Bernett [1955] 1 Q.B. 98; [1954] 3 All E.R. 370; [1954] 3 W.L.R. 737; 98
  Sol. Jo. 805; 1 Digest (Repl.) 723 130
Hichens Harrison, Woolston & Co. v. Jackson [1943] A.C. 266, H.L. 127
Hippisley v. Knee Bros. [1905] 1 K.B. 1; 74 L.J.K.B. 68; 92 L.T. 20; 21 T.L.R. 5;
  49 Sol. Jo. 15; 1 Digest (Repl.) 548 .... 28, 30
Hodges (G.T.) & Sons v. Hackbridge Park Residential Hotel Ltd. [1940] 1 K.B.
  404; [1939] 4 All E.R. 347; 109 L.J.K.B. 190; 162 L.T. 74; 56 T.L.R. 128; 83
  Sol. Jo. 941, C.A.; 1 Digest (Repl.) 582 23
Holt (J.S.) and Moseley (London) Ltd. v. Sir Charles Cunningham & Partners
  (1950) 83 Ll.L.Rep. 141; Digest Cont. Vol. B 13 129
Humble v. Hunter (1848) 12 Q.B. 310; [1843-60] All E.R. Rep. 468; 17 L.J.Q.B.
  350; 11 L.T.O.S. 265; 12 Jur. 1021; 1 Digest (Repl.) 738 .... 71, 72

Industries and General Mortage Co. Ltd. v. Lewis [1949] 2 All E.R. 573; 93 Sol.
  Jo. 577; 1 Digest (Repl.) 553 109
Ireland v. Livingston (1872) L.R. 5 H.L. 395; 41 L.J.Q.B. 201; 27 L.T. 79; 1 Asp.
  M.L.C. 389, H.L.; 39 Digest (Repl.) 687 4
Irvine & Co. v. Watson and Sons (1880) 5 Q.B.D. 414; [1874-80] All E.R. Rep.
  1007; 49 L.J.Q.B. 531; 42 L.T. 800, C.A.; 1 Digest (Repl.) 678 .... 99, 101

Jacques v. Lloyd D. George & Partners Ltd. [1968] 2 All E.R. 187; [1968] 1
  W.L.R. 625; 112 Sol. Jo. 211; 66 L.G.R. 440; 205 Estates Gazette 1207, C.A.;
  Digest Supp. 44
Jebara v. Ottoman Bank [1927] 2 K.B. 254; 96 L.J.K.B. 581; 137 L.T. 101; 43
  T.L.R. 369; 32 Com. Cas. 228, C.A.; on appeal, sub nom. Ottoman Bank v.
  Jebara, [1928] A.C. 269; [1928] All E.R. Rep. 243; 97 L.J.K.B. 502; 139 L.T.
  194; 44 T.L.R. 525; 72 Sol. Jo. 516; 33 Com. Cas. 260, H.L.; 46 Digest (Repl.)
  472 23
"Johannesburg", The [1907] P. 65 14
Joynson v. Hunt & Son (1905) 93 L.T. 470; 21 T.L.R. 692, C.A.; 1 Digest (Repl.)
  637 63

Keen v. Mear [1920] 2 Ch. 574; 89 L.J. Ch. 513; 124 L.T. 19; 40 Digest (Repl.)
  285 3
Keighley, Maxsted & Co. v. Durant [1901] A.C. 240; [1900-3] All E.R. Rep. 40; 70
  L.J.K.B. 662; 84 L.T. 777; 17 T.L.R. 527; 45 Sol. Jo. 536, H.L.; 1 Digest
  (Repl.) 457 74
Kelner v. Baxter (1866) L.R. 2 C.P. 174; 36 L.J.C.P. 94; 15 L.T. 213; 12 Jur. N.S.
  1016; 15 W.R. 278; 1 Digest (Repl.) 459 72
Kendall v. Hamilton (1879) 4 App. Cas. 504; [1874-80] All E.R. Rep. 932; 48
  L.J.Q.B. 705; 41 L.T. 418; 28 W.R. 97, H.L.; 1 Digest (Repl.) 668 96
Keppel v. Wheeler [1927] 1 K.B. 577; 96 L.J.K.B. 433; 136 L.T. 203, C.A.; 12
  Digest (Repl.) 97 4

Lage v. Siemens Bros. & Co. Ltd. (1932) 42 Ll.L.Rep. 252 49
Lamb v. Attenborough (1862) 1 B. & S. 831; 31 L.J.Q.B. 41; 8 Jur. N.S. 280; 10
  W.R. 211; 1 Digest (Repl.) 386 86
Lamb v. Evans [1893] 1 Ch. 218; 62 L.J. Ch. 404; 68 L.T. 131; 41 W.R. 405; 9
  T.L.R. 87; 2 R. 189, C.A.; 37 Digest (Repl.) 431 19
Leadbitter v. Farrow (1816) 5 M. & S. 345; 1 Digest (Repl.) 743 131

Les Affréteurs Réunis Société Anonyme v. Leopold Walford (London) Ltd. [1919]
A.C. 801; 88 L.J.K.B. 861; 121 L.T. 393; 35 T.L.R. 542; 14 Asp. M.L.C. 451;
24 Com. Cas. 268, H.L.; 41 Digest (Repl.) 211 34
L'Estrange v. F. Graucob Ltd. [1934] 2 K.B. 394; [1934] All E.R. Rep. 16; 103
L.J.K.B. 730; 152 L.T. 164; 12 Digest (Repl.) 70 46
Levy v. Goldhill & Co. [1917] 2 Ch. 297; [1916-17] All E.R. Rep. 226; 86 L.J. Ch.
693; 117 L.T. 442; 33 T.L.R. 479; 61 Sol. Jo. 630; 1 Digest (Repl.) 609 .... 32, 63
Lilly, Wilson & Co. v. Smales, Eeles & Co. [1892] 1 Q.B. 456; 40 W.R. 544; 8
T.L.R. 410; 1 Digest (Repl.) 763 138
Lindus v. Melrose (1858) 3 H. & N. 177; 27 L.J. Ex. 326; 31 L.T.O.S. 36; 4 Jur.
N.S. 488; 6 W.R. 441; 1 Digest (Repl.) 745 132
London County Freehold and Leasehold Properties Ltd. v. Berkeley Property and
Investment Co. Ltd. [1936] 2 All E.R. 1039; 155 L.T. 190; 80 Sol. Jo. 652,
C.A.; 1 Digest (Repl.) 684 114
London General Omnibus Co. v. Pope (1922) 38 T.L.R. 270; 1 Digest (Repl.) 726 . 133
Long (Peter) & Partners v. Burns [1956] 3 All E.R. 207; [1956] W.L.R. 1083, 100
Sol. Jo. 619, C.A.; 1 Digest (Repl.) 596 41
Lownie (Murdoch) Ltd. v. Newman [1949] 2 All E.R. 783; 65 T.L.R. 717; 93 Sol.
Jo. 711; 1 Digest (Repl.) 588 37
Lowther v. Harris [1927] 1 K.B. 393; [1926] All E.R. Rep. 352; 96 L.J.K.B. 170;
136 L.T. 377; 43 T.L.R. 24; 1 Digest (Repl.) 386 85
Ludgater v. Love (1881) 44 L.T. 694; 45 J.P. 600, C.A.; 1 Digest (Repl.) 683 114
Luxor (Eastbourne) Ltd. v. Cooper [1941] A.C. 108; [1941] 1 All E.R. 33; 110
L.J.K.B. 131; 164 L.T. 313; 57 T.L.R. 213; 85 Sol. Jo. 105; 46 Com. Cas. 120,
H.L.; 1 Digest (Repl.) 587 35

McCallum v. Hicks [1950] 2 K.B. 271; [1950] 1 All E.R. 864, C.A. 41
McCann (John) & Co. v. Pow [1975] 1 All E.R. 129; [1974] 1 W.L.R. 1643, C.A. .. 8
Mahesan v. Malaysia Government Officers' Co-operative Housing Society Ltd.
[1978] 2 All E.R. 405; [1978] 2 W.L.R. 444, P.C. 107
Maloney v. Hardy and Moorshead (1970) 216 E.G. 1582 .... 8, 105
Manchester Trust v. Furness [1895] 2 Q.B. 539; 64 L.J.Q.B. 766; 73 L.T. 110; 44
W.R. 178; 11 T.L.R. 530; 8 Asp. M.L.C. 57; 1 Com. Cas. 39; 14 R. 739, C.A.;
42 Digest (Repl.) 664 99
Marshall v. Glanville [1917] 2 K.B. 87; 86 L.J.K.B. 767; 116 L.T. 560; 33 T.L.R.
301; 1 Digest (Repl.) 611 53
Martin-Baker Aircraft Co. Ltd. v. Murison [1955] 2 Q.B. 556; [1955] 2 All E.R.
722; [1955] 3 W.L.R. 212; 99 Sol. Jo. 472; 72 R.P.C. 236; Digest Cont. Vo.. A
1251 64
Martin Gale & Wright v. Buswell (1961) 178 E.G. 709 41
Metropolitan Asylum Board (Managers) v. Kingham & Sons (1890) 6 T.L.R. 217;
1 Digest (Repl.) 460 78
Midgley Estates Ltd. v. Hand [1952] 2 Q.B. 432; [1952] 1 All E.R. 1394; [1952] 1
T.L.R. 1452; 96 Sol. Jo. 375, C.A.; 1 Digest (Repl.) 595 42
Miller, Gibb & Co. v. Smith and Tyrer Ltd. [1917] 2 K.B. 141; 86 L.J.K.B.
1259; 116 L.T. 753; 33 T.L.R. 295; 22 Com. Cas. 320, C.A.; 1 Digest (Repl.)
670 129
Motion v. Michaud (1892) 8 T.L.R. 253; on appeal, 8 T.L.R. 447, C.A.; 1 Digest
(Repl.) 636 .... 64, 65
Mullens v. Miller (1882) 22 Ch.D. 194 8

Nash v. Dix (1898) 78 L.T. 445; 1 Digest (Repl.) 724 .... 70, 71
Near-East Relief v. King, Chasseur & Co. [1930] 2 K.B. 40; 99 L.J.K.B. 522; 35
Com. Cas. 104; 36 L1.L.Rep. 91; 29 Digest (Repl.) 105 50
Newsholme Brothers v. Road Transport and General Insurance Co. Ltd. [1929]
2 K.B. 356; [1929] All E.R. Rep. 442; 98 L.J.K.B. 751; 141 L.T. 570; 45

T.L.R. 573; 73 Sol. Jo. 465; 34 Com. Cas. 330; 24 Ll.L.Rep. 247, C.A.; 29
Digest (Repl.) 71 .... **110**
Newtons of Wembley Ltd. *v.* Williams [1965] 1 Q.B. 560; [1964] 2 All E.R. 532;
[1965] 3 W.L.R. 888; 108 Sol. Jo. 619, C.A.; Digest Cont. Vol. B 635 .... **92**
Nicolene Ltd. *v.* Simmonds [1953] 1 Q.B. 543; [1953] 1 All E.R. 822; [1953] 2
W.L.R. 717; 97 Sol. Jo. 247; [1953] 1 Lloyd's Rep. 189, C.A.; Digest Cont.
Vol. A 274 46

Oppenheimer *v.* Attenborough & Son [1908] 1 K.B. 221; [1904-7] All E.R. Rep.
1016; 77 L.J.K.B. 209; 98 L.T. 94; 24 T.L.R. 115; 52 Sol. Jo. 76; 13 Com. Cas.
125, C.A.; 1 Digest (Repl.) 392 .... **88**
Oppenheimer *v.* Frazer and Wyatt [1907] 1 K.B. 519; 76 L.J.K.B. 276; 23 T.L.R.
183; 12 Com. Cas. 147; on appeal, [1907] 2 K.B. 50; [1904-7] All E.R. Rep.
143; 76 L.J.K.B. 806; 97 L.T. 3; 23 T.L.R. 410; 12 Com. Cas. 280, C.A.; 1
Digest (Repl.) 390 87
Overbrooke Estates Ltd. *v.* Glencombe Properties Ltd. [1974] 3 All E.R. 511;
[1974] 1 W.L.R. 1335 .... **116**

Pacific Motor Auctions Pty. Ltd. *v.* Motor Credits (Hire Finance) Ltd. [1965] A.C.
867; [1965] 2 All E.R. 105; [1965] 2 W.L.R. 881; 109 Sol. Jo. 210, P.C., Digest
Supp. 86
Parker *v.* McKenna [1874] 10 Ch. App. 96; [1874-80] All E.R. Rep. 443; 44 L.J.
Ch. 425; 31 L.T. 739; 23 W.R. 271, C.A.; 47 Digest (Repl.) 261 11
Parker *v.* Winlow (1857) 7 E. & B. 942; 27 L.J.Q.B. 49; 1 Digest (Repl.) 730 124
Pearson *v.* Rose & Young Ltd. [1951] 1 K.B. 275; [1950] 2 All E.R. 1027; 66 (pt. 2)
T.L.R. 886; 94 Sol. Jo. 778, C.A.; 1 Digest (Repl.) 388 91
Prager *v.* Blatspiel, Stamp & Heacock Ltd. [1924] 1 K.B. 566; [1924] All E.R. Rep.
524; 93 L.J.K.B. 410; 130 L.T. 672; 40 T.L.R. 287; 68 Sol. Jo. 460; 1 Digest
(Repl.) 327 .... **21**, 23
Prestwich *v.* Poley (1865) 18 C.B.N.S. 806; 144 E.R. 662 83

R. *v.* Braithwaite [1983] 2 All E.R. 87, C.A. **16**
R. *v.* Carr-Briant [1943] K.B. 607; [1953] 2 All E.R. 156; 112 L.J.K. 581; 169 L.T.
175; 107 J.P. 167; 59 T.L.R. 300; 41 L.G.R. 183; 29 Cr. App. Rep. 76,
C.C.A.; 14 Digest (Repl.) 495 15
R. *v.* Manners [1976] 2 All E.R. 96, C.A. **13**
R. *v.* Newbould [1962] 2 Q.B. 102; [1962] 1 All E.R. 693; [1962] 2 W.L.R. 648; 126
J.P. 156; 106 Sol. Jo. 244; 46 Cr. App. Rep. 247; Digest Cont. Vol. A 413 13
Reed (Dennis) Ltd. *v.* Goody [1950] 2 K.B. 277; [1950] 1 All E.R. 919; 66 (pt. 1)
T.L.R. 918; 94 Sol. Jo. 270, C.A.; 1 Digest (Repl.) 594 .... 41, 46
Reigate *v.* Union Manufacturing Co. (Ramsbottom) Ltd. [1918] 1 K.B. 592; [1918-
19] All E.R. Rep. 143; 87 L.J.K.B. 724; 118 L.T. 479, C.A.; 1 Digest (Repl.)
632 .... **57**
Resolute Maritime Inc. and another *v.* Nippon Kaiji Kyokai and others: The
"Skopas" [1983] 2 All E.R. 1 .... **140**
Rhodes *v.* Fielder, Jones and Harrison [1918-19] All E.R. Rep. 846; 89 L.J.K.B.
15; 122 L.T. 128; 43 Digest (Repl.) 425 .... **62**
Rhodes *v.* Forwood (1876) 1 App. Cas. 256; [1874-80] All E.R. Rep. 476; 47
L.J.Q.B. 396; 34 L.T. 890; 24 W.R. 1078, J.L.; 1 Digest (Repl.) 629 .... **59**
Robertson *v.* Wait (1853) 8 Exch. 299; 22 L.J. Ex. 209; 1 W.R. 132; 12 Digest
(Repl.) 51 .... 34, 35
Rogerson *v.* Scottish Automobile and General Insurance Co. Ltd. (1931) 146 L.T.
26; [1931] All E.R. Rep. 606; 48 T.L.R. 17; 75 Sol. Jo. 724; 37 Com. Cas. 23;
41 Ll.L.Rep. 1, H.L.; 29 Digest (Repl.) 518 112
Rothschild *v.* Brookman (1831) 5 Bli. N.S. 165; 2 Dow. & Cl. 188; 1 Digest (Repl.)
535 12

Said v. Butt [1920] 3 K.B. 497; [1920] All E.R. Rep. 232; 90 L.J.K.B. 239; 124 L.T. 413; 36 T.L.R. 762; 34 Digest (Repl.) 231 .... **69**, 71
Salford Corpn. (The Mayor, Aldermen and Burgesses of the Borough) v. Lever [1891] 1 Q.B. 168; 60 L.J.Q.B. 39; 63 L.T. 658; 55 J.P. 244; 39 W.R. 85; 7 T.L.R. 18, C.A.; 1 Digest (Repl.) 549 .... 107, 108
Salomons v. Pender (1865) 3 H. & C. 639; 6 New. Rep. 43; 34 L.J. Ex. 95; 12 L.T. 267; 29 J.P. 295; 11 Jur. N.S. 432; 13 W.R. 637; 1 Digest (Repl.) 540 .... 28, 29
Sarginson Bros. v. Keith Moulton & Co. Ltd. (1943) 73 Ll.L.Rep. 104 5
Scammell v. Ouston [1941] A.C. 251; [1941] 1 All E.R. 14; 110 L.J.K.B. 197; 164 L.T. 379; 57 T.L.R. 280; 85 Sol. Jo. 224; 46 Com. Cas. 190, H.L.; 39 Digest (Repl.) 448 46
Scarf v. Jardine (1882) 7 App. Cas. 345; [1881-5] All E.R. Rep. 651; 51 L.J.Q.B. 612; 47 L.T. 258; 30 W.R. 893, H.L.; 4 Digest (Repl.) 486 .... 121, 135
Shipway v. Broadwood [1899] 1 Q.B. 369; 68 L.J.Q.B. 360; 80 L.T. 11; 15 T.L.R. 145, C.A.; 1 Digest (Repl.) 552 .... **105**
Smart v. Sandars (1848) 5 C.B. 895; 17 L.J.C.P. 258; 11 L.T.O.S. 178; 12 Jur. 751; 1 Digest (Repl.) 434 57
Sorrell v. Finch [1977] A.C. 728; [1976] 2 All E.R. 371, H.L. **104**
Spooner v. Sandilands (1842) 1 Y. & C. Ch. Cas. 390; 1 Digest (Repl.) 801 57
Staffs Motor Guarantee Ltd. v. British Wagon Co. Ltd. [1934] 2 K.B. 305; [1934] All E.R. Rep. 322; 103 L.J.K.B. 613; 151 L.T. 396; 1 Digest (Repl.) 387 .... **86**
Starkey v. Bank of England (Governor & Co.) [1903] A.C. 114; 72 L.J. Ch. 402; 88 L.T. 244; 51 W.R. 513; 19 T.L.R. 312; 8 Com. Cas. 142, H.L.; 1 Digest (Repl.) 763 .... **139**

Tamplin (F.A.) Steamship Co. v. Anglo Mexican Petroleum Products Co. Ltd. [1916] 2 A.C. 397; [1916-17] All E.R. Rep. 104; 85 L.J.K.B. 1389; 115 L.T. 315; 13 Asp. M.L.C. 467; 32 T.L.R. 677; 21 Com. Cas. 299, H.L.; 41 Digest (Repl.) 232 53
Tattersall v. Drysdale [1935] 2 K.B. 174; [1935] All E.R. Rep. 112; 104 L.J.K.B. 511; 153 L.T. 75; 51 T.L.R. 405; 79 Sol. Jo. 418; 52 Ll.L.Rep. 21; 29 Digest (Repl.) 531 112
Teheran-Europe Co. Ltd. v. S.T. Belton (Tractors) Ltd. [1968] 2 Q.B. 545; [1968] 2 Lloyd's Rep. 37, C.A. 128
Thompson v. Davenport (1829) 9 B. & C. 78; Dan. & Ll. 278; 4 Man. & Ry. K.B. 110; 7 L.J.O.S.K.B. 134; 2 Sm. L.C. 300; 1 Digest (Repl.) 669 ..... 100, 101, 102, 124
Thompson v. Havelock (1808) 1 Camp. 527; 34 Digest (Repl.) 115 106
Toulmin v. Millar (1887) as reported in 58 L.T. 96; 3 T.L.R. 836, H.L.; 1 Digest (Repl.) 556 24
Trollope (George) & Sons v. Martyn Bros. [1934] 2 K.B. 436; 103 L.J.K.B. 634; 152 L.T. 88; 50 T.L.R. 544; 78 Sol. Jo. 568; 40 Com. Cas. 53, C.A. 1 Digest (Repl.) 585 47
Trueman v. Loder (1840) 11 Ad. & El. 589; 3 Per. & Dav. 267; 9 L.J.Q.B. 165; 4 Jur. 934; 1 Digest (Repl.) 714 122
Turner v. Goldsmith [1891] 1 Q.B. 544; [1891-4] All E.R. Rep. 384; 60 L.J.Q.B. 247; 64 L.T. 301; 39 W.R. 547; 7 T.L.R. 233, C.A.; 1 Digest (Repl.) 630 .... **60**

UBAF Ltd. v. European American Banking Corp. [1984] 2 All E.R. 226, C.A. **117**
United Australia Ltd. v. Barclays Bank Ltd. [1941] A.C. 1; [1940] 4 All E.R. 20, H.L. 108
Universal Steam Navigation Co. Ltd. v. James McElvie [1923] A.C. 492; 92 L.J.K.B. 647; 129 L.T. 395; 39 T.L.R. 480; 67 Sol. Jo. 593; 16 Asp. M.L.C. 184; 28 Com. Cas. 353, H.L.; 1 Digest (Repl.) 731 .... **123**, 127

Vacuum Oil Co. v. Union Insurance Society of Canton Ltd. (1926) 32 Com. Cas. 53; 25 Ll.L.Rep. 546; 29 Digest (Repl.) 328 .... **111**

Vlassopulos (N. & J.) Ltd. *v.* Ney Shipping Ltd.: The "Santa Carina" [1977] 1
Lloyd's Rep. 478, C.A. **126**

Watson *v.* Davies [1931] 1 Ch. 455; 100 L.J. Ch. 87; 144 L.T. 545; 1 Digest (Repl.)
456 .... **77**
Watteau *v.* Fenwick [1893] 1 Q.B. 346; [1891-4] All E.R. Rep. 897; 67 L.T. 831; 56
J.P. 839; 41 W.R. 222; 9 T.L.R. 133; 37 Sol. Jo. 117; 5 R. 143; 1 Digest (Repl.)
358 .... **67**
Waugh *v.* H.B. Clifford & Sons Ltd. [1982] 1 All E.R. 1095, C.A. **82**
Weiner *v.* Harris [1910] 1 K.B. 285; 79 L.J.K.B. 342; 101 L.T. 647; 26 T.L.R. 96;
54 Sol. Jo. 81; 15 Com. Cas. 39, C.A.; 1 Digest (Repl.) 387 .... **86**
Wilkinson *v.* General Accident Fire and Life Assurance Corporation Ltd. [1967] 2
Lloyd's Rep. 182 .... **112**
Williams *v.* North China Insurance Co. (1876) 1 C.P.D. 757; 35 L.T. 884; 3 Asp.
M.L.C. 342, C.A.; 29 Digest (Repl.) 111 .... **80**
Willis Faber & Co. Ltd. *v.* Joyce (1911) 104 L.T. 576; 27 T.L.R. 388; 55 Sol. Jo.
443; 11 Asp. M.L.C. 601; 16 Com. Cas. 190; 1 Digest (Repl.) 715 .... 81, **121**
Wilson *v.* Harper Son & Co. [1908] 2 Ch. 370; 77 L.J. Ch. 607; 99 L.T. 391; 1
Digest (Repl.) 610 .... **31**, 32
Wragg *v.* Lovett [1948] 2 All E.R. 968, C.A.; 1 Digest (Repl.) 433 .... **2**

Yonge *v.* Toynbee [1910] 1 K.B. 215; [1908-10] All E.R. Rep. 204; 79 L.J.K.B.
208; 102 L.T. 57; 26 T.L.R. 211, C.A.; 1 Digest (Repl.) 761 .... **135**

TABLE OF STATUTES

Bills of Exchange Act 1882
s. 26 132
(1) 131, 132
(2) 132

Civil Aviation Act 1971
s. 62 (2) 13

Coal Industries Nationalisation
Act 1946 14

Companies Act 1862
s. 35 55

Companies Act 1985
s. 35 (1) 55, 73
(2) 73
36 (4) 72

Factors Act 1889 95
s. 1 (1) 85, 89, 90, 93
2 (1) 86, 87, 88, 89, 90, 91, 93, 96
(2) 94
8 94
9 .... 92, 93, 94, 95, 96

Gas Act 1948
s. 1 (a) 15
3 15
4 15
7 15
9 15
10 15
14 (1) 15
41 (1) 15

Landlord and Tenant Act 1954
s. 25 118

Local Government Act 1972
s. 234 (2) 118

Marine Insurance Act 1906
s. 52 (2) 50
61 111
86 80

Military Service Act 1916 53

Misrepresentation Act 1967
s. 2 (1) 140, 141, 142
3 .... 116, 117

Partnership Act 1890
s. 36 122

Prevention of Corruption
Act 1906 ... 13, 15, 16, 17, 18, 19, 110

Prevention of Corruption
Act 1916 .... 13, 15
s. 1 14
2 .... 13, 14, 16, 17, 18, 19, 110
4 (2) 13, 14
(3) 18

Public Authorities Protection Act
1893 .... 14, 15

Public Bodies Corrupt Practices Act
1889 17
s. 1 (1) 18
7 14

Sale of Goods Act 1893
s. 23 93
25 (1) 86

Sale of Goods Act 1979
s. 23 93
24 86
25 (1) 93

Statute of Frauds Amendment
Act 1828
s. 6 .... 117, 118

Theft Act 1968
s. 15 (1) 91
33 (3) 91

War Risks Insurance Act 1939 5

PART I

RELATION BETWEEN PRINCIPAL AND AGENT

A. DUTIES OF AGENT

(1) Duty to obey instructions

The "Hermione"

(1922) 126 L.T. 701

Where an agent receives express instructions from his principal, he is guilty of a breach of duty if he disobeys them.

H.M.S. *Daffodil* rendered salvage services to the *Hermione* which had struck a mine. Commander Noakes, of the *Daffodil*, instructed Stillwell & Sons, who were the ship's agents, to prosecute a salvage claim on behalf of himself and his crew, and to settle it for not less than £10,000. Stillwell & Sons settled the claim with the *Hermione*'s owners for £100 only.

Held, by the Probate, Divorce and Admiralty Division, that the agents were guilty of a breach of duty.

HILL, J. (at page 705)

Taking all these letters up to the 4th September, 1919, coupled with the fact that the plaintiff sent no reply, can it be said that the plaintiff authorised the defendants, or by his conduct induced the defendants to believe that he had given them authority to settle or to make a settlement of the kind which was made? I think not. He had refused to accept £100, and proposed on his return to England to obtain independent advice, "unless something better can be done with reference to this claim". He has later on withdrawn his own absurd figure of £10,000, and asked whether the defendants recommended him to accept £100. He did not assent to the accepting of £100, and in that letter said he expected to be in England shortly, so that the claim might be proceeded with. The defendants expressed in reply their opinion as to the wisdom of accepting the £100, but without receiving a reply, although the time for reply in the ordinary course had gone by, authorised a settlement. I cannot find in those matters, first of all, that the plaintiff authorised the settlement. It is to my mind quite clear he did not. Did he by his silence induce the defendants to believe that he had authorised it? Again, in face of the specific prohibition in the letters, I cannot find that by not replying to the last letter he led the defendants to suppose that

1

they had authority. On this matter I may also add that it was not the want of a reply to their last letter which induced the defendants to do anything, because they had begun the final settlement before any reply could have been received. I think, though as I say, I came to the decision with some hesitation, I must find that the defendants settled in breach of their duty towards the plaintiff. It was said with truth that the defendants were agents, not only of Commander Noakes, but of his officers and crew, and they were also entitled to have some regard to this fact, that Commander Noakes was apparently a person who sometimes expressed very rash opinions, because in one of his letters he stated he did not mind if the whole of the award recovered was used up in costs, he still wanted to fight. It is also quite true that as agents for the officers and crew, the defendants had their interests to consider, but that gave them no authority to settle Commander Noakes's claim against his prohibition; and their only alternative, if they thought he was a wholly unreasonable man, would seem to me to be to communicate with him and the other people for whom they were acting and say: "Well, we cannot go on: we must cease to act as your agent". Therefore, I can see no way by which I can acquit them of a breach of duty.

Wragg v. Lovett

[1948] 2 All E.R. 968

Where an estate agent is instructed to sell property at a stated price, he is authorised to do no more than agree the price with the intending purchaser. He has no authority to make a contract with him.

The defendant authorised Ward & Co., who were estate agents, to sell his house to the plaintiff for £840. The agents entered into a contract with the plaintiff to sell the property to him. Under the contract the agents stated that the defendant sold as beneficial owner, and that the title should commence with a document forming a good root of title dated at least 20 years ago. The plaintiff claimed specific performance of the contract. The defendant pleaded that he had never authorised the agents to enter into the contract.

Held, by the Court of Appeal, that an agent who was instructed to sell property at a stated price, had no authority to enter into a contract with the intending purchaser. But a decree of specific performance would be ordered, for, on the facts, it had been shown that the defendant had authorised the making of the contract.

LORD GREENE, M.R. (at page 969)

We must not be understood as suggesting that when a vendor merely authorises a house agent to "sell" at a stated price, he must be taken to be authorising the agent to do more than agree with an intending purchaser the essential (and, generally, the most essential) term, i.e., the price. The making of a contract is no part of an estate agent's business, and, although, on the facts of an individual case, the person who employs him may authorise him to make a contract, such an authorisation is not lightly to be inferred from vague or ambiguous language. But there remains the question whether or not Ward & Co. were authorised (or, what in law is the same thing, reasonably understood themselves to be authorised) to make this particular contract. It was held by RUSSELL, J., in *Keen* v. *Mear*[1] that, on the facts of that case, the only authority given to the agent was to make an open contract. In the present case, the learned Judge understood that decision as not excluding the making of a contract containing terms not less favourable to the vendor than those of an open contract. It is not, in our view, necessary to express a concluded opinion upon this question. We may, however, point out (i) that the words of RUSSELL, J.[2]

> "But had he authority to sign the particular contract here in question? I think not. It contains a special condition as to title, which might or might not be less favourable to a vendor than the title required under an open contract."

suggest to our minds that he meant to limit the authorisation in such a case to an authorisation to make an open contract and to exclude a consideration whether a term inappropriate to an open contract was or was not more beneficial to the vendor; (ii) that an open contract is a thing certain, whereas the question whether or not a particular stipulation is more or less beneficial to the vendor may, in the complications of English conveyancing, be a question of great difficulty which could only be resolved by litigation; and (iii) we are not clear that the special provision as to the date of completion was, in fact, more beneficial to the vendor than would have been the corresponding provision under an open contract. To say that a simple authority to make a contract allows a house agent to insert any terms he pleases provided they are ultimately held to be more beneficial to the vendor appears to us to be a proposition which requires careful examination.

In the present case, we do not think it necessary to decide this matter. It appears to us that the proper inference from all the facts of the case is that the defendant was satisfied to allow his agents to make whatever contract they thought best and relied on them to protect his interests provided, and provided only, that they obtained the desired statement from the plaintiff as to his intention to remain in the house. Mrs Martin[3] so interpreted her instructions. The action which she took did not appear to Mr Hatch[4] himself as being in the least unusual or improper, but what appears to us to be most important is that the defendant not only did not question the authority of Ward & Co. to make a contract for him, but his solicitor either was or conceived himself to be authorised to write the letter of 3rd August in which he expressly asserted the making of a contract. It may be perfectly true that the defendant had not seen the contract and was ignorant as to its terms, but this appears to us to be immaterial on the facts of this case. If, as we think, he must be taken to have left it to his agents to make such a contract as they thought proper in his interests, the fact that he did not see the contract would be immaterial. Moreover, the fact

---

[1] [1920] 2 Ch. 574.
[2] *Ibid.*, at p. 579.
[3] A partner in the firm of estate agents.
[4] The defendant's solicitor.

that before Mr Hatch wrote the letter of 2nd August the defendant, though plainly aware that a contract had been made, did not ask to see the contract, appears to us to be consistent only with the view that he was not interested in its contents save as regarded the question of the plaintiff's intentions on the matter of residence. That this would have been a reasonable attitude on the defendant's part appears to us to be confirmed by the fact that Mr Hatch saw nothing unreasonable in it and did not even show the contract to the defendant but assumed that it had been authorised.

Ireland v. Livingston

(1872) 27 L.T. 79

If a principal gives ambiguous instructions to the agent, the agent will not be liable for breach of duty if he interprets them in the sense not intended by the principal.

LORD CHELMSFORD (at page 85)

Now, it appears to me that, if a principal gives an order to an agent in such uncertain terms as to be susceptible of two different meanings, and the agent *bona fide* adopts one of them and acts upon it, it is not competent to the principal to repudiate the act as unauthorised because he meant the order to be read in the other sense, of which it is equally capable. It is a fair answer to such an attempt to disown the agent's authority, to tell the principal that the departure from his intention was occasioned by his own fault, and that he should have given his order in clear and unambiguous terms.

(2) Duty to show proper skill and care

Keppel v. Wheeler

(1927) 136 L.T. 203

An agent is under a duty to show proper skill and care. If a better offer is received by an estate agent than the one he has already communicated to his principal, he must inform him of it unless a binding contract to sell the property has been entered into.

Keppel instructed Wheeler, an estate agent, to find someone to purchase his block of flats. On 29th May a prospective purchaser made an offer to buy at £6,150. This offer was communicated to Keppel, who accepted it "subject to contract". On 3rd June an offer of £6,750 was received from another person, but Wheeler did not pass on this information to Keppel.

Held, by the Court of Appeal, that this failure was a breach of duty to show proper skill and care, and Wheeler was liable in damages.

ATKIN, L.J. (at page 206)

It appears to me to be a complete mistake to suppose that when agents are employed to sell a property, their duty ends when they have introduced a purchaser ready and willing to buy the property. It is true that if the transaction goes through, that is all they need do, but up to the time at which there is in fact a concluded agreement between the purchaser and the vendor, it appears to me that the agents still owe a duty to their principal. For instance, supposing after they have introduced a purchaser ready and willing to purchase, but the matter still being in negotiation, they discovered that the person so introduced was a person who was either insolvent, or a person of bad character, or a person who intended to employ the premises for some purpose contrary to law, or perhaps contrary to the conditions in the vendor's agreement, then it appears to me to be plain that it would be their duty to their principal to disclose those facts to him. On the other hand, supposing that the purchaser, while still in negotiation, applied to the agents for further particulars of the property in order to complete the negotiations, which particulars had been entrusted to the agents by the vendor for the purpose of imparting them to prospective purchasers, then it appears to me that they would be committing a breach of their duty to their principal, the vendor, if they declined to give those particulars, and said: "No, we owe no duty to anybody hereafter in respect to that matter". And if the proposed sale went off because of that refusal, it appears to me that their principal would have a substantial cause of complaint against them, a complaint which would amount to a claim for breach of the contract to use reasonable skill and diligence in the obtaining of a purchaser, i.e., a person who would purchase the property.

Sarginson Brothers v. Keith Moulton & Co. Ltd.

(1943) 73 Ll.L.Rep. 104

An agent will be guilty of negligence if he expresses an unqualified opinion on a point of law knowing that his principal will act on it, unless the agent has taken reasonable care to furnish himself with such information as would entitle him to give that opinion.

Insurance brokers informed their clients that their timber was uninsurable under the War Risks Insurance Act 1939. The timber was destroyed by enemy action. The information, however, was incorrect and the timber was insurable. The clients brought an action against them claiming damages for negligence.

Held, at Birmingham Assizes, that the brokers were liable because they had not taken sufficient care to see that the advice given was correct.

HALLETT, J. (at page 107)

In my view, if people occupying a professional position take it upon themselves to give advice upon a matter directly connected with their own profession, then they are responsible for seeing that they are equipped with a reasonable degree of skill and a reasonable stock of information so as to render it reasonably safe for them to give that particular piece of advice. One has a great deal of sympathy, I suppose, with every professional man nowadays, at the way in which his operations are affected by a mass of emergency legislation, emergency regulations and emergency rules and orders. They pour out in an unceasing flow, and I can well understand that it is most difficult for those concerned to keep up to date with them. I can well understand that there is always a danger of their being caught out by something. I do not for one moment say they are bound to be acquainted with everything. I think it is open to them always to say: "Well, this is a difficult matter; I shall have to look this up; I shall have to make inquiries". They can say, if they like: "This is a matter for a solicitor, not for me"; and if they went to a solicitor, he very likely would say: "You had better consult counsel". No one is under obligation to give advice on those difficult matters. If they are going to give advice, they can always qualify their advice and make it plain that it is a matter which is doubtful or upon which further investigation is desirable; but if they do take it upon themselves to express a definite and final opinion, knowing, as they must have known in this case, that their clients would act upon that, then I do think they are responsible if they give that information without having taken reasonable care to furnish themselves with such information, of whatever kind it be, as will render it reasonably safe, in the view of a reasonably prudent man, to express that opinion.

Now, here, it seems to me, applying that limited test, the defendants had not done what was required of them. It seems to me that the materials upon which Mr Shepherd[5] took it upon himself to tell the plaintiffs that their idea of insuring their goods was hopeless, were palpably not such as a prudent man would have acted upon. After all, it was, I think, plain not merely to a lawyer but to a reasonable sensible business man that the case of pattern manufacturers, to put it shortly, might well be different from the case of a builder. If you went to the ordinary man and asked him: "Is a builder and a pattern-maker the same thing"? I think the answer of an ordinary intelligent man in the street would be: "Of course not". I do not think it requires to be a lawyer to know that a pattern-maker is one thing and a builder another, and because he had an opinion about a builder's stock of materials, it seems to me it would be a rash thing to assume that the same would apply to a pattern-maker's stock of materials.

Secondly, they were brokers and consultants. It was quite a simple thing for them to put up any proposed risk to whatever insurance company they thought proper, and find out whether the risk would or would not be accepted by the insurance company; and to say, "because we put up a risk from the builder, therefore it is useless to put up a risk from a pattern-maker", seems to me to be a reasonably clear *non sequitur*.

It seems to me, to sum it up, that this answer, such a vital answer to the plaintiffs, given in such a positive and final manner, was given by Mr Shepherd in perfect good faith; but it was not merely that he gave a mistaken answer, in

---

[5] The defendant company's manager.

which case it may well be that the defendants would be under no liability, but he gave an answer without equipping himself with the information or without taking the steps which a reasonably prudent person would clearly have deemed necessary before that answer could be given with reasonable safety.

(3) Duty to carry out instructions personally

De Bussche v. Alt

(1878) 38 L.T. 370

An agent is not normally entitled to delegate his duties.

THESIGER, L.J. (at page 375)

As a general rule, no doubt, the maxim *delegatus non potest delegare* applies so as to prevent an agent from establishing the relationship of principal and agent between his own principal and a third person; but this maxim, when analysed, merely imports that an agent cannot, without authority from his principal, devolve upon another obligations to the principal which he has himself undertaken to personally fulfil, and that, inasmuch as confidence in the particular person employed is at the root of the contract of agency, such authority cannot be implied as an ordinary incident of the contract. But the exigencies of business do from time to time render necessary the carrying out of the intentions of a principal by a person other than the agent originally instructed for the purpose, and where that is the case, the reason of the thing requires that the rule should be relaxed, so as, on the one hand, to enable the agent to appoint what has been termed a "sub-agent" or "substitute" (the latter of which descriptions, although it does not exactly denote the legal relationship of the parties, we adopt for lack of a better, and for the sake of brevity), and on the other hand, to constitute in the interests and for the protection of the principal a direct privity of contract between him and such substitute; and we are of opinion that an authority to the effect referred to may and should be implied where, from the conduct of the parties to the original contract of agency, the usage of trade, or the nature of the particular business which is the subject of the agency, it may reasonably be presumed that the parties to the contract of agency originally intended that such authority should exist; or where in the course of employment unforeseen emergencies arise which impose upon the agent the necessity of employing a substitute; and that when such authority exists, and is duly exercised, privity of contract arises between the principal and the substitute, and the latter becomes as responsible to the former for the due discharge of the duties which his employment casts upon him as if he had been appointed agent by the principal himself.

John McCann & Co. *v.* Pow

[1975] 1 All E.R. 129

An estate agent, especially where he is appointed as a sole agent, has no authority to delegate his duties to a sub-agent unless he is expressly authorised to do so.

> The defendant appointed the plaintiffs, who were estate agents, to find someone to purchase his flat for about £14,350 and agreed to pay them a reasonable commission for doing so. The plaintiffs advertised the flat adding the fact that they were sole agents. They did, however, send particulars of the flat to Douglas & Co., another firm of estate agents, but did not give them the defendant's name. Douglas & Co. introduced a Mr Rudd, who eventually agreed to buy the flat for £14,200. The plaintiffs claimed commission from the defendant.
>
> *Held*, by the Court of Appeal, that the plaintiffs' claim failed for they had no right to employ Douglas & Co. as sub-agents.

LORD DENNING, M.R. (at page 131)

The general rule is that an agent has no authority to appoint a sub-agent except with the express or implied authority of the principal. There was no express authority here. The question is whether or not there was implied authority at the time, 29th August, when the property was introduced by Douglas to Mr Rudd. It seems to me that an estate agent, and certainly one who claims to be a sole agent, has no implied authority to appoint a sub-agent. The reason is because an estate agent holds a position of discretion and trust. Discretion in his conduct of negotiations. Trust in his handling of affairs. It is his duty, certainly in the case of a sole agent, to use his best endeavours to sell the property at an acceptable price to a purchaser who is satisfactory and who is ready and willing and able to purchase the property. It is his duty also to take care to prepare particulars of the property accurately, and to make no misrepresentation about it. It is his duty to receive applications, to make appointments to view, and to negotiate the best price that can be obtained in the circumstances. Furthermore, he is at liberty in the course of the negotiations to receive a deposit as stakeholder, but not as agent for the vendor. Those functions and duties of an estate agent, certainly of a sole agent, require personal skill and competence. So much so that I think an estate agent has no authority to delegate his responsibilities to a sub-agent, unless he is expressly authorised so to do. That is borne out by the authorities to which we have been referred this morning by counsel for Mr Pow, such as *Mullens* v. *Miller*[6] and *Maloney* v. *Hardy and Moorshead*[7].

Faced with the general principle, counsel for John McCann & Co. sought to avoid it by saying that Douglas & Co. had a very limited kind of sub-agency. They were only entrusted, he said, with a mere ministerial duty. Their part was only to pass particulars to potential purchasers, leaving all the negotiations and so forth to the principal agents, John McCann & Co. He referred to the

---

[6] (1882) 22 Ch.D. 194.
[7] (1970) 216 E.G. 1582.

entertaining case of *Burial Board of the Parish of St Margaret, Rochester* v. *Thompson*[8], where it was held that a sexton was able to appoint a delegate to dig the grave and ring the bell because those acts could be done by any reasonably competent person. But the Court said that when it was an employment to which personal skill was essential—as a painter engaged to paint a portrait—he could not hand it over to some one else to perform.

It seems to me that the functions entrusted to Douglas & Co. were not merely ministerial. They prepared particulars. They said that they took every care to ensure that particulars were correct. If they had been sub-agents, Mr Pow would be liable for any misrepresentations that they made. That would be most unfair seeing that he did not choose them and knew nothing of them. The reason why he would not be liable is because they were not authorised sub-agents at all. So it comes to this. The introduction of Mr Rudd was not made by the agents, John McCann & Co., nor was it made by any authorised sub-agent. It was made by Douglas & Co., who had no authority, express or implied, to act as sub-agents so as to bind Mr Pow or to make him liable to pay commission.

Calico Printers' Association *v.* Barclays Bank

(1931) 145 L.T. 51

Even where an agent has authority to appoint a sub-agent, the general rule is that he remains liable for the sub-agent's negligence.

The sellers sold some cotton to a consignee in Beirut, and despatched the shipping documents including a bill of exchange to Barclays Bank in Manchester. They instructed the Bank that if the documents were not accepted by the consignee, the Bank was to insure the goods. With the knowledge of the sellers, Barclays Bank employed the Anglo-Palestine Bank in Beirut as its agents, and in its turn instructed the Anglo-Palestine Bank to insure the goods if the documents were not accepted. The Anglo-Palestine Bank never presented the bill of exchange for payment, and failed to insure the cotton which was destroyed in a fire. The sellers then sued the Anglo-Palestine Bank for damages for negligence.

Held, by the King's Bench Division[9], that the action failed. Even though Barclays Bank were authorised to appoint a sub-agent, that did not mean that it was authorised to create privity of contract between the sellers and the Anglo-Palestine Bank. Barclays Bank was liable for the negligence of its sub-agent.

WRIGHT, J. (at page 55)

To support the argument that there was privity between the plaintiffs and the Anglo-Palestine Bank, reliance was especially placed on a passage from *Story on Agency*, s. 201, as establishing a general principle that where the employment of a sub-agent was authorised either by express terms or by a known course of

---

[8] (1871) L.R. 6 C.P. 445.
[9] The decision of WRIGHT, J., was subsequently affirmed by the Court of Appeal ((1931) 145 L.T. 51, at p. 58) on another point without affecting the decision on the point set out in the text—for no appeal was lodged against this part of the decision of the learned Judge.

business, or some unforeseen exigency necessitating such employment, there was privity established between the principal and the sub-agent, so that the sub-agent and not the agent became directly responsible to the principal for any negligence or misconduct in the performance of the mandate. But I do not think the English law has admitted any such general principle, but has in general applied the rule that even where the sub-agent is properly employed, there is still no privity between him and the principal; the latter is entitled to hold the agent liable for breach of the mandate, which he has accepted, and cannot, in general, claim against the sub-agent for negligence or breach of duty. I know of no English case in which a principal has recovered against a sub-agent for negligence. The agent does not as a rule escape liability to the principal merely because employment of the sub-agent is contemplated. To creative privity it must be established not only that the principal contemplated that a sub-agent would perform part of the contract, but also that the principal authorised the agent to create privity of contract between the principal and the sub-agent, which is a very different matter requiring precise proof. In general, where a principal employs an agent to carry out a particular employment, the agent undertakes responsibility for the whole transaction, and is responsible for any negligence in carrying it out, even if the negligence be that of the sub-agent properly or necessarily engaged to perform some part, because there is no privity between the principal and the sub-agent.

Thomas Cheshire & Co. *v.* Vaughan Bros. & Co.

(1920) 123 L.T. 487

It is not yet settled whether an agent is responsible for the negligence of a sub-agent (appointed with the principal's authority) if he himself has used reasonable care in the selection of that sub-agent.

ATKIN, L.J. (at page 495)

I also wish to say for myself that in this particular case it has been assumed by everybody that if, in fact, the sub-agent, the insurance broker in London, was negligent, the defendants here, the country insurance brokers, were responsible for that negligence. I express no opinion upon that matter at all. I daresay it is perfectly true. I can imagine circumstances in which an agent in the country employed under such circumstances, as he necessarily must be, if he is contemplating the employment of an agent in London, may not be responsible for the negligence of that sub-agent if, in fact, he himself has used reasonable care in the selection of the agent. But that is a matter which does not arise now, and I only mention it.

(4) Duty not to take advantage of principal or make secret profit

Armstrong *v.* Jackson

[1916–17] All E.R. Rep. 1117

An agent must not allow his duty to conflict with his interest. He must therefore not make a secret profit.[10]

A client instructed a stockbroker to buy 600 shares in a company known as Champion Gold Reefs of West Africa Ltd. The stockbroker did not buy the shares in the open market, but sold him 600 shares which he himself owned.

Held, by the King's Bench Division, that the sale of the shares should be set aside because the broker, in selling his own shares to the client, had allowed his interest to conflict with his duty.

MCCARDIE, J. (at page 1119)

First, as to the claim to avoid the transaction. It is obvious that the defendant gravely failed in his duty to the plaintiff. He was instructed to buy shares, but he never carried out his mandate. A broker, who is employed to buy shares, cannot sell his own shares unless he makes a full and accurate disclosure of the fact to his principal, and the principal, with a full knowledge of such facts, gives his assent to the changed position of the broker. The rule is one not merely of law, but of obvious morality. As was said by Lord CAIRNS, L.C., in *Parker* v. *McKenna*:[11]

"No man can in this Court, acting as an agent, be allowed to put himself into a position in which his interest and his duty will be in conflict."

A broker who secretly sells his own shares is in a wholly false position. As vendor it is to his interest to sell shares, and, moreover, to sell at the highest price. As broker it is his clear duty to the principal to buy at the lowest price, and to give unbiased and independent advice (if such be asked) as to the time when, and the price at which, shares shall be bought, or whether they shall be bought at all. The law has ever required a high measure of good faith from an agent. He departs from good faith when he secretly sells his own property to his principal. The rule has long been the same both at law and in equity; see *Story on Agency*, s. 210. It matters not that the broker sells at the market price, or that he acts without intent to defraud; see *Bentley* v. *Craven*.[12] The prohibition of the law is absolute. It will not allow an agent to place himself in a situation which, in ordinary circumstances, would tempt a man to do that which is not the best for his principal; see *per* Sir JOHN ROMILLY, M.R., in *Bentley* v. *Craven*.[13]

---

[10] See further, *Andrew* v. *Ramsay & Co.* (1903) 89 L.T. 450, which is set out on p. 27, *post*. As to the effect of an agent receiving a secret commission on the relation between the principal and the third party, see pp. 105–110, *post*.

[11] (1874) 10 Ch.App. 96, at p. 116.

[12] (1853) 17 Beav. 204.

[13] *Supra*.

The Court will not enter into discussion as to the propriety of the price charged by the broker, nor is it material to inquire whether the principal has or has not suffered a loss. If the breach of duty by the broker be shown, the Court will set aside the transaction: see *Gillett* v. *Peppercorne*.[14] The rule was strikingly illustrated in *Rothschild* v. *Brookman*.[15] The facts of that case were not dissimilar to the facts of the present action. The House of Lords (affirming the Court below) set aside transactions in which the agent had secretly acted as principal. In giving his opinion Lord WYNFORD (formerly BEST, C.J.) used these words:[16]

> "If any man who is to be trusted places himself in a condition in which he has an opportunity of taking advantage of his employer, by placing himself in such a situation, whether acting fairly or not, he must suffer the consequences of his situation. Such is the jealousy which the law of England entertains against any such transaction."

Boston Deep Sea Fishing and Ice Co. *v.* Ansell

(1888) 59 L.T. 345

Where an agent has received a bribe, he can be dismissed instantly.

> A managing director of a company was paid a sum of money by a third party as an inducement to place an order for ice for use in the company's ships.
> *Held*, by the Court of Appeal, that since he had accepted the bribe, the company was justified in dismissing him without notice.

BOWEN, L.J. (at page 355)

Now, there can be no question that an agent employed by a principal or master to do business with another, and unknown to that principal or master takes from that other a profit arising out of the business which he is employed to transact, is doing a wrongful act inconsistent with his duty towards his master and the continuation of confidence between them. He does the wrongful act, whether such profit be given to him in return for services which he actually performed towards the third party, or whether it be given to him in return for services which he is supposed to perform, or whether it is given to him for his supposed influence, or whether it is given to him on any other ground at all. If it is a profit which arises out of the transaction, it belongs to his master, and he has no right to take it, or keep it, or bargain for it, or to receive it without bargain, unless his master knows it. It is said, if the transaction was one of very old date, that in some way deprives the master of his right to treat it as a breach of faith. As [COTTON, L.J.] has pointed out, the age of the fraud may be a reason in the master's mind for not acting on his rights, but it is impossible to say that, because a fraud has been concealed for six years therefore the master's right

---

[14] (1840) 3 Beav. 78.
[15] (1831) 5 Bli. N.S. 165.
[16] *Ibid.*, at p. 197.

when he discovers it is not to act upon his discovery, and to put an end to the relation of employer and employed with which such fraud was inconsistent. I therefore find it impossible . . . to come to any other conclusion except that the managing director, having been guilty of a fraud on his employers, was rightly dismissed by them, and dismissed by them rightly even though they did not discover the fraud until after the time they had actually pronounced the sentence of dismissal.

R. *v.* Manners

[1976] 2 All E.R. 96

Where an agent employed by a "public body" is charged with receiving a bribe contrary to the Prevention of Corruption Acts 1906 to 1916, the burden of proving that the payment was not received corruptly lies on the accused. An Area Gas Board is such a "public body" for the purpose of the Acts.

The accused, who was employed by the North Thames Gas Board as a pipeline projects engineer, was charged with receiving a bribe from a public works contractor contrary to the Prevention of Corruption Acts 1906 to 1916. The trial Judge directed the jury on the basis that since the Board was a "public body" within the meaning of the Acts, the burden of proving that the payment was not received corruptly lay on the accused. The accused was convicted and appealed against conviction on the ground that the Judge's ruling as to the burden of proof was wrong.

Held, by the Court of Appeal, that the ruling was correct and that the appeal would be dismissed.

LAWTON, L.J. (at page 99)

Earlier in the trial Judge RIGG had ruled that the North Thames Gas Board was a public body within the meaning of those words in the Prevention of Corruption Acts 1889 to 1916 and as defined in s. 4(2) of the 1916 Act. When he came to sum up, the Judge directed the jury as to the burden of proof in accordance with s. 2 of the 1916 Act. No complaint is made about how he did it. What is challenged is that he did it at all. . . .

The question for us has been what the words "public body" meant in 1916, not what the words "public authority" meant in Acts passed many years later. The use of the same or similar words in later Acts may be of some help; but we have reminded ourselves that many considerations affect the wording of Acts.

This is illustrated by the reference to the Prevention of Corruption Acts 1889 to 1916 in s. 62(2) of the Civil Aviation Act 1971. It seems to us likely that this reference was made because the parliamentary draftsman knew of the judgment of WINN, J., in *R. v. Newbould*,[17] which was strongly relied on by counsel for Manners before this Court. WINN, J., ruled that the National Coal Board was not a public body for the purposes of the Prevention of Corruption Acts 1889 to 1916. He based his ruling on the absence of any reference to "public authority"

---

[17] [1962] 2 Q.B. 102.

in the Coal Industry Nationalisation Act 1946 and the application of the *ejusdem generis* rule. He said:[18]

> "In my judgment, it would be a bold, and for the purpose of a criminal trial an unjustifiable, interpretation of the wording in s. 4(2) of the Act of 1916 to extend it beyond the limits indicated by the application to the wording of the guide to construction known as the *ejusdem generis* rule. It seems to me that a rational and sufficient connotation can be given to the words if they are taken to comprise no more than local authorities and public authorities of the general kind, character, genus referred to in the earlier phrase contained in s. 7 of the [Public Bodies Corrupt Practices Act] 1889."

In our judgment, WINN, J., was wrong. Drafting practices in Acts change from time to time and are not a reliable guide to the construction of Acts passed before the new fashions were established. Much more important, however, is our conclusion that the *ejusdem generis* rule does not apply anyway.

Section 7 of the 1889 Act defined "public body" as meaning—

> "any council of a county or council of a city or town, any council of a municipal borough, also any board, commissioners, select vestry, or other body which has power to act under and for the purposes of any Act relating to local government, or the public health, or to poor law or otherwise to administer money raised by rates in pursuance of any public general Act, but does not include any public body as above defined existing elsewhere than in the United Kingdom . . .".

The 1906 Act extended the ambit of the 1889 Act to agents; persons serving under the Crown were deemed to be agents within the meaning of this Act. The 1916 Act was an amending one. It was passed rapidly through Parliament following some criticisms made by LOW, J., of the penalties prescribed by the 1889 and 1906 Acts: see "The Times", 18th September, 1916. Within a few weeks a draft Bill was presented to Parliament; it had two clauses later to become ss. 1 and 2 of the 1916 Act. Section 4(2) got into the Act as a result of an amendment moved by Lord BUCKMASTER in the House of Lords. The reason he gave for moving the amendment is irrelevant to its construction; but nothing in what he said has caused us to hesitate over what meaning we give to the words "local and public authorities of all descriptions" in the subsection.

By 1916 the words "public authority" had often been construed by the Courts for the purpose of applying the Public Authorities Protection Act 1893. In *The Johannesburg*[19] the issue was whether the Tyne Improvement Commission was a public authority for the purposes of that Act. Sir GORRELL BARNES, P., examined the Acts under which the Commission performed its duties. It performed public duties; its powers were directed to public ends; it did not concern itself with making gain or profit save insofar as was necessary to enable it to perform its public duties in accordance with the Acts constituting it. This case was considered by the House of Lords in *Griffiths* v. *Smith*[20] and approved: see the speech of Lord PORTER.[21] These two cases, taken together, support the definition of a public authority given in *Halsbury's Laws of England*:[22]

---

[18] *Ibid.*, at p. 106.
[19] [1907] P. 65.
[20] [1941] A.C. 170.
[21] *Ibid.*, at pp. 205–206.
[22] 30 *Halsbury's Laws* (3rd edn.) p. 682, para. 1317.

"A public authority is a body, not necessarily a county council, municipal corporation or other local authority, which has public or statutory duties to perform, and which performs those duties and carries out its transactions for the benefit of the public and not for private profit."

When this definition is applied to the North Thames Gas Board, it is clear that it is a public body. It was constituted pursuant to s. 1(1)(a) of the Gas Act 1948 to "develop and maintain an efficient, co-ordinated and economical system of gas supply for their area and to satisfy, so far as it is economical to do so, all reasonable demands for gas within their area". There were provisions relating to research (s. 3), training and education (s. 4). The Minister had powers of direction (s. 7). There were to be consultative councils for each area board so that the public interest could be taken into account (s. 9). Annual reports were to be made to the Minister (s. 10). Section 14(1) is a most significant one because Parliament considered it necessary to exclude the operation of the Public Authorities Protection Act 1893. This would not have been necessary if Parliament had not intended to make area boards public authorities in all other respects. Finally, by s. 41(1) each area board had a duty so "to exercise and perform their functions under this Act as to secure that the revenues of the Board are not less than sufficient to meet their outgoings properly chargeable to revenue account, taking one year with another". This is not trading for gain or profit.

In our judgment Judge RIGG's ruling was correct.

R. v. Carr-Briant

[1943] 2 All E.R. 156

Where a person makes a gift to an agent employed by a Government department or public body contrary to the Prevention of Corruption Acts 1906–1916, the burden of showing that it was not made corruptly lies on that person, and can be discharged by evidence satisfying the jury of the probability of that which he is required to establish.

The accused, who was a company director, was charged with corruptly giving £60 to a person employed by the War Department as an inducement for showing favour to the company contrary to the Prevention of Corruption Acts 1906–1916. The Judge directed the jury that the accused had to satisfy them beyond reasonable doubt that he had not given the money corruptly. The accused was convicted, and appealed against conviction on the ground (*inter alia*) that there had been a misdirection of the jury as to the burden of proof.

Held, by the Court of Criminal Appeal, that there had been a misdirection. The burden of proof could be discharged by the accused producing evidence satisfying the jury of the probability that the gift had not been made corruptly.

HUMPHREYS, J. (at page 157)

The appellant contended that the Judge misdirected the jury as to the extent of the burden of proof placed upon an accused person by the terms of the

Prevention of Corruption Act 1916, s. 2. That section provides, *inter alia*, that, where, in any proceedings against a person for an offence under the Prevention of Corruption Act 1906, it is proved that any consideration has been given to a person in the employment of a Government department by the agent of a person holding a contract from a Government department, the consideration shall be deemed to have been given corruptly as such inducement or reward as is mentioned in the Act, unless the contrary is proved. The Judge directed the jury on this point as follows:

"What has the accused to do? He has not only to discharge the burden of proof to the contrary of corruption, he has not only to prove that he gave it without a corrupt motive, but he has to do so beyond all reasonable doubt. Indeed, it has been held that, if the jury are left in doubt by the evidence given on behalf of the accused, they must convict him. That is the law by which I am bound and by which you and every subject of this country are bound . . . Are you satisfied beyond all reasonable doubt? If you are not satisfied, find him guilty. If you have any doubt about it, find him guilty. Only if you are completely satisfied that in all these circumstances, having regard to the nature of Baldock, the man, the time when the loan was made—only if you are completely satisfied that it was given innocently, simply as an act of extraordinary friendship, will you find him not guilty. Otherwise you will find him guilty".

That is to say, the Judge laid down the proposition of law that the onus of proving his innocence lay on the accused, and that the burden of proof resting on him to negative corruption was as heavy as that resting in a normal case upon the prosecution.

In our judgment, in any case where, either by statute or at Common Law, some matter is presumed against an accused person "unless the contrary is proved", the jury should be directed that it is for them to decide whether the contrary is proved; that the burden of proof required is less than that required at the hands of the prosecution in proving the case beyond a reasonable doubt: and that the burden may be discharged by evidence satisfying the jury of the probability of that which the accused is called upon to establish.

R. *v.* Braithwaite

[1983] 2 All E.R. 87

The word "consideration" in the Prevention of Corruption Act 1916, s. 2 (which states that where "any money, gift or other consideration" has been paid or given to an employee of a public body, it is deemed to have been paid or given corruptly unless the contrary is proved) is used in its legal sense and connotes the existence of something in the nature of a contract or bargain between the parties.

Braithwaite, an employee of the British Steel Corp., which was a "public body" within the meaning of the Prevention of Corruption Act 1916, s. 2, was charged with receiving nine motor car tyres as an inducement or reward for showing favour to a third party contrary to the Prevention of Corruption Act 1906, s. 1. The trial Judge directed the jury that since there had been a receipt of the tyres, that amounted in law to "consideration" and, therefore, under the Prevention of Corruption Act 1916, s. 2 the burden of proof shifted to the accused to show that he had not received them corruptly.

The accused appealed on the ground that the jury had been misdirected for the word "consideration" meant a gratification which did not include money or a gift.

Held, by the Court of Appeal, Criminal Division, that the appeal would be dismissed for there had been no misdirection for the word "consideration" was used in its legal sense and connoted the existence of something in the nature of a contract or bargain between the parties.

LORD LANE, L.C.J. (at page 91)

Section 1 of the Prevention of Corruption Act 1906 reads as follows:

"(1) If any agent corruptly accepts or obtains, or agrees to accept or attempts to obtain, from any person, for himself or for any other person, any gift or consideration as an inducement or reward for doing or forbearing to do, or for having after the passing of this Act done or forborne to do, any act in relation to his principal's affairs or business, or for showing or forbearing to show favour or disfavour to any person in relation to his principal's affairs or business; or if any person corruptly gives or agrees to give or offers any gift or consideration to any agent as an inducement or reward for doing or forbearing to do, or for having after the passing of this Act done or forborne to do, any act in relation to his principal's affairs or business, or for showing or forbearing to show favour or disfavour to any person in relation to his principal's affairs or business; or if any person knowingly gives to any agent, or if any agent knowingly uses with intent to deceive his principal, any receipt, account, or other document in respect of which the principal is interested, and which contains any statement which is false or erroneous or defective in any material particular . . . he shall be guilty of [an offence], and shall be liable on conviction . . .

(2) For the purposes of this Act the expression 'consideration' includes valuable consideration of any kind . . ."

I then turn to s. 2 of the 1916 Act, which deals with the presumption of corruption in certain cases. It reads as follows:

"Where in any proceedings against a person for an offence under the Prevention of Corruption Act, 1906 [which is this case], or the Public Bodies Corrupt Practices Act, 1889, it is proved that any money, gift, or other consideration has been paid or given to or received by a person in the employment of Her Majesty or any Government Department or a public body by or from a person, or agent of a person, holding or seeking to obtain a contract from His Majesty or any Government Department or public body, the money, gift, or consideration shall be deemed to have been paid or given and received corruptly as such inducement or reward as is mentioned in such Act unless the contrary is proved."

The effect of that is that when the matters in that section have been fulfilled, the burden of proof is lifted from the shoulders of the prosecution and descends on the shoulders of the defence. It then becomes necessary for the defendant to show, on a balance of probabilities, that what was going on was not reception corruptly as inducement or reward. In an appropriate case it is the judge's duty to direct the jury first of all that they must decide whether they are satisfied so as to feel sure that the defendant received money or gift or consideration, and then to go on to direct them that if they are so satisfied, then under s. 2 of the 1916 Act the burden of proof shifts.

In the present case [the trial] judge, to put the matter shortly, on the view that he took of the law, directed the jury that since in each case there had admittedly been a receipt of goods or service, that amounted in law to consideration, and therefore, on the very concessions made by the defence, without further ado the burden of proof shifted. It is quite unnecessary in those circumstances for us to read the passages in the directions to the jury, in which [the] judge set out that matter and directed the jury. The sole question in the appeal is whether that interpretation of the word "consideration" in s. 2 of the 1916 Act is correct. The [accused] submit it is not.

We were referred to the wording of the earlier Act, the Public Bodies Corrupt Practices Act 1889. Section 1(1) of that Act, which Counsel . . . prays in aid in order to test the interpretation of the word "consideration", runs as follows: "Every person who shall by himself or by or in conjunction with any other person, corruptly solicit or receive, or agree to receive, for himself, or for any other person, any gift, loan, fee, reward, or advantage whatever as an inducement to, or reward for, or otherwise on account . . ."

Those words, counsel points out, are a great deal fuller than the words which appear in the 1906 Act, and he seeks by that means to elicit the meaning of the word "consideration" in the 1906 Act.

It is submitted by the [accused] that the word "consideration" therefore means a gratification which does not include money or a gift, or alternatively, as Counsel . . . any benefit not including money or a gift which is capable of being an inducement or reward. Secondly, it is submitted on behalf of the [accused] that the word "gift" in s. 2 of the 1916 Act is pointless if the argument of the Crown is correct. Thirdly it is submitted that where there is an ambiguity it must be resolved in favour of the defendant. We have been referred to *Maxwell on the Interpretation of Statutes.*[23] It is perhaps unnecessary for us to refer to the specific passage which counsel for the second appellant drew to our attention. Finally it is submitted on behalf of [the accused] that the onus of proof in cases such as this should only shift where there is something which emerges from the prosecution case which calls for or demands an explanation from the defendant.

First of all what is the meaning of the word "consideration", particularly in the light of the definition contained in the 1906 Act, namely " 'consideration' includes valuable consideration of any kind"? That is picked up in s. 4(3) of the 1916 Act as follows: ". . . 'consideration' in this Act [has] the same meaning as in the Prevention of Corruption Act, 1906 . . ." In our view the meaning of the word "consideration" must be the legal meaning of it and not any common or garden meaning; that really goes without saying. On that basis one turns to the classic definition which is to be found in *Currie* v. *Misa* per LUSH, J.[24] delivering the judgment of the Court of Exchequer Chamber: "A valuable consideration, in the sense of the law, may consist either in some right, interest, profit, or benefit accruing to the one party, or some forbearance, detriment, loss, or responsibility, given, suffered, or undertaken by the other . . ."

If one turns, as we think we are entitled, to see what the *Shorter Oxford*

---

[23] 12th edn., 1969.
[24] (1875) L.R. 10 Exch. 153, at p. 162.

English Dictionary has to say about consideration, the only meaning of it which is relevant to the present circumstances is meaning No. 6: "*Law.* Anything regarded as recompense or equivalent for what one does or undertakes for another's benefit; *esp.*, in the law of contracts, 'the thing given or done by the promisee in exchange for the promise'."

In our judgment the word "consideration" connotes the existence of something in the shape of a contract or a bargain between the parties. In the context of the present case, take E as the employee of the public body and A as the agent of the contractor. E the employee, promises to pay A, the agent of the contractor, £x. The consideration for that promise is that the contractor will supply tyres for E's car, or will do work on E's car, as the case may be. That is the consideration, namely the work done on the car or the supplying of the tyres for the car. If that is correct, then on proof of the receipt of the tyres or the doing of the work, the defendant is called on for an explanation. In our view the word "gift", according to the Crown's argument, is not otiose. The word "gift" is the other side of the coin, that is to say it comes into play where there is no consideration and no bargain. Consideration deals with the situation where there is a contract or a bargain and something moving the other way. Indeed if one looks at the word "money" in the 1916 Act, although it does not appear in the 1906 Act, it would be a very strange thing if the receipt of money was to bring s. 2 into play even though value is given for it, whereas the receipt of goods did not bring s. 2 into play where there was value given for the receipt of goods. Consequently the first submission on behalf of the [accused] in our opinion, fails.

Likewise it seems to us that there is no ambiguity which would bring into operation the principles set out in *Maxwell on the Interpretation of Statutes*. As suggested earlier in this judgment, it seems to us that this case demonstrates the very reason for the passing of the 1916 Act. Given that the advantage of the tyres or the repairs work is proved, it is almost impossible for the Crown to prove that no payment was ever made in return. Indeed in answer to the accused's final point, in our view there was indeed something which called for an explanation in these circumstances, and that is the reason for s. 2 of the 1916 Act.

For these reasons we have come to the conclusion that on this main point the judge in each case was correct.

(5) Duty not to disclose confidential information

Lamb *v.* Evans

(1893) 68 L.T. 131

An agent must not make use of confidential information which he has acquired during the course of the agency.

The owner of a trades directory employed two commercial travellers to canvass traders for the purpose of obtaining advertisements for insertion in it. At the end of their period of employment they proposed to use the information and materials, which they had acquired during the agency, in assisting a rival publication. The owner sought an injunction to prevent them from so acting.

Held, by the Court of Appeal, that the injunction would be granted.

BOWEN, L.J. (at page 135)

It is a question of whether the plaintiff, whatever the property in the documents may be, or whatever the property in the materials may be, had not sufficient special property in the matter to entitle him to restrain the use of them against him when they were really obtained in the course of the employment of his agents for his own use. That depends entirely, I think, upon the terms upon which the employment was constituted, upon which the fiduciary relation of principal and agent came into existence. I think my Brothers have already during the course of the argument expressed what I fully believe, that there is no distinction between law and equity as regards the law of principal and agent. The Common Law, it is true, treats the matter from the point of view of an implied contract, because it assumes that there is a promise to do that whichever is part of the bargain, or can be fairly implied as part of the good faith which is necessary to make the bargain effectual. What is an implied contract or an implied promise in law? Why, it is that promise which the law implies and authorises to infer in order to give the transaction that minimum of equity which the parties must have intended it should have, without which the transaction would be unintelligible and would be futile. Take this business and let us see, because I agree that there may be cases in which the terms would differ, and the terms as to the use which might be made of the materials obtained might be necessarily different. But take this business as a business of an ordinary kind. An employer gives his agent the means, by employing him, of obtaining in his name and for the purposes of the contract certain materials and certain information which have been committed for the purposes of that contract to writing. Is it intelligible that the bargain made between the principal and agent should be any other than one which implies that the agent was not, having obtained this under the cover of this agency, to turn round and use the information and materials against his employer as soon as the agency was determined? It seems to me that in this case the proper inference to be drawn would be that it was part of the understanding that these materials were not to be used otherwise than for the purposes of the employment in the course of which they were obtained.

B. PRINCIPAL'S REMEDIES FOR AGENT'S BREACH OF DUTY

Christoforides *v.* Terry

[1924] All E.R. Rep. 815

When an agent is guilty of a breach of duty, three separate remedies are open to the principal.

LORD SUMNER (at page 820)

Principals have three rights as against agents who fail in their duty—they can recover damages for want of skill and care, and for disregard of the terms of the mandate; they can obtain an account and payment of secret and illicit profits, which have come to the hands of their agents as agents; and they can resist an agent's claims for commission[25] and for indemnity[26] against liability incurred as a mandatory by showing that the agent has acted as a principal himself and not merely as an agent. Each remedy is distinct and is directed to a specific irregularity.

C. AGENCY OF NECESSITY

Prager *v.* Blatspiel, Stamp & Heacock Ltd.

[1924] All E.R. Rep. 524

For an agency of necessity to arise (1) the agent must have been unable to communicate with his principal; (2) there must be a commercial necessity; and (3) the agent must act bona fide *in the interests of all parties.*

The plaintiff was a fur dealer in Bucharest. In 1915 and 1916 he instructed the defendants, who were fur merchants in London, to buy some furs for him, and send them to Bucharest. They bought the skins but could not forward them to him because Rumania had been defeated and occupied by German troops. So in 1917 and 1918 they sold the furs. At the end of the war the plaintiff brought an action against them claiming damages for conversion. The defendants contended that they had sold the furs as agents of necessity.

Held, by the King's Bench Division, that the action succeeded, for the defendants were not agents of necessity. They could not communicate with the plaintiff, but there was no commercial necessity for the sale of the furs, for they could have placed them in cold storage. In addition, they had not acted *bona fide*.

---

[25] As to right to commission, see pp. 23–47, *post.*
[26] As to right to indemnity, see pp. 48–50, *post.*

McCardie, J. (at page 528)

I must refer briefly to several other features of the doctrine of agency of necessity in a case where, as here, the agent has, without orders, sold the goods of his principal. In the first place, it is, of course, clear that agency of necessity does not arise if the agent can communicate with his principal.

The basis of this requirement is, I take it, that, if the principal's decision can be obtained, the agent should seek it ere acting. In the present case it is admitted that the agents could not communicate with the principal. In the next place it is essential for the agent to prove that the sale was necessary.

In the third place, I think that an alleged agent of necessity must satisfy the Court that he was acting *bona fide* in the interests of the parties concerned. I hold, in the first place, that there was no necessity to sell the goods. They had been purchased by the plaintiff in time of war and not of peace. He bought them in order that he might be ready with a stock of goods when peace arrived. He had refused, by letters to the defendants, several profitable offers for some of them prior to the cessation of correspondence between the defendants and himself. The goods were not perishable like fruit or food. If furs are undressed, they may deteriorate somewhat rapidly in the course of a year or two, but these furs were dressed and not undressed. Dressed furs deteriorate very slowly. They lose somewhat in colour and suppleness year by year. The measure of deterioration depends on whether they are properly stored. If put into cold storage the deterioration is very little. Even if kept in an ordinary fur warehouse the deterioration is but slight, that is, if care be used. The great bulk of the furs here were of the best quality. I see no adequate reason for the sale by the defendants, for I am satisfied that there was nothing to prevent the defendants from putting them into cold storage and certainly nothing to prevent them from keeping them with proper care in their own warehouse. The expense of cold or other storage would have been but slight compared with the value of the furs. The plaintiff had given nearly £1,900 for them, and they steadily rose in value. The contra account of the defendants was less than £400. The margin, therefore, was of the most ample description. The defendants could and ought to have stored the goods till communication with Rumania was restored. I have said that the value of the furs was rising. Broadly speaking it may be said that from 1917 on to 1919 there was a steady and sometimes a rapid rise in the value of furs. This arose from the shortage of supply. The slight deterioration of the furs was far outweighed by the general and striking increase in market prices. I can see no point of time at which the defendants could honestly and fairly say: "In the interests of the plaintiff it is imperative that we sell his goods". That the furs were deteriorating but slightly is, I think, plain, and particularly when I observe the prices at which the defendants sold them. The defendants could not have formed the view at any time given that there was a necessity for sale, for they sold the goods by about 17 different sales, ranging from October, 1917, to 20th September, 1918. If the defendants honestly believed in the necessity of sale, they could at any time have sold the whole. In view of the military position in September, 1918, the sales in that month are significant. I hold that there was no commercial necessity for the sale. In the second place I decide, without hesitation, that the defendants did not act *bona fide*. I need not repeat the observations I have already made as to the absence of necessity for the sale. But I must add a few further words. I hold that the defendants were not, in fact, agents of necessity, that the sales of the plaintiff's goods were not justified, and that the defendants acted dishonestly.

Jebara *v.* Ottoman Bank

(1927) 137 L.T. 101

An agency of necessity may arise from an original agency, but it is more difficult for this to happen where there is no pre-existing agency.

SCRUTTON, L.J. (at page 105)

The expansion desired by MCCARDIE, J.[27] becomes less difficult when the agent of necessity develops from an original and subsisting agency, and only applies itself to unforeseen events not provided for in the original contract, which is usually the case where a ship-master is agent of necessity. But the position seems quite different when there is no pre-existing agency as in the case of a finder of perishable chattels or animals, and still more difficult when there is a pre-existing agency, but it has become illegal and void by reason of war, and the same reason will apply to invalidate any implied agency of necessity. How can one imply a duty in an enemy to protect the property of his enemy? Will he not be violating his duty to his own country if he takes active steps to preserve an enemy's property? I do not feel strong enough to expand the Common Law to this extent, and I do not see that MCCARDIE, J., has considered the effect of illegality and invalidity by reason of war in his doctrine.

D. RIGHTS OF AGENT

(1) Commission[28]

(A) GENERAL RULES APPLICABLE TO ALL AGENTS

G. T. Hodges & Sons *v.* Hackbridge Park Residential Hotel Ltd.

[1939] 4 All E.R. 347

In order to earn commission the agent must prove that he was the "effective cause" of the transaction which has been brought about.

---

[27] In *Prager* v. *Blatspiel, Stamp and Heacock Ltd.* [1924] All E.R. Rep. 524, at p. 527.

A firm of estate agents were instructed by their client to find a purchaser for his hotel. They found a Colonel Cannon who was looking for some land for erecting a hall with a sports ground. Negotiations took place for a sale at about £12,500 but came to nothing. Colonel Cannon had been acting for the War Office, which acquired it later under a compulsory purchase order for between £7,000 and £8,000. The agents claimed their commission from their client.

Held, by the Court of Appeal, that they were not entitled to it as they were not the "effective cause" of the sale.

SCOTT, L.J. (at page 349)

The [agents] have no evidence to show that they earned any commission, even if they have material upon which, had there been a voluntary sale, I think there would have been evidence of their being entitled to a commission. In the absence of a voluntary sale, however, there was no contractual relationship between what they did and the transfer of the estate under compulsion to the Government as the purchaser. It makes the rule laid down by Lord WATSON in *Toulmin* v. *Millar*[29] directly applicable. In that case, which was a claim for commission on the sale of an estate by the plaintiff, who was a London estate agent, Lord WATSON says:[30]

> "It is impossible to affirm, in general terms, that A. is entitled to a commission if he can prove that he introduced to B. the person who afterwards purchased B.'s estate, and that his introduction became the cause of the sale. In order to found a legal claim for commission, there must not only be a causal, there must also be a contractual relation between the introduction and the ultimate transaction of sale."

It is just that gap which existed in the facts of this case. In a certain sense, [the agents] had been the causal connection between the [client] and the War Office, the compulsory purchaser, but there was no contractual relationship between [them] and the [client] which would entitle [them] to say: "According to the terms of my employment by you, I have found for you a ready and willing purchaser at a price which you have voluntarily accepted". It is just those elements which are the elements necessary under the contract to entitle the [agents] to [their] commission and which in this case were absent by reason of the facts.

The facts, quite shortly, were that [the client] said: "I am not willing to sell for less than £12,500". The next event in the transaction was, no doubt, that that figure was reported to the War Office, who said: "That is ridiculous. We are not going to pay that. We will give notice to treat under the compulsory powers in the Acquisition of Land Act". That led to the fixing of the compensation. In my opinion, the Judge[31] erred in thinking that, because in effect [the agents] may

---

[28] For the effect of the termination of the agency on the agent's right to commission, see further, pp. 57–61, *post*.

[29] (1887) 58 L.T. 96.

[30] *Ibid.*, at p. 96.

[31] In the Court below.

have been the originating cause, [they were] therefore contractually entitled to commission.

Alpha Trading Ltd. *v.* Dunnshaw-Patten Ltd.

[1981] 1 All E.R. 483

The Court will imply a term that once the principal has entered into a contract with a third party he will not break it and thereby deprive the agent of the commission to which, if the contract had been performed, the agent would have been entitled.

The defendants, an international trading company, agreed to pay the plaintiffs, another international trading company, a commission of U.S. $1.50 per tonne if the plaintiffs introduced to them a buyer for 10,000 tonnes of cement. The plaintiffs found a purchaser, who entered into a contract with the defendants to purchase that quantity. Subsequently the defendants were unwilling or unable to perform the contract, and defaulted on it. The plaintiffs brought an action against the defendants claiming damages for loss of commission under the agency agreement.

Held, by the Court of Appeal, that the claim succeeded, for it was an implied term of the agency agreement that the defendants would not break their contract with the purchaser and deprive the plaintiffs of the commission due to them.

TEMPLEMAN, L.J. (at page 490)

The plaintiff agents contracted to provide, and did provide, for the defendant vendors a purchaser for 10,000 metric tonnes of cement at $49.50 per tonne in consideration of the vendors agreeing to pay the agents' commission of $1.50 per tonne out of the purchase price. The vendors entered into the stipulated contract with the purchaser, but the purchase price was never paid because the vendors, in breach of their contract with the purchaser, failed to supply the cement and thereby released the purchaser from its obligation to pay the purchase price.

The agents claim damages on the grounds that the vendors are in breach of an implied term in the contract between the agents and the vendors, an implied term that the vendors would perform their contract with the purchaser so as to become entitled to the purchase price out of which the commission was to be paid.

The vendors deny that any term is to be implied. By repudiating their contract with the purchaser, they painlessly released themselves from their contract with the agents.

Counsel for the defendant vendors submitted that there was no room or necessity for any implied term. The commission was only payable out of the purchase price paid by the purchaser. The purchase price was never paid. Therefore, the commission never became payable.

In the present case, the agents performed their part of their bargain with the vendors by providing a purchaser who was ready and willing to contract with the vendors. The vendors utilised and took advantage of the services provided by the agents by entering into a contract with the purchaser on terms acceptable to the vendors and, no doubt, designed and intended by the vendors to produce a profit for themselves.

In my judgment, it is necessary to imply a term to prevent the vendors from making use of the agents' services without being under any liability to the agents to ensure, so far as the vendors were concerned, that the agents then received the stipulated reward for the agents' services, which were supplied to and utilised by the vendors. An agent does not provide services and agree to accept and postpone payment for his services restricted to the purchase price on terms that the vendor, who accepts, exploits and makes use of the agent's services, is free to deprive the agent of the reward promised for the services of the agent if the vendor thinks fit to do so. If there was no implied term in the present case, the vendors could have sold their cement to the purchaser provided by the agents if the market price of cement went down, thus increasing the benefit of the contract with the purchaser so far as the vendors were concerned.

On the other hand, if the market price of cement remained stable or went up, the vendors were free in the absence of an implied term to sell to a third party, to repudiate their contract with the purchaser furnished by the agents, and in the result would be $1.50 per tonne better off at the expense of the agents.

If the vendors are right, they were entitled to keep $1.50 per tonne in their pocket by selling to a third party while retaining power to complete their contract with the purchaser provided by the agents, if that contract in the event yielded the vendors a higher rate of profit than any available contract with a third party. In other words, the agents' commission depended on the vendors not discovering that it was worth their while to break their contract with the agents' purchaser and thereby deprive the agent of the commission which was earned by the services provided by the agent and exploited and utilised by the vendors.

In my judgment, it is necessary to imply a term which prevents a vendor, in these circumstances, from playing a dirty trick on the agent with impunity after making use of the services provided by that agent in order to secure the very position and safety of the vendor. It is necessary to imply a term which prevents the vendor from acting unreasonably to the possible gain of the vendor and the loss of the agent. In my judgment, the term properly to be implied in the present circumstance is that the vendors will not deprive the agents of their commission by committing a breach of the contract between the vendors and the purchaser which releases the purchaser from its obligation to pay the purchase price.

. . .

In the present case, I can see no uncertainty, no difficulty and no hardship in implying a term that, if the principal enters into a contract with a third party procured by the agents, then the principal agrees that he will not deprive the agent of his commission by committing a breach of the contract which releases the third party from his obligation to pay the purchase price which is the sole agreed source of the agent's commission.

In my judgment, it is necessary to imply a term in the present case because no agent would agree and no principal would attempt to insist that the principal should be able to take the benefit of the agent's work and the advantages of the contract with the third party and yet retain the right to defeat the agent's claim for commission by breaking his contractual obligations to the third party.

Fullwood *v*. Hurley

(1928) 138 L.T. 49

An agent is not entitled to commission from both parties unless he has made a full disclosure of the position to both of them, and has obtained their consent to being paid such a commission.

A hotel broker was employed by a vendor to sell a hotel, and was paid his agreed commission for doing so. He claimed a second commission from the purchaser in respect of his services as broker.

Held, by the Court of Appeal, that he was not entitled to such a commission, for he had not made a full disclosure to each party that he was acting for both of them, and had not obtained the consent of both parties to his being paid a double commission.

SCRUTTON, L.J. (at page 51)

If Messrs Fullwood or any public-house broker want to get two commissions, they must fulfil the two conditions of the law by making a full disclosure to each party of the exact nature of their interest before they make the alleged agreement, and, if they get a second commission, of obtaining the consent of each party. It is not enough to say that it is the usual or customary brokerage, because the law has held that a custom to the effect that an agent shall have double brokerage without informing his principal is unreasonable, and shall not be enforced; and anybody who does want to get double commission where he has two different interests in himself which may clash, must fulfil to the strictest extent the requirements of the law.

. . . I rest my judgment on the ground that an agent who wants to make two contracts for double commission, must do so in the clearest possible terms and with the clearest possible information to each of his principals what he is doing, otherwise he cannot sue under an alleged agreement.

Andrew *v*. Ramsay & Co.[32]

(1903) 89 L.T. 450

Where an agent has received a secret commission, he cannot retain such commission or his ordinary commission in respect of the transaction for which he has been employed by the principal.

A client instructed a firm of auctioneers to sell some property for him. They found a purchaser, and the purchaser paid them a secret commission. The client discovered that this payment had been made, and claimed that the sale should be set aside, and also that he was entitled to be repaid £50 which they had retained as their ordinary commission.

Held, by the King's Bench Division, that the sale should be set aside, and that the auctioneers must hand over the £50.

---

[32] As to the effect of an agent receiving a secret commission on the relation between the principal and the third party, see pp. 105–110, *post*.

LORD ALVERSTONE, C.J. (at page 451)

Then the next point is that the defendants are not bound to hand over the £50, because the plaintiff acted on the contract and took the benefit of the defendants' services, and that there was no such failure of consideration as would entitle the plaintiff to recover this sum. I think that that entirely loses sight of the principle laid down in *Salomons* v. *Pender*[33] where it was held that an agent, who was employed to sell property and who had sold it to a company in which he was himself interested as a shareholder and director, was not entitled to any commission from his employer in respect of the sale. The principle of that case seems to me to govern this case, and, in my opinion, it is sufficient to do so. That case turned on the fair principle that where the person who is acting as agent is not in a position to say to his principal, "I have been acting as your agent and I have done my duty by you", he is not entitled to recover any commission from that principal. . . . It appears to me that this case is only one instance in which an agent who has acted improperly while acting as such agent is unable to recover his commission from his principal. It is impossible to say what the result of the sale might have been if the agent had acted honestly. The purchaser was willing to give £20 more than the price which the plaintiff actually received, and it may be that he would have given more than that; and it is therefore impossible to say or to estimate in any way what the plaintiff may have lost by the improper conduct of the defendants. A principal is entitled to have an honest agent, and if it turns out that the agent is not honest, then the agent is not to be entitled to his commission. If the agent, either directly or indirectly, enters into collusion with the opposite party, then he is not entitled to his commission.

Hippisley *v.* Knee Bros.

(1905) 92 L.T. 20

Commission may be payable by the principal even where the agent is guilty of a breach of duty, if the breach of duty was only incidental and had no bearing on the transaction which the agent has caused to be brought about.

Hippisley employed Knee Brothers, who were auctioneers, to sell some pictures for him at a commission of £20, and agreed to pay them out-of-pocket expenses. They arranged for advertisements concerning the pictures to be printed. They received a discount of 10% from the printers (in accordance with the usual trade practice), but charged Hippisley the full price of the cost of the printing. Throughout they had acted *bona fide*. Hippisley claimed the discount, and refused to pay them their commission.

Held, by the Court of Appeal, that the discount was recoverable, but that the commission was payable, for the duty to account for the rebate was only incidental and had no bearing on their duty in relation to the sale of the pictures.

---

[33] (1865) 12 L.T. 267.

LORD ALVERSTONE, C.J. (at page 23)

I think that an honest neglect to account for a commission or rebate allowed in some matter which has no direct bearing on the main duty or business of the agent does not come within the principle of *Andrew* v. *Ramsay and Co.*,[34] *Salomons* v. *Pender*,[35] and other cases which have been relied on by the plaintiff. In this case the discounts were allowed in respect of matters incidental to the work which the defendants had to do on behalf of the plaintiff in relation to the sale of his goods. It cannot be suggested that the plaintiff has suffered in any way in the sale of his goods by reason of the defendants' conduct in the matter of the discounts. I must say that I think that the law which has been applied in the cases referred to should be applied in all cases where an agent employed to do certain work receives a secret commission in relation to the performance of his duty to his employer from any one other than his employer. In this case the neglect to account had no effect whatever on the performance of his duty by the agent. It was purely incidental and had nothing to do with the duty.

KENNEDY, J. (at page 24)

Where the remuneration is to be paid for an inseparable duty, even if that duty may involve very different classes of acts to be performed, then if the agent is unfaithful in any part of his duty, by reason of his taking a secret profit—and I use the word "unfaithful" as meaning a breach of the obligation, whether he may think it right or wrong—it may be that he forfeits his commission. But where it is possible to separate the classes of duties to be performed by the agent, it may not follow that unfaithfulness in one part of his duties would disentitle him to receive his commission on the other part which he had performed faithfully. I am of opinion that where the duties are separable, as they were in the present case, it does not follow that an agent, by unfaithful performance of one duty, forfeits his right to the whole of the remuneration which he has earned in the proper discharge of his other duties. I think this case is a good example of that.

Harrods Ltd. *v.* Lemon

[1931] All E.R. Rep. 285

Where an agent is guilty of a breach of duty disentitling him from claiming commission, he will still be able to obtain it if the principal has waived the breach of duty.

Harrods Ltd. had two separate departments:—(i) an estate agency department; and (ii) a building department. Mrs Lemon asked them in their capacity of estate agents to

---

[34] (1903) 89 L.T. 450. This case is set out at p. 27, *ante.*
[35] (1865) 12 L.T. 267.

sell a property for her. The intending purchaser employed Harrods Ltd. as surveyors to inspect the drains for him. Harrods Ltd. found out that they were acting in two capacities, so they made a full disclosure of this to Mrs Lemon, and suggested that she should have an independent surveyor. She declined to do so, and completed the purchase through Harrods Ltd., but refused to pay Harrods Ltd. any commission as they were guilty of a breach of duty since they had acted for both parties.

Held, by the Court of Appeal, that commission was payable because she had waived the breach of duty.

LORD HANWORTH, M.R. (at page 289)

Have the plaintiffs, then, lost the right to commission? It is right that I should repeat, on behalf of Messrs Harrods, that they make it quite plain that they regret that they acted in an equivocal position. Mr Ford, who negotiated the sale to Mrs Campbell, says this: "It would be wrong for us to act for both vendor and purchaser"; and he also says this: "I never said anything to Mrs Campbell or Mrs Lemon about the drains, and knew nothing about their condition". The manager of the estate office, Mr Robinson Steele Smith, agrees that the telegram of 12th July would tend to diminish the price and would be in the interest of the purchaser. Reliance has been placed on a decision of Lord ALVERSTONE as justifying the view that the commission is not recoverable. In *Hippisley* v. *Knee Bros.*[36] he said:[37]

> "If the Court is satisfied that there has been no fraud or dishonesty upon the agent's part, I think that the receipt by him of a discount will not disentitle him to his commission unless the discount is in some way connected with the contract which the agent is employed to make or the duty which he is called upon to perform".

It is said that there was a conflict, and, therefore, that the principle of *Hippisley* v. *Knee Bros.*[38] does not apply. But it must be remembered that the offer was made that Harrods should drop out of it, and that was not accepted. It appears to me that after that acceptance of the situation, it is not possible for the defendant to impute to Harrods that they have lost their right to commission, when she has accepted their services with full knowledge, and rejected the opportunity to put the matter right by having an independent surveyor. If the facts were different, if the whole transaction had gone off and this was an action by Mrs Lemon for a loss of part of the price, different considerations might have applied. If the eventualities contemplated in the letter which I read, of 17th July, had been carried out, again we might have had to apply a different set of rules. But all that we have to consider here is whether, in the present circumstances, after the knowledge was conveyed to Mrs Lemon and she acted as she did, it can be said that Messrs Harrods have lost their right to commission. It appears to me, reaffirming the principles which I have already laid down, and which are not in any way contested by Messrs Harrods, that they are entitled to be paid for their services.

---

[36] [1905] 1 K.B. 1. This case is set out at p. 28, *ante*.
[37] [1905] 1 K.B. 1, at p. 8.
[38] *Supra*.

Wilson *v.* Harper Son & Co.

(1908) 99 L.T. 391[39]

Whether commission in respect of orders from customers introduced by him will continue to be payable to the agent's estate after his death is a matter of construction in each case.

On 9th August, 1890, the defendants, Harper Son & Co., who carried on business as iron founders, wrote a letter to a Mr Wroe in which they stated:—"We have turned up your letter in which you offer to secure for us some orders for malleable castings for 5% commission on all goods supplied to customers introduced by you. We shall be pleased to pay you 5% as long as we do business with those you place on our books". Wroe introduced customers who did business with Harper Son & Co., and was duly paid commission until his death in 1906. The plaintiff, who was his executor, claimed commission on all orders received by the defendants from these customers after Wroe's death.

Held, by the Chancery Division, that commission was payable, and that the action succeeded.

NEVILLE, J. (at page 393)

There are interviews in the meantime between Mr Wroe and members of the firm, and his letter receives no answer until the 9th August, when the firm write and say to Mr Wroe, "Since you were here last week", etc. . . . Now, that seems to me to be the beginning and the end of the transaction which concerns the present case; and I think it is only the letter of the 9th August that is sometimes spoken of as a commission note. It was simply saying to a man, "If you introduce business I will pay you 5% upon the business introduced"; and it seems to me that all question as to duration is set at rest by the words which have been used here: "So long as we do business with those you place on our books". I think that these words show quite clearly that the commission was not only in respect of orders given through the agent, if you like to call him so, as in one of the cases that has been cited to me, but that there was a commission of 5% to be paid as the price of an introduction for all business done by the firm with the customers introduced. Now it seems to me quite impossible to say that you are to read in business documents of this kind an implied limitation that no remuneration is to be paid to the executors of one of the contracting parties; because if you read the word "you" as meaning "you", and not your representatives after your death, the result would be that earned commission—that is, commission in respect of orders already executed—would not be payable because there is nobody to receive; the man is dead, and you are not bound to pay his executors. It appears to me, therefore, that you must read the agreement to pay "you" in the ordinary sense in which those words are used—that is, to pay you, and after your death to

---

[39] This case should be contrasted with *Crocker Horlock Ltd.* v. *B. Lang & Co. Ltd.* [1949] 1 All E.R. 526 (see p. 32, *post*), where it is emphasised that whether commission is payable after the termination of the agency relationship is a matter of construction in each case.

pay your executors. I think what you are to pay is quite clear. You are to pay 5% as the orders received from firms introduced by Mr Wroe. Therefore it seems to me that it does not matter whether he was dead or alive, because after he is dead the thing comes to an end in this way, that no further customers can be introduced by anybody on the terms of this document. It seems to me it might have been determined at any time by notice by Harper and Sons, and from that moment no commission could be recovered in respect of any fresh business introduced; but I do not think that would affect the right to receive commission in respect of business from firms introduced, and I do not think that death puts an end to that any more than the notice of determination of the agreement by Harper and Sons would have done in Mr Wroe's lifetime.

Crocker Horlock Ltd. *v.* B. Lang & Co. Ltd.[40]

[1949] 1 All E.R. 526

Whether commission "on all orders and all repeats" is payable after the termination of the agency is a matter of construction in each case.

The plaintiffs were the representatives of the defendants, who were clothing manufacturers, and on 20th April, 1944, received a letter from them stating:—"We confirm the arrangement that you represent us for the London area for the wholesale trade. Commission to be 5% on all orders, whether received direct or indirect, and on all repeats. Payable on the 20th of each month on all goods actually dispatched and invoiced". The period of the contract was six months from 1st May, 1944, subject to a "renewal for a further period, say, of three years should you reach the minimum figure of £1,000 between now and November 1944". The business obtained by the plaintiffs exceeded £1,000 in the trial period, and the agreement continued until it was terminated by the defendants in July, 1947. The plaintiffs contended that they were entitled to commission on all repeat orders received after the agency had been determined.

Held, by the King's Bench Division, that the claim failed, for, as a matter of construction, the word "repeats" meant repeat orders which were received during the period of the agency and not afterwards.

MORRIS, J. (at page 529)

I have not referred at length to the decisions in the various cases to which I have referred, for it seems to me that when one notes the divergent phrases used in the different cases, it does become entirely plain that the question is one of construction, and that there is always danger in seeking to draw too much guidance from a decision in regard to other words in other contexts. Counsel for the defendants drew my attention to the fact that in *Levy* v. *Goldhill*,[41] PETERSON, J., in his judgment, laid emphasis more than once on the difference

---

[40] This case should be contrasted with *Wilson* v. *Harper Son & Co.* (1908) 99 L.T. 391 (see p. 31, *ante*), where it was held, as a matter of construction, that commission was payable even after the death of the agent.

[41] [1917] 2 Ch. 297.

between cases where the agreement was for a definite, and cases where it was for an indefinite, period. Counsel for the plaintiffs submits that it would be an erroneous test to say that merely because an agreement has a fixed term there cannot be a provision that commission is payable after the end of the term. I think counsel is correct in that submission. Everything must turn on a consideration of the exact words used.

Referring again to the words of the letter of 20th April, it is first to be noted that the provision is that commission is to be 5% "on all orders". There is a further provision as to when the commission is to be paid—"on the 20th of each month on all goods actually despatched and invoiced"—but the provision is that payment is to be "on all orders". Then the agreement goes on: "whether received direct or indirect, and on all repeats". It would be rather a surprising result if the sentence to which I am now referring contemplated, by its first part, the contract period, and by its second part, after the word "indirect", a period after the end of the contract. It seems to me that this wording denotes that the commission is to be 5% on all orders, and then, by way of specifying and making clear what orders are referred to, the letter goes on to say that they are orders, whether received directly or indirectly, and all "repeats". It is to be observed that there is no mention in this letter of introducing a customer. It would have been very easy, if the parties had so wished, to provide that commission was payable at a particular rate on all orders given by a customer introduced, but that language is not found. It is cogently submitted by counsel for the plaintiffs that the words "on all repeats" are not really necessary, but it seems to me that those words are put there further to define and fully to clarify the meaning of the word "orders". A situation might otherwise have arisen in which a customer gave an order and then later sent a repeat order, and some question might have arisen whether commission was payable on the latter. To avoid ambiguity those words were put in. If counsel for the plaintiffs is right in his submission as to what these words mean, the result would follow that, if a customer was introduced by the plaintiffs, and gave no order during the contract period, but did give an order after the contract period, no commission would be payable because it would not be a "repeat". That would seem to me to be rather a surprising result if the intention was to relate the remuneration to orders that resulted from customers introduced by the plaintiffs.

It is not strictly necessary to decide the question whether this agreement provided for commission on an order that came from the London area irrespective of any work on the part of the plaintiffs, but, as that has been argued and as it may be closely allied to what I have to decide, I think it is desirable to state my view on it. The agreement provides for commission to be 5% on all orders, but that still leaves open the question whether the reference is to all orders in the London area or to all orders in the London area from customers introduced by the plaintiffs. The agreement does not have the words, "from customers introduced by the plaintiffs"; it simply has the words "on all orders". That must have some limitation, but the limitation, as it seems to me, is the limitation of the words "London area", and the agreement, therefore, in my judgment, means that the commission is to be one of 5% on all orders coming from the London area during the period of the contract. If the minimum business had not been reached during the six months' period, in my judgment, there would have been an end when the six months' period terminated, of any obligations on the part of the defendants, save for orders received during the six months.

For the reasons which I have indicated, my conclusion is that by these agreements the parties provided that the plaintiffs' remuneration was to be 5% or 2½%, on all orders, whether received directly or indirectly, and on all repeats, meaning "including all repeats", and that that remuneration was the remuneration payable during the contract period and that the parties have not provided by this contract for any payment after that period came to an end.

Les Affréteurs Réunis Société Anonyme *v.* Leopold Walford (London) Ltd.

(1919) 121 L.T. 393

Where a charter-party states that commission is to be paid to a shipbroker who has negotiated it, the shipbroker, although not a party to the contract, can enforce the commission clause against the shipowner by getting the charterer to sue the shipowner, for in such a case by the custom of the trade the charterer is a trustee for the shipbroker in respect of the commission.

> A time charter-party stated that "a commission of 3% on the estimated gross amount of the hire" of a vessel should be paid to the shipbrokers who had negotiated it. The shipbrokers were not a party to the contract.
> *Held*, by the House of Lords, that the charterers, as trustees for the shipbrokers, could enforce the commission clause against the shipowners.

LORD BIRKENHEAD, L.C. (at page 394)

A charter-party is, of course, a contract between owners and charterers, and it is elementary that, so far as the brokers are concerned, it is *res inter alios acta*; but the parties in the present case by an interlocutory and very sensible arrangement have agreed that the matter shall be dealt with as if the charterers were co-plaintiffs. The question, therefore, is, can the charterers succeed in such circumstances as the present in such an action against owners?

It was decided nearly seventy years ago in the case of *Robertson* v. *Wait*[42] that charterers can sue under an agreement of this character as trustees for the broker. I am unable to distinguish between the decision in *Robertson* v. *Wait*[43] and the decision which in my view should be reached in the present case.

So far as I am aware, that case has not before engaged the attention of your Lordships' House, and I think it right to say plainly that I agree with that decision, and I agree with the reasoning, shortly as it is expressed, upon which the decision was founded.

---

[42] (1853) 8 Exch. 299. ·
[43] *Supra.*

It appears to me plain that for convenience and under long-established practice the broker in these cases in effect nominates the charterer to contract on his behalf, influenced probably by the circumstance that there is always a contract between charterer and owner in which this stipulation, which is to enure to the benefit of the broker, may very conveniently be inserted. I take the view that in these cases the broker in effect, and on ultimate analysis, nominates the charterer to contract on his behalf. I agree, therefore, with the conclusion arrived at by all the learned Judges in *Robertson* v. *Wait* that in such cases the charterer can sue as trustee on behalf of the broker.

(B) ESTATE AGENTS' COMMISSION

Luxor (Eastbourne) Ltd. *v.* Cooper

[1941] 1 All E.R. 33

The liability to pay commission to an estate agent depends upon the exact terms of the contract. Little help is afforded by decisions in other cases. There is a presumption against adding implied terms.[44]

LORD RUSSELL OF KILLOWEN (at page 43)

A few preliminary observations occur to me. (1) Commission contracts are subject to no peculiar rules or principles of their own. The law which governs them is the law which governs all contracts and all questions of agency. (2) No general rule can be laid down by which the rights of the agent or the liabilities of the principal under commission contracts are to be determined. In each case, these must depend upon the exact terms of the contract in question, and upon the true construction of those terms. (3) Contracts by which owners of property, desiring to dispose of it, put it in the hands of agents on commission terms are not (in default of specific provisions) contracts of employment in the ordinary meaning of those words. No obligation is imposed on the agent to do anything. The contracts are merely promises binding on the principal to pay a sum of money upon the happening of a specified event, which involves the rendering of some service by the agent. There is no real analogy between such contracts and contracts of employment by which one party binds himself to do certain work and the other binds himself to pay remuneration for the doing of it.

LORD WRIGHT (at page 48)

However that may be, what is in question in all these cases is the interpretation of a particular contract. I deprecate in general the attempt to enunciate decisions on the construction of agreements as if they embodied rules of law. To

---

[44] In view of the principles established in this case, only a few of the cases concerning estate agents' commission are included in this casebook. *It is to be emphasised that they relate to the question of the proper interpretation of the particular contract involved.*

some extent decisions on one contract may help by way of analogy and illustration in the decision of another contract, but, however similar the contracts may appear, the decision as to each must depend on the consideration of the language of the particular contract, read in the light of the material circumstances of the parties in view of which the contract is made . . .

The general presumption is that the parties have expressed every material term which they intended should govern their agreement, whether oral or in writing. It is well-recognised, however, that there may be cases where obviously some term must be implied if the intention of the parties is not to be defeated, some term of which it can be predicated that "it goes without saying", some term not expressed, but necessary to give to the transaction such business efficacy as the parties must have intended. This does not mean that the Court can embark on a reconstruction of the agreement on equitable principles, or on a view of what the parties should, in the opinion of the Court, reasonably have contemplated. The implication must arise inevitably to give effect to the intention of the parties. These general observations do little more than warn Judges that they have no right to make contracts for the parties. Their province is to interpret contracts. However, language is imperfect, and there may be, as it were, obvious interstices in what is expressed which have to be filled up.

Bentall, Horsley and Baldry *v.* Vicary

(1930) 144 L.T. 365

Where a principal has appointed an agent a "sole agent", the principal can sell the property himself without incurring a liability to pay the agent damages for breach of contract.

A client desiring to sell a certain property placed it in the hands of a firm of estate agents, appointing them as "sole agents". While they were still endeavouring to find a purchaser, he sold it himself to a third party.

Held, by the King's Bench Division, that he was entitled to do so without having to pay the agents damages for breach of contract. No term could be implied into the contract that he would not sell the property himself.

McCARDIE, J. (at page 367)

Are the plaintiffs entitled to damages for breach of contract? This raises a question of some importance. The plaintiffs were appointed "sole agents" for the sale of the property for a period of six months. There was ample consideration for this agreement by reason of the arrangement as to advertising expenses. But what is the effect of the words I have just set out? The plaintiffs submit that those words gave to them and to them *alone* the right to sell the property, and that therefore the defendant committed a breach of contract by himself disposing of it. To put it another way, the plaintiffs argue that it was an implied term of the contract that the defendant should not himself sell the property and so deprive the plaintiffs of the commission they might perhaps be able to earn . . .

It is quite open to a property owner to agree that an estate agent shall have the sole right to dispose of the property and that no one else, whether another agent or the owner himself, shall deal with the property during the contract period. If, however, such a bargain is intended, then clear words must be used. In the present case I hold that the defendant committed no breach of contract by himself selling the property.

Murdoch Lownie Ltd. *v.* Newman

[1949] 2 All E.R. 783

Where an estate agent is to be paid commission "in the event of business resulting", commission is not payable unless he introduces a person who signs a binding contract to purchase the property concerned.

An owner of a hotel agreed to pay commission to an estate agent "in the event of business resulting". The agent introduced a Mr Graham, who signed an agreement to buy the hotel for £35,000 "subject to his being able to arrange a mortgage" of £25,000 if the owner were not willing to lend him that sum. The owner subsequently changed his mind, and paid Graham £1,550 to be released from the agreement. The agent claimed commission.

Held, by the King's Bench Division, that the action failed, for commission was not payable unless the person introduced by the agent signed a binding contract.

SLADE, J. (at page 785)

I now come to the second question: "What, on the true construction of that contract, is the event on the happening of which the right to commission accrues to the plaintiffs?" Three constructions were put before me in the course of the argument. Taking them in ascending order they were that the right to commission accrued (a) on the introduction by the plaintiffs to the defendant of a party who was ready, willing and able to purchase the property on terms acceptable to the defendant, the vendor; (b) on the introduction by the plaintiffs to the defendant of a party who entered into a binding contract with the vendor for the purchase of the property; and (c) on the introduction of a party who not only entered into a binding contract for the purchase of the property, but who actually completed the purchase. Counsel for the plaintiffs contended that (a) was the proper construction of the contract, and alternatively, if he failed on that, that (b) was the proper construction. Counsel for the defendant, on the other hand, contended that (c) was the proper construction, or, if he failed on that, that the proper construction was (b).

In my judgment, the words "in the event of business resulting" are neither clear nor unequivocal. Indeed, I go further and say that they are ambiguous, and, as the argument in this Court shows, susceptible of at least three possible constructions. They are, moreover, the words of the plaintiffs themselves, and, if all other canons of construction failed, I should construe them by resolving any ambiguity in favour of the principal and against the agent who proffered them. I do not, however, find it necessary to employ the legal maxim applicable to cases of that kind in the present case, because I am satisfied that the words "in the event of business resulting" on their true construction require at least that the right to commission shall not accrue until the agent has introduced to the principal a person who has entered into a binding contract to purchase the property. I shall deal later with what I mean by "a binding contract to purchase the property". I am fortified in my view that the words "in the event of business resulting" are by no means unequivocal by reference to later passages in the agreed correspondence which seem to me to indicate that the plaintiffs themselves were not sure what the words meant. Whatever the expression "binding contract" may mean, it must, in my view, at least mean a contract which is binding on the party introduced by the agent so that the principal gets something definite from the party introduced by the agent in return for the commission which he is called on to pay. In some of the reported cases a "binding contract" is looked on from the point of view of whether it binds the vendor. I think that "binding contract" means a contract which binds both parties, i.e., which is a contract and is clothed with the necessary form required to make it an enforceable contract in law. But whether that be so or not, I am satisfied that the expression envisages a contract which, as against the party introduced by the agent, the vendor is entitled to have specifically performed or for whose breach he is at least entitled to recover damages. In the case of this document it is manifest that the defendant may say nothing and that Mr Graham may make no inquiry up till the date fixed for completion, and may even not have taken the necessary steps by that date to form a company to become mortgagor to the defendant. That date may arrive and the defendant may attend with his solicitor at the place fixed for completion, only to be met by Mr Graham with the statement: "I am sorry. I have done my very best to find a mortgagee, but I have not been able to do so". On any view of the matter, it is a highly unsatisfactory position from the point of view of the defendant, and, in my judgment, not the position which was contemplated by the words: "You shall pay us commission in the event of business resulting". What business can be said to have resulted from that state of affairs?

Bennett, Walden & Co. *v.* Wood

[1950] 2 All E.R. 134

Where an estate agent is to be paid commission "on securing an offer", no commission is payable unless the person introduced makes a firm offer and not merely one which is "subject to contract".

> The plaintiffs were estate agents, who had agreed to act as the defendant's agents to negotiate a sale of his house, and were to be paid commission "in the event of our securing for you an offer". The person whom they introduced signed an agreement to buy the house "subject to contract". The defendant proceeded no further in the matter. The plaintiffs thereupon sued him for commission.
>
> *Held*, by the Court of Appeal, that commission was not payable. The word "offer" meant a *firm* offer which by acceptance created a contract. An offer "subject to contract" lacked that essential characteristic.

Sir Raymond Evershed, M.R. (at page 137)

Applying the proper test of construction, *viz.*, what is the ordinary, straight-forward, meaning of the language, it seems to me reasonably clear that the answer here is that by "offer" is meant a firm offer. In the ordinary sense of the term in business matters an offer is something which by acceptance creates a bargain. An offer "subject to contract" lacks that essential characteristic, for its acceptance does not create a contract. *Prima facie* when the word "offer" in such a document as this is used, what is meant is something, which, if accepted, gives rise to a contractual relationship. I think that that view is supported by the use of the word "securing"—making sure—for something which amounts to no more than a step in the negotiations provides no kind of assurance or security for the principal. Counsel for the plaintiffs conceded that a contract in this form was not intended to provide and ought not to be construed so as to provide the opportunity of more than one commission in respect of the same subject-matter for the agent, but, if there is here to be no such requirement as I have indicated, namely, if "offer" means, not a firm offer, but a mere proposal, then there will be the greatest possible difficulties in identifying the particular proposal which attracts the commission. It is true that that has not arisen in this case, but it is a legitimate way to test the matter.

It seems to me, therefore, tolerably plain that by "offer" is here meant what I have described as a firm offer. I do not think the result of that is necessarily to produce the same result as would have been produced had the words been "find a purchaser". I am not saying what would be the precise result if a firm offer had been made here, and for one reason or another the contracts so confirmed had broken down at a later stage. I certainly do not, as at present advised, assent to the view that the construction I put on this document makes this formula synonymous with the other formulae I have mentioned.

If I am right so far, then plainly the document of 17th January lacked the essential characteristic.

Graham & Scott (Southgate) Ltd. *v.* Oxlade

[1950] 1 All E.R. 856

Where commission is to be paid on the introduction of a person "able and willing" to purchase, no commission will be payable if the person introduced makes an offer to purchase "subject to contract".

The defendant agreed to pay commission to the plaintiffs, who were estate agents, in the event of their introducing a person "willing and able to purchase" his property. The plaintiffs introduced a Mrs Smith, who made an offer to purchase it "subject to contract and satisfactory survey". They now claimed commission from the defendant.

Held, by the Court of Appeal, that commission was not payable, for the plaintiffs had not introduced a person who was "willing" to purchase, Mrs Smith had not made an unqualified offer to purchase for it had been made "subject to contract and satisfactory survey", and the defendant by accepting the offer could not constitute a binding contract.

COHEN, L.J. (at page 861)

I think that the agent may prove that a person he has introduced is willing to purchase the property by showing that that person has made an unqualified offer or expressed an unqualified intention to make an offer notwithstanding that such an offer until accepted could be withdrawn. On the other hand, if the evidence shows that the offer is qualified by a condition inserted to prevent the other party turning the offer into a contract by acceptance, I think it is impossible to say that the agent has discharged the onus which rests on him of proving that the person he has introduced was willing to purchase the property.

In the present case there was some evidence that Mrs Smith was keen on purchasing. She had continually increased her offer to meet the rising appetite of the defendant, and she was described by her husband as anxious to purchase, but she never made an unqualified offer and her anxiety was at all material times qualified by "subject to satisfactory survey". Such an offer meant that Mrs Smith had constituted herself the arbitrator whether the survey was satisfactory, and the principal could not by accepting her offer constitute a binding contract. In these circumstances I think the learned Judge[45] was right in his conclusion, and that the plaintiffs had not established that Mrs Smith was a "person willing to purchase the property".

Christie Owen & Davies Ltd. *v.* Rapacioli

[1974] 2 All E.R. 311

Where commission is to be paid on the introduction of a "person ready, able and willing to purchase", commission will be payable if a person who is able to purchase is introduced and expresses his readiness and willingness by an offer to purchase even though such offer has not been accepted, and can be withdrawn.

> The defendant agreed to pay commission to the plaintiffs, who were estate agents, if they introduced a person "ready, able and willing to purchase" the lease of a restaurant for £20,000 or such sum as was acceptable to the defendant. The plaintiffs introduced a Mr Abbas, who offered to buy the lease for £17,700. This offer was accepted by the defendant. Subsequently Mr Abbas signed his part of the contract, and sent it to the defendant. The defendant refused to continue with the sale. The plaintiffs claimed commission.
>
> *Held*, by the Court of Appeal, that they were entitled to it, for Mr Abbas was a person "ready, able and willing to purchase".

CAIRNS, L.J. (at page 318)

It seems to me that the trend of the authorities supports the three propositions enunciated by counsel for the plaintiffs. (1) The decision whether the commission is payable depends on the terms of the contract and on ordinary rules of construction. (2) When the agreement between principal and agent is

---

[45] ROXBURGH, J., in the Court below: [1950] 1 All E.R. 91.

for commission to be payable on the introduction of a person ready, able and willing to purchase, the commission is payable if a sale actually results, but may become payable when the transaction becomes abortive. (3) Commission is payable when a person who is able to purchase is introduced and expresses readiness and willingness by an unqualified offer to purchase, though such offer has not been accepted and could be withdrawn.

In connection with the third proposition, it is to be assumed that the offer is one within the terms that the agent has been authorised to invite; also, that the offer is not withdrawn by the applicant, but is refused by the vendor. In my judgment, on the facts in this case, the plaintiffs bring themselves within that proposition and are entitled to the commission claimed.

ORR, L.J. (at page 319)

The contract in this case was that commission should be payable in the event of the plaintiffs effecting an introduction of a person ready, able and willing to purchase at the named price, or at any other price that the defendant might agree to accept. It is not a case in which an offer made by a person so introduced was later withdrawn (*Dennis Reed Ltd.* v. *Goody*[46]), or in which the offer was expressed to be "subject to contract" (*Martin Gale & Wright* v. *Buswell*[47]), or qualified by some condition (*Graham and Scott (Southgate) Ltd.* v. *Oxlade*[48]). In those circumstances, in my judgment, on the authorities to which CAIRNS, L.J., has referred, the entitlement to commission arose when the person introduced by the plaintiffs made a firm offer for the purchase of the property in question on terms acceptable to the vendor. The views expressed by DENNING, L.J., in *McCallum* v. *Hicks*[49] and *Dennis Reed Ltd.* v. *Goody*[50] and by HODSON, J., in the latter case, that the entitlement does not arise until some later date, whether it be the signing of a contract or the completion of a sale, cannot, with great respect, be accepted as correct.

The result is that where a prospective vendor binds himself, on the terms with which we are here concerned, to more than one estate agent, he may find himself liable to pay more than one commission.

Peter Long & Partners *v.* Burns

[1956] 3 All E.R. 207

Where an estate agent is to be paid commission on the introduction of a person "ready, able and willing to purchase", and the person introduced signs a contract to purchase, commission is not payable if the contract is voidable on the ground of an innocent misrepresentation, for such a contract is not a "binding" one.

---

[46] [1950] 2 K.B. 277, C.A.
[47] (1961) 178 E.G. 709.
[48] [1950] 2 K.B. 257, C.A. See p. 39, *ante.*
[49] [1950] 2 K.B. 271, C.A.
[50] *Supra.*

The defendant employed the plaintiffs, who were estate agents, to sell a garage business for her, and to pay them commission "upon their introducing a person ready, able and willing to enter into a binding contract to purchase" the business. A Mrs Pritchard was induced to sign a contract to purchase by an innocent misrepresentation by a representative of the plaintiffs that under a road widening scheme two or three feet might be taken from the front of the garage. Later, Mrs Pritchard discovered that the scheme involved the compulsory purchase of the bulk of the garage site, and that it would be impossible to continue the business on what remained. Mrs Pritchard refused to complete. The plaintiffs claimed commission from the defendant.

Held, by the Court of Appeal, that the action failed for the words "binding contract" meant a contract which could be enforced by the vendor against the purchaser, and in the present case the contract was unenforceable because there had been an innocent misrepresentation on the part of the plaintiffs' representative.

MORRIS, L.J. (at page 211)

Counsel argues that, on the signing of the contract in this case, there was at that moment a binding contract even though it was a contract that was voidable. It seems to me, however, that in the present context the words "binding contract" mean a contract which can be enforced by the vendor against the purchaser. It is much too narrow a construction to say that the reference is to some contract which might temporarily have been regarded as a contract or a binding contract. The reference is to a contract that remains binding. I respectfully agree with the judgment of the Lord Chief Justice[51] on this point. I agree further with the Lord Chief Justice that commission is payable in a case of this kind when the contract is shown to be a binding contract in this sense. The result is that commission is not necessarily payable as soon as a contract is signed but only when it is shown to be a binding contract, and it may in many cases not be possible to prove that a contract is a binding contract until completion has taken place. Mention was made of the case in this Court of *Midgley Estates Ltd.* v. *Hand.*[52] In that case a contract was entered into by the plaintiffs, estate agents, and the defendant vendor under which it was agreed that the agents' commission should be paid as soon as the purchaser introduced by them

> "shall have signed a legally binding contract effected within a period of three months from this date".

The person introduced signed a legally binding contract within the three months, paid a deposit, and was permitted by the vendor to enter into occupation of the premises, but he was unable financially to complete the purchase and his deposit was forfeited. The agents claimed their commission, but the County Court Judge held that as the person they had introduced was not able to complete the purchase, they had not earned their commission. On appeal to this Court, it was held that although, generally speaking, when a vendor puts his property into the hands of an agent for sale, he contemplates that if a completed sale resulted, and not otherwise, he will be liable to pay the

---

[51] In the Court below: [1956] 2 All E.R. 25.
[52] [1952] 1 All E.R. 1394.

agent's commission out of the purchase price, the question depends on the construction of each particular contract. If its terms are clear, and not ambiguous, the Court will give effect to them. The plaintiff agents having introduced, within the stipulated period of time, a person who had bound himself to purchase the property by a legally binding contract, they had earned their commission, and the subsequent fate of the contract of sale did not affect their right to it. In that case, however, no suggestion was made that the contract was not binding, and, as the Lord Chief Justice pointed out, the difference between that case and the present is that in that case no one suggested that it was a contract that could be rescinded. It seems to me, therefore, that here, since there was an innocent misrepresentation as to an important matter, Mrs Pritchard was entitled to resile, and so there was no binding contract.

Drewery and another *v*. Ware-Lane

[1960] 3 All E.R. 529

A "prospective purchaser" means a person who has the buying of the property genuinely in prospect or in contemplation and is prepared to make a bona fide *offer with regard to it.*

> The plaintiffs, who were estate agents, undertook to offer the defendant's leasehold house for sale at £2,250. The defendant agreed to pay them commission "if and when (a) a prospective purchaser signs your purchaser's agreement, and (b) I sign your vendor's agreement". They introduced a Mr Sinho, who offered to pay £2,160 for the house, and the offer was accepted. He signed the "purchaser's agreement", and the defendant signed the "vendor's agreement". Both agreements were "subject to contract". Mr Sinho was unable to complete the purchase unless he obtained a mortgage, and no further progress was made. The defendant then sold the house to another person. Mr Sinho was prepared to go on with the purchase if the house had not been sold. The plaintiffs claimed commission from the defendant.
> *Held*, by the Court of Appeal, that commission was payable, for the plaintiffs had introduced a person who was a "prospective purchaser" within the meaning of the clause set out above, for he had the buying of the property genuinely in prospect or contemplation, and was prepared to make a *bona fide* offer with regard to it.

ORMEROD, L.J. (at page 532)

As far as I know, there is no authority on what is meant by "a prospective purchaser". Had the word "prospective" not been put in before "purchaser", it might very well be that, in view of the authorities, the plaintiffs might have been in some difficulty. It appears to me, however, that the word "prospective" does not connote necessarily either the term "ready" or "willing" or "able"; it means a man who has the question of buying this property in prospect or in contemplation and is prepared to make an offer with regard to it. This means that there must be a *bona fide* prospect. In the ordinary way it would be accepted that such an offer would be *bona fide* and it would be for the defendant to prove, if he sought to set it up, that the offer was not a *bona fide* offer.

In the present case the evidence is not disputed that Mr Sinho made an offer to purchase this property for £2,160; he signed an agreement to purchase for that sum, subject to contract; he stated in evidence that he was prepared to go on and would have gone on, had the defendant not put an end to negotiations by his letter of 12th January, and, indeed, he showed that he wished to be a purchaser of a house because a very short time later he bought another house for a sum rather more than the sum which he was prepared to pay for this house. It seems to me that, in the circumstances, it would be extremely difficult to describe Mr Sinho as anything other than a prospective purchaser and, if in fact he was a prospective purchaser, I find it difficult to see how any different construction can be put on cl. 4(a) of the letter of authority. The evidence was that the defendant, before he signed the letter of authority, read it, that he read also the vendor's agreement and he knew, therefore, that he was agreeing to sell the property for £2,160, subject to contract. The evidence of Mr Lowman, which was not accepted by the learned County Court Judge, was that the defendant also saw and read the agreement which was signed later in the day by the purchaser. That was not accepted by the learned County Court Judge, but it is clear that the defendant had the opportunity of reading it had he so wished to do.

The question in this case is a short one: it is purely a question of construction of cl. 4 of the letter of authority. As I see it, the clause does not admit of anything other than that, if two things happen—that is, if the vendor signs the vendor's agreement as put forward to him by the plaintiffs, and if a prospective purchaser signs their purchaser's agreement—the commission is payable. That happened in this case, and it appears to me that the appeal must be dismissed. It may very well be that it is undesirable that agreements of this kind should be signed by prospective vendors, and it may be wise for a prospective vendor to examine with very great care an agreement which he signs in these circumstances. That is not a matter for this Court. We have to consider the agreement which is put before us and consider what is the proper construction to be put on its terms.

Jaques v. Lloyd D. George & Partners Ltd.

[1968] 2 All E.R. 187

A clause stating that an estate agent is entitled to commission if he is instrumental in introducing a person "willing to sign a document capable of becoming a contract to purchase" is so uncertain that it is unenforceable.

A tenant of a café with a lease which had seven years to run instructed estate agents to sell it for him. They agreed to do so, and one of their representatives told him that if they found a suitable purchaser and the deal went through, he would have to pay them a commission of £250. He signed a form which stated: "Should we be instrumental in introducing a person willing to sign a document capable of becoming a contract to purchase at a price, which at any stage of the negotiations has been agreed by me, I agree to pay you a commission of £250". The meaning of this clause was not explained to him. The agents introduced a Mr Sullivan, who signed a contract of sale subject to the tenant's landlord granting a licence to assign and Sullivan supplying satisfactory references. The references were not satisfactory, and the landlord did not grant the licence. The matter was not proceeded with, and the agents claimed that they were entitled to commission.

Held, by the Court of Appeal, that they were not entitled to commission because (1) the terms of the agreement as to the payment of commission were so uncertain that they were unenforceable; and (2) the agents could not rely on the agreement because their representative had misrepresented the effect of the clause which the tenant had signed.

LORD DENNING, M.R. (at page 190)

We have had many cases on commission claimed by estate agents. The common understanding of mankind is that commission is only payable by the vendor when the property is sold. It is payable out of the purchase money; but some agents have sought, by their printed forms, to get commission even though the property has not been sold or the purchase money received. At first, it was "when a binding contract is signed". Next, it was if they introduced a person "ready, able and willing to purchase". Then they missed out "able" and wanted commission if they only got a "prospective" purchaser or a "willing" purchaser who was unable to purchase. Now we have got to the widest clause that I have yet seen.

> "Should you be instrumental in introducing a person willing to sign a document capable of becoming a contract to purchase . . ."

Can an estate agent insert such a clause and get away with it? I think not. I regard this clause as wholly unreasonable and totally uncertain. Suppose a man signed a piece of paper which had just got on it the address of the premises and the price. That could be said to be "a document capable of becoming a contract", even though there was not an offer contained in it. So, also, if a man signed a document which was expressly "subject to contract"; or even signed a blank form with all the blanks to be filled in. It might be said to be "a document capable of becoming a contract". Even if the man was quite unable to complete, he might still be a person "willing" to sign. So we are faced with the question in this case: to what extent can estate agents go in putting a form before vendors to sign?

The principles which, in my opinion, are applicable are these: When an estate agent is employed to find a purchaser for a business or a house, the ordinary understanding of mankind is that the commission is payable out of the purchase price when the matter is concluded. If the agent seeks to depart from that ordinary and well-understood term, then he must make it perfectly plain to his client. He must bring it home to him so as to make sure he agrees to it. When his representative produces a printed form and puts it before the client to sign, he should explain its effect to him, making it clear that it goes beyond the usual understanding in these matters. In the absence of such explanation, a client is entitled to assume that the form contains nothing unreasonable or oppressive. If he does not read it and the form is found afterwards to contain a term which is wholly unreasonable and totally uncertain, as this is, then the estate agent cannot enforce it against the innocent vendor. Applying this principle, I think that the clause in this case was wholly unreasonable and totally uncertain. It can and should be rejected, leaving the agent to his commission on the usual basis, namely, that, if the sale goes through, he gets his commission. That follows from the principle laid down by the House of Lords in *Scammell* v. *Ouston*,[53] together with the corollary stated by this Court in *Nicolene Ltd.* v. *Simmonds*.[54] The other principle is that an estate agent cannot rely on the printed form when his representative misrepresents the content or effect of the form. In *Dennis Reed Ltd.* v. *Goody*,[55] the representative said it was "merely a routine matter" when he asked the seller to sign. In the present case, he said: "If we find a suitable purchaser and the deal goes through, you pay £250". That is equivalent to a representation that the usual terms apply. It was a misrepresentation of the effect of the document. No person can hold another to a printed form which has been induced by a misrepresentation, albeit an innocent misrepresentation. I well remember SCRUTTON, L.J., in *L'Estrange* v. *F. Graucob Ltd.*[56] saying with emphasis: ". . . In the absence of fraud, *or, I will add, misrepresentation*, the person signing it is bound".

Applying this other principle, I think that the agent misrepresented the effect of the document, and for this reason it can and should be avoided, leaving the agent to claim for commission on the usual basis.

Blake & Co. *v.* Sohn and another

[1969] 3 All E.R. 123

An estate agent cannot claim damages for loss of commission if the person introduced by him rescinds a contract for the sale of the property because the vendor cannot make a good title to it, unless the agent can prove that it was an implied term of his instructions that the vendor would make out such title.

The plaintiffs were estate agents, who had been employed by the defendants to find a purchaser for a hotel which they owned. There was some adjoining land over which the defendants had an easement, and the plaintiffs considered that the defendants had a squatter's title to the land. The plaintiffs introduced a person who signed a contract to buy the hotel and the adjoining land, which was essential for its commercial development. The defendants, in fact, could not make out a good title to the land, and the contract was rescinded. The plaintiffs now claimed from the defendants damages for the loss of their commission on the ground that it was an implied term of their instructions that the defendants would make out a good title.

Held, by the Queen's Bench Division, that the action failed for there was no fault on the defendants' part rendering them liable in damages, and they had not impliedly contracted to make out a good title.

---

[53] [1941] 1 All E.R. 14.
[54] [1953] 1 All E.R. 822.
[55] [1950] 1 All E.R. 919, at pp. 924, 925.
[56] [1934] All E.R. Rep. 16, at p. 19.

NIELD, J. (at page 129)

Attention is also called to *George Trollope & Sons* v. *Martyn*[57] and in particular to a passage in which SCRUTTON, L.J., said:[58]

> "In my opinion the proposition that if the employer prevents the agent from earning his commission, he is liable, is much too wide. The prevention must be a fault or a default, in the sense that it is a breach of an express contract, or of some contract that must of necessity be implied, as where the employer has no title to the property he contracts to sell, or in breach of contract does not perform a term of the contract. In my opinion the 'prevention' by the employer must be 'wrongful', a 'default', a breach of his contract with the purchaser to entitle the agent to base an action upon it. Mr Bowstead heads his Art. 65 'if he wrongfully prevents'."

Finally, I turn to consider—I think that I can do so very briefly—the alternative claim under para. 9 of the statement of claim. The plaintiffs, in order to succeed on this, would have to show that the defendants, when instructing the plaintiffs to find a purchaser for the property, were promising contractually to be able to make out a good title. The only authority for this is the dictum of SCRUTTON, L.J., in *Trollope's* case,[59] and I find that I am not able to act on that in the light of all the other authorities to which I have had my attention directed.

Having considered all these cases and others which were cited to me, and having considered all the facts and the history of this matter and the principles which appear to me to be applicable, I am satisfied that this claim must fail. In the first place, I have to construe the bargain which was made between the plaintiffs and the defendants. That I must do in accordance with the first principle which I have ventured to advance and, in order to do that, to determine whether the event has happened on the happening of which it is agreed that commission should be payable. I am satisfied that that event has not happened. Secondly, there is no justification here for implying the term which I am asked to imply. Thirdly, it seems to me to be now settled that, in the normal course of things, commission is payable from the purchase price; that is to say, the completion of the sale is a condition precedent to payment of commission, unless there is unequivocal qualification. Here there is none; and, finally, what I am satisfied of is that there is no default on the part of the defendants amounting to such default as would entitle the plaintiffs to commission, in the light of all the circumstances.

---

[57] [1934] 2 K.B. 436.
[58] *Ibid.*, at p. 443.
[59] *Supra.*

(2) Indemnity[60]

Anglo Overseas Transport Ltd. *v.* Titan Industrial Corporation (United Kingdom) Ltd.

[1959] 2 Lloyd's Rep. 152

Where an agent has incurred personal liability to a third party in the course of carrying out his principal's instructions, he is entitled to an indemnity from his principal to the extent of that liability.

A firm of forwarding agents were employed by some shippers of goods to reserve shipping space for them on a vessel sailing from the port of London. The agents did so, but the space was unfilled because the goods were late in arriving at the port, and they had to pay to the shipowners damages for dead freight since, by the custom of the port, they incurred personal liability in these circumstances. They claimed an indemnity from their principals in respect of the sum they had to pay.

Held, by the Queen's Bench Division (Commercial Court), that the agents were entitled to an indemnity.

BARRY, J. (at page 160)

The only question which is relevant to the issue now under consideration is whether there is a custom in the London freight market whereby companies in the position of the plaintiff company may, at their option, contract as principals and involve themselves in personal liability under contracts which they make. I am abundantly satisfied on the evidence that in the London freight market it is certainly a usage or custom that forwarding agents and brokers should involve themselves in personal liability to the ship's agents with whom they are dealing.

It is, I think, impossible to see how business in this market could be conducted if no such personal liability was undertaken by the forwarding agents or brokers. There may well be delays in the completion of liner booking notes, or the ship's agents may have no knowledge at all of the identity or repute of the owners of various goods for which shipping space is booked, and it seems to me that, unless the ship or the ship's agents were entitled to look to the brokers who are booking the cargo space on their vessels, no shipowner would know whether he was going to be provided with a proper cargo or not until the moment when the ship was due to sail, and if no cargo was forthcoming, the shipowner or ship's agents would have no recourse to anyone except to shippers unknown to them in many cases, and whose credit they have no opportunity of investigating. . . .

In those circumstances, it cannot be, and is not questioned, that they are entitled to be indemnified against the expenses to which they have been put in connection with this transaction.

---

[60] As to the effect of the termination of the agency on the agent's right to an indemnity, see pp. 61–62, *post*.

Lage *v.* Siemens Brothers & Co. Ltd.

50

(1932) 42 Ll.L.Rep. 252

An agent cannot claim an indemnity in respect of expenses which he ~~~
on behalf of his principal if he is guilty of a breach of duty.

The plaintiffs were employed by the defendants as their ship's agents for their cable laying vessel *Faraday* at Rio de Janeiro. The defendants shipped about 1,803 miles of wire on her so that it could be used for a submarine cable from the island of Fernando Noronha to a point three miles off shore from Rio. About 1,800 miles of wire (which was not entered on her manifest because it was not being imported into Brazil) was used in this operation. The other three-mile length of wire was entered on the manifest and was to be used for linking up the off shore end of the cable with the city. The defendants were fined by the Rio Customs authorities because the three-mile length of wire had not passed through the Customs House, and no duty had been paid on it. The plaintiffs paid the fine for them, and now claimed an indemnity from them.

Held, by the King's Bench Division, that the action failed, for, on the facts, the plaintiffs had failed to discharge their duties as agents either with regard to informing the Customs authorities of the circumstances in which the three-mile length of wire was to be laid, or subsequently in not taking steps to avoid the imposition of the fine when that was threatened.

MCKINNON, J. (at page 262)

The plaintiffs, as I have said, claim that they are entitled to an indemnity against the liability that they have incurred as agents for the defendants. It is true that that is the fact, but clearly I do not think it is disputed by [counsel] that they cannot claim that indemnity if the liability arose by reason of their failure to discharge with reasonable diligence their duties as agents, or, secondly, if, after the imposition of the fine was threatened, they could have avoided that imposition by the exercise of reasonable care, skill and diligence in taking steps to have it remitted, as I hear from Mr de Barros it could be remitted if a reasonable explanation had been given. It is quite obvious to me that the plaintiffs took no reasonable steps to procure that the Customs were given that explanation. So far as I can see, in no communication to the Customs at any time did they even point out the simple story about the manner of discharge of this 41 tons, which, as I have said, must have been known to hundreds of people in Rio de Janeiro. I think that on that ground alone the plaintiffs fail to be entitled to the indemnity in this case.

Barron *v.* Fitzgerald

(1840) 6 Bing. N.C. 201

Where an agent has not complied with his principal's instructions, he is not
entitled to an indemnity in respect of liabilities which he has incurred.

In 1832 Fitzgerald instructed Barron and Stewart, who were partners, to insure his life for seven years in their names and to pay the first and subsequent premiums. They did so, but in 1834 Barron and Stewart renewed the policy in the names of Barron, Stewart and Smith who had joined the partnership. They paid the premiums down to 1838. Barron now claimed an indemnity from Fitzgerald in respect of all the premiums paid since 1834.

Held, by the Court of Common Pleas, that the action failed. Barron had not complied with his principal's instructions, and therefore had no right to an indemnity.

MAULE, J. (at page 206)

I agree also that the plaintiff must be nonsuited, because the letter of April 1832 gave him no authority to pay the premiums for which he now seeks to recover: that letter authorised him to pay premiums on a policy in the names of Barron and Stewart, and for the benefit of those two. I should not be disposed to construe such an authority very strictly; but the insertion of another name might make a great difference to the defendant, and therefore the policy should have been effected in the names specified by him. As the authority has been exceeded, the rule for a nonsuit must be made.

(3) Lien

Near-East Relief *v.* King, Chasseur & Co.

(1930) 36 Ll.L.Rep. 91

By s. 53(2) of the Marine Insurance Act 1906: "Unless otherwise agreed, the broker has, as against the assured, a lien upon the policy for the amount of the premium . . .; and where he has dealt with the person who employs him as a principal, he has also a lien on the policy in respect of any balance on any insurance account which may be due to him from such person, unless when the debt was incurred he had reason to believe that such person was only an agent."

The plaintiffs instructed the Marine and General Insurance Agency to insure a cargo from Beirut to America. The Marine and General Insurance Agency employed the defendants, who were marine insurance brokers, to effect the policy for them. The defendants had a general cover with the Argonaut Insurance Co., and declared the insurance under this cover. The Argonaut Insurance Co. issued a policy to them. The goods were lost when the vessel foundered, and the plaintiffs demanded the policy from the defendants so that they could claim against the Argonaut Insurance Co. But the defendants refused to surrender the policy because they contended that they had contracted with the Marine and General Insurance Agency as principals, and since the Agency owed them a sum of money on an insurance account, they had a lien on the policy under s. 53(2) of the Marine Insurance Act 1906.

Held, by the King's Bench Division, that the policy must be surrendered to the plaintiffs, for the defendants had no lien on it under s. 53(2) because it had been proved that they knew that the Marine and General Insurance Agency were acting as agents only.

WRIGHT, J. (at page 93)

Counsel has relied on a number of matters as pointing to that inference and to justify that conclusion. The name of the instructing company, the Marine and General Insurance Agency, in itself suggests that it was a concern engaged as insurance agents and engaged in effecting insurances for other parties. In 1924 a printed form of circular blank, obviously intended for circulation among possible clients, was sent by the Agency to the defendants, and that clearly indicated that the business they were doing was that of insurance agency business. Their practice was to effect open covers with the Argonaut Insurance Company, and they sent a certificate to the defendants certifying that they had the right of declaring insurances under that cover, and in that certificate there appears this clause: "Declarations are posted per registered post to Messrs King, Chasseur & Co., London, on the date of acceptance of the risk by Messrs Marine and General Insurance Agency and/or branch and/or agents". That is, in my judgment, clear indication that when this certificate was received by the defendants, the business which the Agency was doing was an insurance agency business.

When this particular risk came through and was dealt with, it was dealt with in the ordinary form. In the covering slip the name of the plaintiffs was not mentioned and would not have been in the ordinary course of business, but the printed certificate headed "Marine and General Insurance Agency" begins: "This is to certify that the undermentioned interest has been declared for insurance in London on open cover effected by Messrs King, Chasseur & Co., London, with Lloyd's and/or British companies for the account of Near East Relief." That certificate as soon as the loss was known was sent to the defendants, and there is no record anywhere in writing that the defendants were in any way surprised to receive it or raised any objection to its correctness or otherwise. That certificate clearly showed that the interest of the Agency in the insurance was as agents and nothing else. When the certificate was received by the defendants, they posted it on without any comment at all in writing to the underwriters, the Argonaut Insurance Company. Their letter, which is dated 3rd January, 1928, by which time they were fully aware of the position, says: "With reference to the loss of the steamship *Braga* we have now received a claim from Near East Relief for the total loss of their goods. The claim amounts to £625. Please let us have an early cheque in settlement. Enclosed please find documents". In the letter the defendants sent the original policy which they had in their possession and the certificate of insurance; they also sent other relevant documents.

The defendants wrote on the same day to the plaintiffs' representatives: "We thank you for your letter of yesterday's date enclosing documents in support of claim for total loss per steamship *Braga*. The documents are being presented to the underwriters and we will advise you in due course of any further requirements. In the meantime we beg to advise you settlement will be made through the issuers of the certificate in question". This is much relied on, but it does not seem to me to affect the position, but merely indicates that the defendants wanted an actual cash settlement to take place between the plaintiffs and the Agency, and not between themselves and the plaintiffs.

All these considerations to my mind constitute an almost overwhelming body of reasons to justify the conclusion that when the debt in question was incurred, the defendants had reason to believe that the Marine and General Insurance Agency were only agents in the matter of this insurance.

Against that, I have to consider very carefully the evidence given by one of the directors of the defendants who has been called, and who expressed a very limited degree of knowledge of the business between the Marine and General Insurance Agency and his company. I can only hope that the other directors have more knowledge of the business. He says that he thought that the Marine and General Insurance Agency were merchant insurance people. I confess, with great respect to his evidence, that I find it quite impossible to accept his view of the position. I do not know whether he has persuaded himself of that in the meantime or whether he is saying what is definitely untrue. I think probably not the latter, but I have heard his evidence and considered it very carefully, and I am quite unsatisfied with it; and I find as a fact that at the time that this insurance was taken up and the debt was incurred the defendants had reason to believe that the Marine and General Insurance Agency were only agents; and if that is so, it is clear on the authorities and the statute that they cannot justify their claim to a general lien.

E. TERMINATION OF AGENCY

(1) Modes of termination

Gillow & Co. v. Lord Aberdare

(1892) 9 T.L.R. 12

The relationship of principal and agent is terminated by the completion of the transaction for which the agent is employed.

The defendant employed the plaintiffs, who were agents, (i) to let his house furnished; or (ii) to let it unfurnished for a term of at least five years; or (iii) to sell the ground lease. The plaintiffs let the house furnished and were paid commission. They now claimed further commission for negotiating the sale of the ground lease to a Mr Tooth.

Held, by the Court of Appeal, that the action failed. The relationship of principal and agent was terminated when the plaintiffs let the house furnished. They had no authority to sell the ground lease to Tooth, and, in any case, the sale had not been brought about through them but through another agent.

LORD ESHER, M.R. (at page 12)

The respondent had instructed the appellants to do one of three things. They did one by letting the house furnished. They had then sent in their claim for their commission on such letting, and this had been paid. They had had no authority to let to a tenant and then at the end of this tenancy to enter into absolutely new negotiations on behalf of the respondent for the sale of the lease to him or anybody else. It was not contended that they had ever made any arrangement to give the tenant an option of purchase, and all Mr Tooth had said to them about purchasing the house had been that if he liked it, he might buy it. The sale to the tenant had not been brought about by the introduction of the plaintiffs, with whom Mr Tooth, indeed, had refused to have any dealings, but had been the result of independent action on his part in going to another firm of house agents and in making an offer to the respondent through them for the ground lease.

Marshall *v.* Glanville

(1917) 116 L.T. 560

The relationship of principal and agent is terminated by the happening of an event rendering further continuance of it impossible.

> In 1915 the plaintiff was employed by the defendant as a commercial traveller, and after the passing of the Military Service Act 1916 became liable to serve in the Armed Forces. He was to have been called up on 16th July, 1916, but on 14th July he joined the Royal Flying Corps. He claimed six months' commission from the defendant as damages for dismissal without notice.
>
> *Held*, by the King's Bench Division, that no commission was payable because the contract was frustrated by the operation of the Act of 1916.

MCCARDIE, J. (at page 561)

The effect of the enlistment of the plaintiff and the operation of the Military Service Act was to sweep away the basis of the arrangement between the parties. From July, 1916, the plaintiff could not lawfully fulfil his duty to the defendants, and the defendants could not lawfully avail themselves of his services. The agreement therefore came to an end. The true principle was laid down in the *Tamplin Steamship Company* v. *Anglo-Mexican, &c., Company*,[61] and the question was: Did the parties make their bargain on the footing that a particular state of things would continue to exist? Here it is clear that the parties contracted on the footing that it would continue to be lawful to perform and to accept the contemplated services, but from July, 1916, that footing no longer existed, and the contracts therefore came to an end.

A state of war is presumed by the law to be of such a permanent character as to put an end to contracts which depended on the continuance of the existence of such a state of things as prevailed in time of peace. The facts here wholly negative the suggestion that the contracts were only suspended.

---

[61] [1916] 2 A.C. 397.

Campanari *v*. Woodburn

(1854) 15 C.B. 400

The relationship of principal and agent is terminated by the death of the principal.

Woodburn promised the plaintiff that if the plaintiff succeeded in selling a picture for him, he would pay him £100. After Woodburn's death the plaintiff succeeded in selling the picture, and now claimed the £100 from Woodburn's administratrix.

Held, by the Court of Common Pleas, that the action failed, for the relationship of principal and agent had been terminated by the principal's death.

JERVIS, C.J. (at page 407)

As alleged on the face of the declaration, it does not appear that the original contract between the plaintiff and the intestate conferred upon the former an authority which was irrevocable: it simply states that it was agreed between the plaintiff and the intestate that the plaintiff should endeavour to sell a certain picture of the intestate, and that, if the plaintiff succeeded in selling the same, the intestate should pay him £100. So far, therefore, as appears in the declaration, it was a mere employment of the plaintiff to do the act, not carrying with it any irrevocable authority. It is plain that the intestate might in his lifetime have revoked the authority, without rendering himself liable to be called upon to pay the £100, though possibly the plaintiff might have had a remedy for a breach of the contract, if the intestate had wrongfully revoked his authority after he had been put to expense in endeavouring to dispose of the picture. In that way, perhaps, the plaintiff might have recovered damages by reason of the revocation. His death, however, was a revocation by the act of God, and the administratrix is not, in my judgment, responsible for anything. It was no fault of hers that the contract was not carried out. It must be taken to have been part of the original compact between the plaintiff and the intestate, that, whereas, on the one hand, he would receive a large sum if he succeeded in selling the picture, so, on the other hand, he would take the chance of his authority to sell being revoked by death or otherwise.

(2) Authority coupled with interest

Re Hannan's Empress Gold Mining and Development Co. Ltd.: Ex parte Carmichael

(1896) 75 L.T. 45

Where an authority is coupled with an interest, it is irrevocable.

Phillips was a promoter of a company to which he was going to sell a mining property. In February, 1896, he received from Carmichael an underwriting letter by which Carmichael agreed to subscribe for 1,000 shares in the company should the public not take them up. Carmichael was to be paid an underwriting commission for so doing.

The company was incorporated on 24th March. On 30th March Carmichael wrote to Phillips repudiating any authority contained in the underwriting letter to apply for shares on his behalf. But on 2nd April, Phillips applied for shares for Carmichael, and the company allotted them to Carmichael accordingly. Carmichael then applied for his name to be removed from the register of shareholders.

Held, by the Court of Appeal, that the authority given to Phillips to apply for shares for Carmichael was coupled with an interest, for its purpose was to enable Phillips to obtain the purchase price for the mine. It was therefore irrevocable, and Carmichael's name could not be removed from the register.

LINDLEY, L.J. (at page 46)

In this case the appellant's [i.e., Carmichael's] counsel ask us to regard this as a complex transaction, treating this document as consisting of two parts, a contract and an authority; and they contend that there is power for the appellant to revoke that authority. But when I come to consider the document and see the purpose for which the authority was given, it appears to me that the illustration put forward is not in point at all. Now, let us look at the document. It is called an "underwriting contract" . . . What is the true meaning of it? It is part of the bargain that the appellant shall for valuable consideration take certain shares in the company; and in order to enable Phillips to better carry out the transaction the appellant authorises him to make any further or other application for shares on the appellant's behalf, and he agrees not to revoke the contract. Phillips, acting upon that, does apply in the appellant's name for shares in the company. Why is the appellant not to be held to be a member of the company? Can it be said that under these circumstances his name was, in the words of s. 35 of the Companies Act 1862,[62] "without sufficient cause entered in the register of members of the company". It appears to me that there was ample cause for entering his name in the register. And the contention that the appellant had power to revoke the authority appears to me to be entirely futile. STIRLING, J.,[63] read a passage from the judgment in the case of *Clerk* v. *Laurie*,[64] where WILLIAMS, J., referring to the case of *Gaussen* v. *Morton*[65] as to the meaning of an authority coupled with an interest, said this: "What is meant by an authority coupled with an interest being irrevocable is this—that where an agreement is entered into on a sufficient consideration, whereby an authority is given for the purpose of securing some benefit to the donee of the authority, such an authority is irrevocable". That is the principle on which STIRLING, J., decided the present case, and that is the principle on which I think that this appeal ought to be decided. It appears to me quite obvious that the appellant's attempt to revoke the authority which he gave to Phillips fails utterly . . .

---

[62] Now replaced by Companies Act 1985, s. 359(1).
[63] In the Court below: (1896) 74 L.T. 550.
[64] (1857) 2 H. & N. 199.
[65] (1830) 10 B. & C. 731.

LOPES, L.J. (at page 46)

I am of the same opinion. The question is whether the appellant had any power to revoke the authority given by him to Phillips. If it is an authority coupled with an interest, it would be irrevocable. Therefore what we have to see is whether there is any interest coupled with the authority. What was the object which the parties had in view? It was to enable Phillips to obtain some benefit. He was vendor to the company, and the object of the underwriting contract was to secure a sufficient capital to provide funds for the purchase of the property, and so forth. Now, in the words of WILLIAMS, J., in the case of *Clerk* v. *Laurie*,[66] where an authority is given for the purposes of securing some benefit to the donee of the authority, such an authority is irrevocable.

Frith *v.* Frith

(1906) 94 L.T. 383

An authority coupled with an interest is constituted by an agreement which is entered into for valuable consideration, and either forms part of a security or is given for the purpose of securing some benefit to the donee of the authority.

> The defendant had been appointed by a power of attorney to take possession of and manage a property belonging to the plaintiff. The property was mortgaged in favour of a third party, and the defendant gave him a personal guarantee that he would pay the mortgage debt. The power of attorney did not mention the guarantee nor the mortgage debt. The plaintiff revoked the defendant's authority and sought to recover the property, but the defendant refused to deliver it up to him on the ground that the power of attorney constituted an authority coupled with an interest and could not be revoked.
>
> *Held*, by the Judicial Committee of the Privy Council, that the claim succeeded. The authority was not coupled with an interest and could be revoked.

LORD ATKINSON (at page 386)

It cannot be disputed that the general rule of law is that employment of the general character of the appellant's in this case can be terminated at the will of the employer. The proper conduct of the affairs of life necessitates that this should be so. The exception to this rule within which the appellant must bring himself, if he is to succeed, is that where "an agreement is entered into for sufficient consideration, and either forms part of a security, or is given for the purpose of securing some benefit to the donee of the authority, such authority is irrevocable": (*Story on Agency*, s. 476). It cannot be contended that the ordinary case of an agent or manager employed for pecuniary reward in the shape of a fixed salary comes within this exception, though his employment confers a benefit upon him. And their Lordships are of opinion that the position of the appellant under the instruments appointing him attorney over this estate

---

[66] *Supra.*

is in law that of an ordinary agent or manager employed at a salary, and nothing more, because the authority which was conferred upon him contains no reference to the special interest in the occupation of his post which his guarantee to Astwood might have given him, was not expressed or intended to be used for the purpose of subserving that interest, and has no connection with it. For these reasons their Lordships think that the authority given to the appellant was revocable. Several cases have been cited by the appellant's counsel in support of his second contention. On an examination of them it will be found that the essential distinction between this case and those cited is this, that in each of the latter power and authority were given to a particular individual to do a particular thing, the doing of which conferred a benefit upon him, the authority ceasing when the benefit was reaped, while in this case, as already pointed out, nothing of that kind was ever provided for or contemplated. In *Carmichael's Case*[67] the donor of the power, for valuable consideration, conferred upon the donee authority to do a particular thing in which the latter had an interest—namely, to apply for the shares of the company which the donee was promoting for the purpose of purchasing his own property from him, and the donor sought to revoke that authority before the benefit was reaped. In *Spooner* v. *Sandilands*[68] the donor charged his lands with certain debts due and to accrue due to the donees, and put the latter into the possession of those lands and into receipt of the rents and profits of them, for the express purpose of enabling the donees to discharge thereout these same debts; and it was sought to eject the donees before their debts were paid. In *Clerk* v. *Laurie*[69] a wife pledged to a bank dividends to which she was entitled to secure advances made to her husband. It was held that while the advances remained unpaid, she could not revoke the bank's authority to receive the dividends. In *Smart* v. *Sandars*[70] it was decided that the general authority of a factor in whose hands goods were placed for sale, to sell at the best price which could reasonably be obtained, could not be revoked after the factor had made advances on the security of the goods to the owner of them, and while these advances remained unpaid.

(3) *Effect of termination on agent's right to commission*

Reigate *v.* Union Manufacturing Co. (Ramsbottom) Ltd.

(1918) 118 L.T. 479

Where a principal has employed an agent for a fixed term, it will depend on the circumstances whether the principal is entitled to terminate the contract by ceasing to carry on business without having to pay further commission.

---

[67] I.e. *Re Hannan's Empress Gold Mining and Development Co. Ltd.: Ex parte Carmichael* (1896) 75 L.T. 45. See p. 54, *ante.*

[68] (1842) 1 Y. & C. 390.

[69] (1857) 2 H. & N. 199.

[70] (1848) 5 C.B. 895.

SCRUTTON, L.J. (at page 483)

This case adds another to the long line of cases in which the Courts have had to consider whether, with a contract made with a business firm or company, it is possible to terminate the carrying on of the business by the firm or company and so terminate the contract. A very large number of cases have been decided and a great amount of time has been taken up in endeavouring to see whether any principle can be extracted from these cases which will guide the Courts in future cases. . . .

Before you consider what has been decided in other cases, the first thing is to see what the parties have agreed to in the case under consideration; and, secondly, before troubling about seeing what you are to imply into the contract, the first thing is to see what the parties have expressed in the contract; and, when you have understood what the parties have expressed in the words there used, you are not to add implications because you think it would have been a reasonable thing to have put in the contract, or because you think you would have insisted on such a term being in the contract. You must only imply a term if it is necessary in the business sense to give efficacy to the contract; that is, if it is such a term that you can be confident that if at the time the contract was being negotiated someone had said to the parties, "What will happen in such a case?" they would have both replied, "Of course, so-and-so. We did not trouble to say that; it is too clear".

Unless you can come to some such conclusion as that, we ought not to imply a term which the parties themselves have not expressed when they have expressed other terms.

L. French & Co. Ltd. *v.* Leeston Shipping Co. Ltd.

[1922] All E.R. Rep. 314

Where a principal has employed an agent for a fixed term, it will depend on the circumstances whether the principal is entitled to terminate the contract by ceasing to carry on business without having to pay further commission.

A firm of shipbrokers effected a time charter-party for 18 months between the shipowners and the charterers. One of its clauses provided that the shipbrokers should be paid a commission of 2½% on "hire paid and earned under it". After four months of the period had expired, the shipowners sold the vessel concerned to the charterers, and refused to pay any further commission to the shipbrokers as the charter-party was terminated by the sale.

Held, by the House of Lords, that no further commission was payable. No term could be implied that the shipowners would not terminate the charter-party by the sale of the vessel.

LORD BUCKMASTER (at page 315)

I agree that it is always a dangerous matter to introduce into a contract by implication provisions which are not contained in express words, and it is never done by the Courts except under the pressure of conditions which compel the introduction of such terms for the purpose of giving what Lord BOWEN once described as "business efficacy" to the bargain between the parties. There is no need whatever in the present case for the introduction of any such term. The contract works perfectly well without any such words being implied, and, if it were intended on the part of the shipbroker to provide for the cessation of the commission which he earned owing to the avoidance of the charter-party, he ought to have arranged for that in express terms between himself and the shipowner.

Rhodes v. Forwood

[1874–80] All E.R. Rep. 476

Where a principal has employed an agent for a fixed term, it will depend on the circumstances whether the principal is entitled to terminate the contract by ceasing to carry on business without having to pay further commission.

A colliery owner appointed an agent to act for him on a commission basis for seven years in respect of all coal sent by the owner to Liverpool for sale. Four years later the owner sold the colliery, and refused to pay the agent any further commission.

Held, by the House of Lords, that no further commission was payable. No term could be implied into the contract that the owner would not sell the colliery and so disable himself from supplying coal to the agent.

LORD CAIRNS, L.C. (at page 481)

If all the coal after it was got out of the colliery might have been sold elsewhere, if the colliery might not have been worked at all, if the prices required to be fetched at Liverpool might have been such that the coal could not have been sold even after it went to Liverpool, if all that was in the power of the colliery owner and it could not be contended that there was any provision in this contract against any of those risks, why is it to be assumed with regard to the risk of the colliery owner selling the colliery to a purchaser, that there is an implied undertaking against that one risk? An agreement of this kind is obviously made upon the chances of risks of the sort I have referred to, none of which is expressed in the agreement. That which is in the mind of the parties, the principal, on the one hand, and the agents, on the other, is, supposing it to be convenient that the business should go on, and the coal find its way to the port of Liverpool, all that we require to stipulate for is that, on the one hand, the principal should have the security that his agents will be sufficiently energetic to sell a certain quantity of coal in the year, and, on the other hand, that the agents should be able, if a sufficient quantity of coal is not put into their hands for sale, to terminate the engagement. . . .

The simple point here appears to me to be, as it is admitted that there is no express contract which has been violated: Can your Lordships say that there is any implied contract which has been violated? I can find none. I cannot find any implied contract that the colliery owner would not sell his colliery.

LORD CHELMSFORD (at page 482)

But what is there in the agreement to prevent its coming positively to a premature end, either by the agents giving up business, or the owner giving up the colliery? The mere agreement for seven years, or the provisions for the determination of it on either side, will not be sufficient, and if it had been intended that the relations of the parties should absolutely continue for seven years, it ought to have been provided for. Not having been provided for, it cannot, in my opinion, be taken to have been intended. It was conceded that the appellant was not bound to send his coals to Liverpool. By sending them elsewhere he would voluntarily disable the agreement itself; what difference in point of fact can there be in disabling himself from performing it by parting with the colliery?

Turner *v.* Goldsmith

(1891) 64 L.T. 301

Where a principal has employed an agent for a fixed term, it will depend on the circumstances whether the principal is entitled to terminate the contract by ceasing to carry on business without having to pay further commission.

> Turner was employed on commission as a traveller by Goldsmith, who was a shirt manufacturer, for a period of five years. A clause in the contract stated that he was to do his utmost to sell "any shirts or other goods manufactured or sold by" Goldsmith. After two years from the date of the contract, Goldsmith's factory was burnt down, and Goldsmith went out of business. Turner then sued him for breach of the agreement, and claimed damages for loss of commission.
>
> *Held*, by the Court of Appeal, that the action succeeded. The agreement to pay commission was not conditional on the continued existence of the factory, for there was no proof that it was impossible for Goldsmith to have continued his business elsewhere. Turner's employment was not confined to articles *manufactured* by Goldsmith. It applied to all goods *sold* by him.

LINDLEY, L.J. (at page 302)

Then it was said that there is no undertaking by the company to go on manufacturing. It is true that there is no express, nor, so far as I see, any implied undertaking by the company to manufacture even a single shirt; they might buy the articles in the market. The defendant's place of business was burnt down; the defendant has given up business, and has made no effort to resume it. The plaintiff then says, "I am entitled to damages for your breach of the agreement to employ me for five years". The defendant pleads that the agreement was conditional on the continued existence of his business. On the face of the agreement there is no reference to the place of business, and no condition as to the defendant's continuing to manufacture or sell. How then can such a condition as the defendant contends for be implied?

The contract will be treated as subject to an implied condition, that it is to be in force only so long as a certain state of things continues, in those cases only where the parties must have contemplated the continuing of that state of things as the foundation of what was to be done. Here the parties cannot be taken to have contemplated the continuance of the defendant's manufactory as the foundation of what was to be done; for, as I have already observed, the plaintiff's employment was not confined to articles manufactured by the defendant. The action, therefore, in my opinion, is maintainable.

KAY, L.J. (at page 303)

If it had been shown that not only the manufactory but the business of the defendant had been destroyed by *vis major*, without any default of the defendant, I think that the plaintiff could not recover. But there is no proof that it is impossible for the defendant to carry on business in articles of the nature mentioned in the agreement. The contract is peculiar; it is to employ the plaintiff for five years certain, with power to either party to determine the employment at the end of that time by notice. The defendant has ceased to employ the plaintiff within the five years, and contends that a condition is to be implied that the manufactory must continue to exist. The plaintiff is not seeking to import anything into the contract; the defendant seeks to import the implied condition I have mentioned. I cannot import any such condition. If it had been proved that the defendant's power to carry on business had been taken away by something for which he was not responsible, I should say that there was no breach of the agreement; but here it was not taken away, and our decision is quite consistent with the class of cases where the parties have been excused from the performance of a contract because it was considered to be subject to an implied condition.

(4) Effect of termination on agent's right to indemnity

Chappell *v.* Bray

(1860) 6 H. & N. 145

Once an agent has acted on the authority given him by the principal and incurred liability towards a third party, he is entitled to an indemnity even though the principal later revokes his authority.

The plaintiff was a part owner of a vessel. He was authorised by his co-owners, of whom the defendant was one, to give orders for her repair and lengthening. He entered into a contract with a shipbuilder, and work was commenced. Later the defendant gave him notice that he would not pay for any of the work. The work was completed and paid for by the plaintiff, who now claimed an indemnity from the defendant in respect of a proportion of the cost.

Held, by the Court of Exchequer, that the action succeeded. Once the plaintiff had acted on his authority and had incurred liability towards the shipbuilder, he was entitled to an indemnity, and his right to it could not be affected by the termination of his authority by the defendant.

WILDE, B. (at page 152)

Then, the plaintiff having made out a *prima facie* case, the remaining question is, whether there is evidence that his authority was revoked. The proof of that ought to have come from the defendant. An authority cannot be revoked if it has passed an interest and has been executed. Here it had been executed; for the work was commenced, and consequently there was no power of revocation.

Rhodes *v*. Fielder, Jones & Harrison

(1919) 122 L.T. 128

Once an agent has properly incurred a liability to a third party even though such liability is not a truly legal liability, he is entitled to an indemnity even though the principal later revokes his authority.

> The plaintiff, who was a country solicitor, employed the defendants, who were London agents, to act for him in a case to be heard in the House of Lords. Counsel were briefed, and the case was won. Certain fees were due to counsel and the plaintiff told the defendants not to pay them, but they did so out of the plaintiff's money which was in their hands. The plaintiff brought an action for the recovery of the sum paid to counsel by the defendants.
>
> *Held*, by the King's Bench Division, that the action failed. The fees had been properly paid by the defendants, although counsel could not sue for them. Consequently the defendants were entitled to an indemnity, even though their authority to pay the fees had been revoked.

LUSH, J. (at page 129)

I now come to the . . . point taken by the plaintiff, which was that after the case had been heard in the House of Lords and after consultations had been held with counsel the plaintiff revoked his authority to the defendants to pay these fees; and it was argued that where the country solicitor instructs his London agents to brief counsel, and in the usual way the London agents, without their authority being in any way fettered, have consultations with counsel and incur liabilities towards counsel, the country solicitor can revoke his authority to his London agents and leave them either to default or pay the counsel's fee out of their own pockets.

I can only say that in my opinion such a position is entirely unsustainable. It is, of course, true that the London agents could not be sued by counsel for their fees, but that does not dispose of the question. If the London agents did not pay these fees, they would be placing themselves in a very serious position. A solicitor having undertaken to pay fees to counsel and then refusing to pay them, would in my view be guilty of misconduct. It is therefore impossible for the country solicitor to say after instructing his London agents that he can revoke his authority. The respondents did what they did at the request of the plaintiff, and made themselves responsible as honourable members of their profession for the payment of these fees. I think therefore that the Master was perfectly right in holding that there was no power to revoke the authority given.

(5) Period of notice of termination

Levy *v.* Goldhill & Co.

(1917) 117 L.T. 442

Where an agent is employed for an indefinite period, the principal is entitled to terminate the agreement without giving him notice of termination unless there is an express term in the contract or a trade custom to the contrary.

In May, 1915, the plaintiff was appointed by the defendants, who traded in sponges, brushes and hardware, to travel and obtain orders for them on a commission basis for an indefinite period. In March, 1916, the defendants wrote a letter to him terminating the agreement, and gave him no notice. He now claimed damages for wrongful dismissal on the ground that he was entitled to reasonable notice of the termination of the agreement.

Held, by the Chancery Division, that the action failed. The relationship was one of principal and agent, and not that of master and servant, and he was not entitled to notice of the termination of the agreement.

PETERSON, J. (at page 445)

Part of the plaintiff's claim in the present action is for damages for wrongful dismissal, on the ground that he was entitled to reasonable notice. It was not attempted to prove a custom of the trade, but it was said the plaintiff was entitled to reasonable notice. Now, in this case there was, in my opinion, no employment in the strict sense of the term. The plaintiff was not the servant in any way of the defendant; he was not bound to do any work whatever. The agreement merely provided that if the plaintiff introduced customers, and if the orders were accepted by the defendant, then the plaintiff should be entitled to half of any profits which were derived from those orders. There was no obligation on the part of the plaintiff to do work for the defendant, nor was there any obligation on the part of the defendant to provide work for the plaintiff, but there was merely a provision that the defendant would, in a certain event, pay certain remuneration to the plaintiff. In those circumstances *Joynson* v. *Hunt*[71] appears to me to be very much in point. That was a case which came before the Court of Appeal. The defendants wrote a letter to the plaintiff in these terms: "In reply to your favour, I beg to say we will give you the 2½ per cent. commission on all business you do for us in London, whether you send the buyers to buy or orders come through the post, or you take them and send them direct. You let us know to whom you show our samples, and, if business results from the transaction, we will forward your commission quarterly as you suggest. This refers to orders executed". The question in that case was whether the plaintiff was entitled to notice. The plaintiff tendered the evidence of witnesses to prove that there was a custom in the glove trade that six months' notice must

[71] (1905) 93 L.T. 470, C.A.

be given to terminate the agency of a commission agent. The learned Judge held that the defendants were entitled to terminate the agency without notice, and rejected the evidence of the alleged custom. The plaintiff appealed, and the Court of Appeal held the learned Judge was right in rejecting the evidence as to custom, on the ground that the custom would be inconsistent with the terms of the written agreement. COLLINS, M.R., said this:[72]

> "Having examined carefully the terms of this particular contract, I have come to the conclusion that the learned Judge was right in excluding evidence of the alleged custom. I think that the pleading in the statement of claim is somewhat misleading, inasmuch as it suggests an agreement between principal and agent to employ the agent, and sets up a custom in that employment. It seems to me to allege an employment of the plaintiff by the defendants as their agent, carrying with it the usual incidents of that employment. Then the defence sets out the exact terms of the bargain, which are admitted. It seems to me that those terms exclude the essential factor of employment by the defendants of the plaintiff as their agent as part of the agreement. Those terms are contained in a letter from the defendants to the plaintiff as follows" (then he reads the letter): "Now that letter, it seems to me, does not import any requirement by the principal to the agent to do anything, or any undertaking that the agent shall be employed or that the agent shall do anything to obtain orders. It is contended that by custom this arrangement cannot be terminated except by notice. It seems to me that that would be inconsistent with the terms of the express agreement. The written agreement excludes any employment by the defendants of the plaintiff, and any obligation on the plaintiff to do any work at all. An implied term as to notice would be quite inconsistent, the terms of the express contract being such as to negative any added obligation to give notice to terminate the arrangement. The letter only expresses willingness to pay a certain commission if the defendants choose to accept any orders which the plaintiff may choose to obtain for them."

ROMER and MATHEW, L.JJ. came to the same view. There are earlier cases to the same effect—namely, *Alexander* v. *Davis and Co.*,[73] *Henry* v. *Lowson*,[74] and *Motion* v. *Michaud*.[75]

In my opinion, therefore, on this part of the case the plaintiff is wrong, as he was not entitled to any notice whatever. There was no case of employment of the plaintiff, and therefore no wrongful dismissal.

Martin-Baker Aircraft Co. Ltd. *v.* Murison

[1955] 2 All E.R. 722

Where the relationship between the principal and agent is more that of master and servant, the agent is entitled to reasonable notice.

The plaintiffs, who were manufacturers of aircraft ejection seats, appointed the defendant to be their sole selling agent for their products in North America. The contract of appointment stated that he agreed (i) to use his best endeavours to promote

---

[72] *Ibid.*, at p. 471.
[73] (1885) 2 T.L.R. 142.
[74] (1885) 2 T.L.R. 199.
[75] (1892) 8 T.L.R. 447, C.A.

and extend the sale of the products throughout the territory; (ii) not to sell in the territory products which might be competitive with those manufactured by the plaintiffs; and (iii) to act as the plaintiffs' general consultant in relation to the marketing of their products in the territory. A question arose as to whether the agreement could be determined summarily or whether reasonable notice was necessary.

Held, by the Queen's Bench Division, that reasonable notice was necessary. The agreement fell more within the analogy of master and servant cases where the agreement was terminable by reasonable notice, for the defendant had to expend a great deal of time and money, and was subject to restriction as to the sale of other persons' products which might be competitive. In the circumstances 12 months' notice of termination was reasonable.

McNAIR, J. (at page 735)

I turn now to the question whether the agency agreement—to use that term without prejudicing the position for the moment—is also determinable. If it were a pure agency agreement and nothing more, there is much to be said for the view that it would be determinable summarily at any moment. An agreement of this nature, however, has to be looked at as a whole and the whole of its contents considered, and if one finds (as one finds here) that the person who is described as sole selling agent has to expend a great deal of time and money, and is subject to restriction as to the sale of other persons' products which may be competitive, it seems to me that it is a form of agreement which falls much more closely within the analogy of the strict master and servant cases where, admittedly, the agreement is terminable by reasonable notice, though not determinable summarily except in the event of misconduct.

I was urged to hold that this agency was terminable summarily on the basis of the decision in *Motion* v. *Michaud*,[76] before DAY, J., and in the Court of Appeal,[77] where it was held that an agreement, under which the plaintiff was appointed purely as a commission agent for the sale of the defendants' brandies in England, was determinable summarily or at will. DAY, J., decided that it was so, but in the course of his judgment he said[78]

"... there was no evidence of anything in the nature of service or of a contract only determinable by notice. The plaintiff was an independent merchant who sold wines for his own profit, and also sold champagne and beer for other people upon commission, and he undertook to see what he could do in the way of selling the defendants' brandies upon similar terms. He was in no sense their servant, and was not bound to devote any time or energy to the business on their behalf. No action in the nature of wrongful dismissal was maintainable in respect of such a relation."

The judgment of Lord ESHER, M.R., in the Court of Appeal is very shortly reported, and I cannot find any help in the determination of principle. It appears to me from the language of DAY, J., that, if he had had to consider the case now

---

[76] (1892) 8 T.L.R. 253.
[77] (1892) 8 T.L.R. 447, C.A.
[78] (1892) 8 T.L.R., at p. 253.

before me, he would clearly have taken the view, having regard to the form of the provisions of the agreement, that, although called an agency agreement, it was determinable only by reasonable notice.

PART II

RELATION BETWEEN PRINCIPAL
AND THIRD PARTY

(1) Rights and liabilities of undisclosed principals

Watteau *v*. Fenwick

[1891–4] All E.R. Rep. 897

A principal is liable to a third party in respect of any acts falling within the usual authority of the agent. A secret limitation of the agent's authority is of no effect.

Humble owned the Victoria Hotel. He sold it to Fenwick, who employed him as manager, and allowed his name to remain over the door. Fenwick forbade Humble to buy cigars on credit. But he bought some on credit from Watteau, who discovered the existence of Fenwick, and claimed their price from him.

Held, by the Queen's Bench Division, that the claim succeeded. It was within the usual authority of a manager of a hotel to buy cigars on credit, and a principal, whether disclosed or not, was liable for the acts of an agent acting within his authority. A secret limitation of such authority was of no avail when the principal was sued by the third party.

WILLS, J. (at page 898)

The plaintiff sues the defendants for the price of cigars supplied to the Victoria Hotel, Stockton-upon-Tees. The house was kept not by the defendants, but by a person named Humble. This person's name was over the door of the house. The plaintiff gave credit to him and to him alone, and had never heard of the defendants. The business, however, was really the defendants', and they had put Humble into it to manage it for them, and had forbidden him to buy cigars on credit. The cigars, however, were such as would usually be supplied to and dealt in at such an establishment. The learned County Court Judge held that the defendants were liable. I am of opinion that he was right.

There seems to be less of direct authority on the subject than one would expect. But I think the Lord Chief Justice during the argument laid down the correct principle, namely, once it is established that the defendant was the real principal, the ordinary doctrine as to principal and agent applies—that the principal is liable for all the acts of the agent which are within the authority usually confided to an agent of that character, notwithstanding limitations, as between the principal and the agent, put upon that authority. It is said that it is only so where there has been a holding out of authority, which cannot be said of a case where the person supplying the goods knew nothing of the existence of a

67

principal. But I do not think so; otherwise in every case of undisclosed principal, or at least in every case where the fact of there being a principal was undisclosed, the secret limitation of authority would prevail, and defeat the action of the person dealing with the agent and then discovering that he was an agent and had a principal.

Archer *v.* Stone

(1898) 78 L.T. 34

Where an agent acting for an undisclosed principal makes a false representation as to his principal's name, and knows that if he told the other contracting party of his principal's real name, no contract would be entered into, the contract is not enforceable against the other party by the undisclosed principal.

> Stone was the owner of a leasehold shop. In no circumstances did he wish to sell it to a Mr Smith, Mrs Smith or her sister, Miss Walker. Archer, acting for Mr Smith, approached Stone with a view to buying the property. Stone asked him if he was intending to buy it for Smith, and Archer said "No". Stone agreed to sell the property to Archer for £900. Archer then assigned the contract to Mrs Smith and Miss Walker. Stone found out that Archer had really been buying the property for Smith, and refused to proceed further. Archer, Mrs Smith and Miss Walker claimed specific performance of the contract.
>
> *Held*, by the Chancery Division, that a decree of specific performance would not be granted, for Archer's misrepresentation had induced Stone to agree to sell the property which he would not have done if he had known the truth, and consequently the contract was not enforceable.

NORTH, J. (at page 35)

I believe that Archer did definitely say that he was not purchasing for Smith or his nominees. The case was opened that he was justified in saying that he was not buying for Smith because he was buying for Mrs Smith and her sister. I am not sure that that is so as a matter of fact. I have seen the documents, and the agreement dated the day after the transaction is signed by Mr and Mrs Smith, and not by Miss Walker at all. I think the purchase was intended to be at least partly for Smith, though I have no doubt the money was to be found by the ladies. Then we come to the question of law. It is clear to my mind that the statement that, if Stone had known the property was to be bought by Smith or any of his party, he would not have sold, is true, and I am satisfied that all the parties concerned knew this, and put their heads together to outwit Stone. Under these circumstances I think the law is clear. It is true that a man may with impunity tell a lie in gross in the course of negotiations for a contract. But he cannot, in my opinion, tell a lie appurtenant. That is to say, if he tells a lie relating to any part of the contract or its subject-matter, which induces another person to contract to deal with his property in a way which he would not do if he knew the truth, the man who tells the lie cannot enforce his contract.

Said v. Butt

(1920) 124 L.T. 413

An undisclosed principal cannot enforce a contract where the personality of the contracting party is a material element.

Said wished to see a play on its first night at the Palace Theatre. He knew that the theatre owners would not sell a ticket to him because of previous differences between them over the production of one of his operas. He therefore asked a friend to buy a ticket for him. When he got to the theatre, Butt (the managing director) refused to allow him to proceed to his seat. Said brought an action for damages against Butt for wrongfully inducing the owners of the theatre to commit a breach of contract for the sale of the ticket.

Held, by the King's Bench Division, that the action failed. No contract existed on which Said could have sued the owners of the theatre because the personal element in the contract was strikingly present—and the owners had made it clear that in no circumstances would they contract with Said, especially as it was the first performance of the play.[1]

MCCARDIE, J. (at page 416)

A first night, therefore, is a special event, with special characteristics. As the plaintiff himself stated in evidence, the management only disposes of first night tickets for the stalls and dress circle to those whom it selects. I may add that it is scarcely likely to choose those who are antagonistic to the management, or who have attacked the character of the theatre officials. . . .

In my opinion, the defendant can rightly say, on the special circumstances of this case, that no contract existed on 23rd December, 1919, upon which the plaintiff could have sued the Palace Theatre Limited. The personal element was here strikingly present. The plaintiff knew that the Palace Theatre Limited would not contract with him for the sale of a seat for 23rd December. They had expressly refused to do so. He was well aware of their reasons. I hold that by the mere device of utilising the name and services of Mr Pollock, the plaintiff could not constitute himself a contractor with the Palace Theatre Limited against their knowledge, and contrary to their express refusal. He is disabled from asserting that he was the undisclosed principal of Mr Pollock. It follows, therefore, that the plaintiff has failed to prove that the defendant caused any breach of a contract between the Palace Theatre Limited and himself.

Dyster v. Randall & Sons

(1926) 135 L.T. 596

An undisclosed principal is entitled to enforce a contract made by his agent with a third party, where the agent has made no misrepresentation, and any personal

---

[1] See further, E. R. Hardy Ivamy, *Show Business and the Law* (1955), pp. 126–7.

qualification possessed by the agent did not form a material ingredient in the contract.

> The plaintiff had been in the employment of the defendants, who were auctioneers. They were engaged in the development of a building estate at Chatham. The plaintiff knew that the defendants would not entertain any offers he might make for the plots of land if he approached them direct. So he procured a friend of his named Crossley to buy the plots for him without disclosing the fact that he was acting as his agent. Crossley did so, but when the defendants found out that he was acting as agent for the plaintiff, they cancelled the agreement. The plaintiff now applied for a decree of specific performance. The defendants contended that he had deceived them in regard to the person with whom they were contracting, and that there was accordingly no contract.
>
> *Held*, by the Chancery Division, that the decree would be granted. There had been no misrepresentation by Crossley. Mere non-disclosure as to the person actually entitled to the benefit of a contract for the sale of real estate did not amount to misrepresentation, even though he knew that the other party would not enter into the contract, which was not one in which any personal qualifications possessed by Crossley formed a material ingredient, if the disclosure were made.

LAWRENCE, J. (at page 598)

It is essential to bear in mind that the agreement which the plaintiff seeks to enforce is not one in which any personal qualifications possessed by Crossley formed a material ingredient, but is a simple agreement for sale of land in consideration of a lump sum to be paid on completion. It is an agreement which the defendants would have entered into with any other person. It is well settled that the benefit of such an agreement is assignable and that the assignee can enforce specific performance of it. If Crossley had entered into the agreement on his own behalf (as the defendants believed he had), he could immediately have assigned it to the plaintiff and the defendants would have been bound to convey the plots to the plaintiff. Moreover, as Crossley had not before signing the agreement disclosed the fact that he was acting as agent, he was liable under it as principal, and the defendants could have compelled him to complete the purchase.

Further, it is to be noted that, in this case, there was no direct misrepresentation such as there was in *Archer* v. *Stone*.[2] Crossley was not asked by the defendants whether he was buying for the plaintiff, and he made no statement to the defendants on the subject. The real question, therefore, is whether Crossley's silence in the circumstances amounted to a misrepresentation which renders the agreement unenforceable in this Court. In my judgment, mere non-disclosure as to the person actually entitled to the benefit of a contract for the sale of real estate does not amount to misrepresentation, even though the contracting party knows that if the disclosure were made, the other party would not enter into the contract, *secus* if the contract were one in which some personal consideration formed a material ingredient: (see *Nash* v. *Dix*,[3] and

---

[2] (1898) 78 L.T. 34. See p. 68, *ante.*
[3] (1898) 78 L.T. 445.

Said v. *Butt*[4]). In *Nash* v. *Dix*[5] NORTH, J., held that the ostensible purchaser was acting on his own account and not as agent, but it appears to me that the learned Judge would have arrived at the same conclusion if the alleged agency had been established. In *Said* v. *Butt*[6] McCARDIE, J., relied entirely on the personal consideration which entered into the contract, and would obviously have decided otherwise if the personal element had been absent.

I therefore hold that the first ground relied upon by the defendants does not afford a good defence to the plaintiff's claim for specific performance.

Fred. Drughorn Ltd. *v.* Rederiakt. Transatlantic

[1918–19] All E.R. Rep. 1122

Evidence that the agent contracted on behalf of an undisclosed principal is admissible, provided that the evidence does not contradict the terms of the contract.

> A charter-party was signed by the shipowners and Lundgren as "charterer". Lundgren in fact was acting for an undisclosed principal. The undisclosed principal claimed that he was entitled to sue on the charter-party.
>
> *Held,* by the House of Lords, that he could do so. Evidence was admissible to show that Lundgren had contracted as agent on his behalf, for it did not contradict the terms of the contract.

VISCOUNT HALDANE (at page 1123)

Evidence of authority of an outside principal is not admissible if to give such evidence would be to contradict some term in the contract itself. It was held in *Humble* v. *Hunter*[7] that where a charterer dealt with somebody described as "the owner", evidence was not admissible to show that somebody else was the owner. That is perfectly intelligible. The question is not before us now, but I see no reason to question that where one has the description of a person as the owner of property, and it is a term of the contract that he should contract as owner of that property, one cannot show that another person is the real owner. That is not a question of agency—that is a question of property. In the same way in *Formby Bros.* v. *Formby*[8] the term was "proprietor", and "proprietor" was treated, in the opinion of the Court of Appeal, as on the same footing as the expression "owner". But we are not dealing with that case here. The principle remains, but the question is whether the principle applies to a charter-party where the person who says that he signed only as agent describes himself as the charterer. There may be something to be said from the heading of the charter-party in this case, and the reference to the company which claims to have been

---

[4] (1920) 124 L.T. 413. See p. 69, *ante.*
[5] *Supra.*
[6] *Supra.*
[7] (1848) 12 Q.B. 310.
[8] (1910) 102 L.T. 116.

his principal, for the proposition that, reading the document as a whole, there is evidence that he intended to convey that he was acting as agent for somebody else; but, whether that is so or not, the term "charterer" is a very different term from the term "owner" or the term "proprietor". A charterer may be and *prima facie* is merely entering into a contract. A charter-party is not a lease—it is a chattel that is being dealt with, a chattel that is essentially a mere subject of contract, and, although rights of ownership may be given under it, *prima facie* it is a contract for the hiring or use of the vessel. Under these circumstances it is in accordance with ordinary business common-sense and custom that charterers should be able to contract as agents for undisclosed principals who may come in and take the benefit of the charter-party.

But it is said that in this charter-party the terms are such as to exclude that notion. Why is that said to be so? Because the term "charterer" is used. I have already commented upon that. It is said that the term "charterer" was meant simply to describe a particular person who is to carry out the nomination of arbitrators and everything else which is contained in the charter-party—to give orders which can only be given by one person, and that for the working out of the charter-party it is essential to treat the person so contracting as designated as a person whose identity cannot be varied or contradicted. The answer to that is that the principal may take that place, and that the company, in this case acting through its agent, whoever that agent may be, will be in the same position as the charterer contracting originally. There is nothing in that proposition inconsistent with the stipulations of this charter-party, and, therefore, it appears to me that the qualifying principle of *Humble* v. *Hunter*,[9] that you shall not contradict the instrument by giving evidence of agency, has no application in this case.

(2) Ratification

Kelner v. Baxter

(1866) 15 L.T. 213

A principal cannot ratify the agent's act, if the principal was not in existence at the time when the act was done. In such circumstances the agent will be personally liable to the third party.

On 27th January a wine merchant supplied goods to the promoters of a projected company. On 1st February a meeting of the directors and promoters purported to ratify the contract of sale. On 20th February the company was formed. The price of the goods was not paid, so the merchant sued the promoters.

Held, by the Court of Common Pleas, that they were personally liable.[9a] The

---

[9] (1848) 12 Q.B. 310.

[9a] The effect of this decision has been given statutory force by the Companies Act 1985, s. 36(4) which states:—"Where a contract purports to be made by a company, or by a person as agent for a company, at a time when the company has not been formed, then subject to any agreement to the contrary the contract shall have effect as a contract entered into by the person purporting to act for the company or as agent for it, and he shall be personally liable on the contract accordingly".

purported ratification of the contract was a nullity as the company was not at that time in existence.

ERLE, C.J. (at page 214)

The action was for goods sold and delivered upon a written contract for sale. The words of the agreement were "Kelner to Baxter, Calisher, and Dales. I propose to sell stock, etc., for £900". The defendants as members of the projected company accepted this offer, and signed their names. The difficulty arises because the plaintiff addressed this proposal to the defendants on behalf of the company, and the question to be decided is whether there is anything on the face of the agreement to limit the personal liability of the defendants. If the company had been in existence at the time the agreement was signed, the defendants might have pledged its responsibility; but the document becomes wholly inoperative, if not binding on the parties themselves. The company was at that time a nonentity; and when it afterwards came into existence, it was a new creature just acquiring rights and liberties. The proposal to form a company does not create that company. Two consenting parties are necessary to a contract, therefore the mere ratification of the purchase by the company subsequently did not make a new contract.

BYLES, J. (at page 214)

The rule of law is, however, that people contracting as agents are personally responsible, where no other responsibility is created. Here the defendants personally bound themselves until the company was formed, and afterwards the company ratified the contract. The ratification, however, can have no effect unless the plaintiff agreed to it.

Ashbury Railway Carriage and Iron Co. Ltd. *v.* Riche

(1875) 33 L.T. 450

A principal cannot ratify an act done on his part by the agent if the principal has no capacity to do the act himself.

A company had power under its memorandum "to sell or lend all kinds of railway plant and to carry on the business of mechanical engineers and contractors". Its directors agreed to purchase a concession from Riche to construct a railway in Belgium, and this agreement was ratified by the company. Later the company repudiated the contract.

Held, by the House of Lords, that it was entitled to do so. The agreement was *ultra vires* the company, so the purported ratification was a nullity.[9b]

[9b] But the other party can hold the company liable where the Companies Act 1985, s. 35 applies. This section states: "(1) In favour of a person dealing with a company in good faith, any transaction decided on by the directors is deemed to be one which is within the capacity of the company to enter into, and the power of the directors to bind the company is deemed to be free of any limitation under the memorandum or articles. (2) A party to a transaction so decided on is not bound to enquire as to the capacity of the company to enter into it or as to any such limitation on the powers of the directors and is presumed to have acted in good faith unless the contrary is proved."

LORD CAIRNS, L.C. (at page 452)

The question is . . . the competency and power of the company to make the contract. I am of the opinion that this contract was, as I have said, entirely beyond the objects of the memorandum of association. If so, it was thereby placed beyond the powers of the company to make the contract. If so, it is not a question whether the contract ever was ratified or not ratified. If it was a contract void at its beginning, it was void for this reason—because the company could not make the contract. If every shareholder said, "That is a contract which we desire to make, which we authorise the directors to make, to which we sanction the placing the seal of the company", the case would not have stood in any different position to that in which it stands now. The company would thereby by unanimous assent have been attempting to do the very thing which by the [Companies] Act they were prohibited from doing. But if the company *ad ante* could not have authorised a contract of this sort being made, how could they subsequently have sanctioned the contract after in point of fact it had been made? [Counsel] endeavoured to contend that when a company had found that something had been done by the directors which ought not to have been done, they might be authorised to make the best they could of a difficulty into which they had thus been led, and therefore might acquire a power to sanction the contract being proceeded with. I am unable to sanction that suggestion. It appears to me it would be perfectly fatal to the whole scheme of legislation to which I have referred, if you were to hold, in the first place, that directors might do that which even the company could not do, and that then the company, finding out what had been done, could sanction subsequently what they could not have authorised antecedently.

Keighley, Maxsted & Co. *v.* Durant

[1900–3] All E.R. Rep. 40

An undisclosed principal cannot ratify.

> Keighley, Maxsted & Co. instructed Roberts, a corn merchant, to buy wheat from Durant on a joint account at 45/3d. per quarter. Roberts could not buy at this price, but he agreed to purchase wheat from Durant at 45/6d. per quarter, but did not disclose that he was buying on joint account. Keighley, Maxsted & Co. purported to ratify the agreement. The price was not paid to Durant, who thereupon claimed to hold Keighley, Maxsted & Co. liable on the contract.
>
> *Held*, by the House of Lords, that the action failed. The purported ratification was ineffective because Roberts had not disclosed the fact that he was acting for a principal. Only a principal whose existence had been disclosed could ratify.

LORD SHAND (at page 46)

The question . . . is whether, where a person has avowedly made a contract for himself—first, without a suggestion that he is acting to any extent for another (an undisclosed principal), and, secondly, without any authority to act for another, he can effectually bind a third party as principal, or as a joint obligant with himself, to the person with whom he contracted, by the fact that in his own mind merely he made a contract in the hope and expectation that his contract would be ratified or shared by the person as to whom he entertained that hope and expectation. I am clearly of opinion that he cannot. The only contract actually made is by the person himself and for himself; and it seems to me to be conclusive against the argument for the respondent, that if his reasoning were sound, it would be in his power, on an averment of what was passing in his own mind, to make the contract afterwards, either one for himself only, as in fact it was, or one affecting or binding on another as a contracting party, even although he had no authority for this. The result would be to give one of two contracting parties in his option, merely from what was passing in his own mind, and not disclosed, the power of saying that the contract was his alone, or a contract in which others were bound to him. That I think he certainly cannot do in any case where he had no authority when he made the contract to bind anyone but himself.

LORD DAVEY (at page 47)

The argument seems to be that, as the law permits an undisclosed principal on whose behalf a contract has been made to sue and be sued on the contract, and as the effect of ratification is equivalent to a previous mandate, a person who ratifies a contract intended, but not expressed, to be made on his behalf, is in the same position as any other undisclosed principal. Further, it is said that, whether the intention of the contractor be expressed or not, its existence is mere matter of evidence, and when once it is proved, the conclusion ought to follow. ROMER, L.J.,[10] held that on principle it ought to be held that ratification (in the case before the Court) is possible, and that to hold the contrary would be to establish an anomaly in the law, and, moreover, a useless one. I cannot agree. There is a wide difference between an agency existing at the date of the contract, which is susceptible of proof, and a repudiation of which by the agent would be fraudulent, and an intention locked up in the mind of the contractor, which he may either abandon or act on his own pleasure, and the ascertainment of which involves an inquiry into the state of his mind at the date of the contract. Where the intention to contract on behalf of another is expressed in the contract, it passes from the region of speculation into that of fact, and becomes irrevocable.

LORD LINDLEY (at page 53)

That ratification, when it exists, is equivalent to a previous authority is true enough (subject to some exceptions which need not be referred to). But before the one expression can be substituted for the other, care must be taken that ratification is established. It was strongly contended that there was no reason

---

[10] In the Court of Appeal: [1900] 1 Q.B. 629.

why the doctrine of ratification should not apply to undisclosed principals in general, and that no one could be injured by it if it were so applied. I am not convinced of this. But in this case there is no evidence of the fact that at the time when Roberts made his contract, he was really acting as distinguished from intending to act for the defendants as possible principals, and the decision appealed from, if affirmed, would introduce a very dangerous doctrine. It would enable one person to make a contract between two others by creating a principal and saying what his own undisclosed intentions were, and these could not be tested.

Bolton & Partners Ltd. *v.* Lambert

(1889) 60 L.T. 687

A principal can ratify an unauthorised acceptance by his agent of an offer made by a third party even though, in the meanwhile, the third party has withdrawn the offer.

On 8th December Lambert made an offer to Scratchley, a director of Bolton & Partners Ltd., to take from them a lease of certain property. This offer was accepted by Scratchley on 13th December, though he had no authority to do so. On 13th January Lambert withdrew his offer. Later the company purported to ratify the contract, and claimed specific performance of the agreement.

Held, by the Court of Appeal, that the action succeeded. The ratification dated back to the time of acceptance of the offer by the director, and the purported withdrawal of the offer was ineffective.

COTTON, L.J. (at page 691)

But it is said that there could be a withdrawal by the defendant on 13th January on this ground: the offer of the defendant had been accepted by Mr Scratchley, a director of the plaintiff company, but it is said that Mr Scratchley was not authorised to bind the company by acceptance of the offer, and, therefore, that until the company ratified Mr Scratchley's act there was no acceptance on behalf of the company binding on the company, and that the defendant could withdraw his offer. Is that so? The rule as to ratification by a principal of acts done by an assumed agent is that the ratification is thrown back to the date of the act done, and that the agent is put in the same position as if he had authority to do the act at the time the act was done by him.

. . . I think the proper view is that the acceptance by Mr Scratchley did constitute a contract subject to its being shown that Mr Scratchley had authority to bind the company. If that were not shown, there would be no contract on the part of the company; but when and as soon as authority was given to Mr Scratchley to bind the company, the authority was thrown back to the time when the act was done by Mr Scratchley, and prevented the defendant withdrawing his offer, because it was then no longer an offer, but a binding contract.

LINDLEY, L.J. (at page 691)

The question is, what is the consequence of the withdrawal of the offer after acceptance by the assumed agent, but before the authority of the agent was ratified? Is the withdrawal in time? It is said, on the one hand, that the ordinary principle of law applies, *viz.*, that an offer may be withdrawn before acceptance. That proposition is, of course, true. But the question is, acceptance by whom? It is not a question whether a mere offer can be withdrawn, but the question is, whether, when there has been, in fact, an acceptance which is in form an acceptance by a principal through his agent, though the person assuming to act as agent has not then been so authorised, is it or is it not too late to withdraw? I can find no authority in the books to warrant the contention that an offer which has been in form accepted by a principal, through an agent or otherwise, can be withdrawn. The true view, on the contrary, appears to be that the doctrine as to the retrospective action of ratification is applicable.

Watson *v.* Davies

(1931) 144 L.T. 545

A principal cannot ratify an unauthorised acceptance of an offer by his agent of an offer made by a third party if the acceptance is made "subject to ratification by the principal", and the third party in the meanwhile has withdrawn the offer.

On 7th January the chairman of a charity accepted an offer to sell property to it "subject to ratification" by its Board of Management. On 14th January the proposed vendor revoked the offer, but on the afternoon of that day the Board ratified the chairman's action. The Board brought an action for the specific performance of the contract.

Held, by the Chancery Division, that the action failed. Since the acceptance of the offer was "subject to ratification", the purported ratification only took effect from the time of ratification, and by that time the offer had been effectively withdrawn.

MAUGHAM, J. (at page 548)

Reference to [*Bolton & Partners Ltd.* v. *Lambert*[11]] will show that the contract was one entered into by a Mr Scratchley on behalf of a company called Bolton & Partners Limited. He had told the defendant that he would refer the defendant's written offer to his directors and he had subsequently written to the defendant stating—erroneously—that the directors had accepted the latter's written offer. On the face of the documents there was therefore a complete contract, and it was held by the Court of Appeal that the defect arising from the circumstance that Mr Scratchley had not obtained a proper authority to bind the company could be cured by a ratification, and this even though the defendant, the other party to the bargain, had purported to withdraw his offer. The ratification was

---

[11] (1889) 60 L.T. 687. This case is set out at p. 76, *ante*.

held to date back, the maxim applicable being *omnis ratihabitio retrotrahitur et priori mandato equiparatur*. In a case where the agent for one party to a negotiation informs the other party that he cannot enter into a contract binding his principal except subject to his approval, there is in truth no contract or contractual relation until the approval has been obtained. The agent has incurred no responsibility. In *Bolton & Partners Ltd.* v. *Lambert*[12] the decision of the Court was, I think, formed on the view that there was a contractual relation of some kind which could be turned into a contract with the company by a ratification, whilst in the absence of ratification there was a right of action against the agent for breach of warranty of authority. It was admitted that there could be no ratification of a legal nullity. An acceptance by an agent subject to ratification by his principal is legally a nullity until ratification, and is no more binding on the other party than an offer which can, as in the present case, be withdrawn before acceptance.

Managers of the Metropolitan Asylums Board *v.* Kingham & Sons

(1890) 6 T.L.R. 217

To enable a principal to sue on a contract made by an agent without his authority, the principal must ratify by the date on which performance under the contract is to commence, or if no date is fixed, the principal must ratify within a reasonable time.

> On 15th September, 1888, the defendants offered to supply eggs to the plaintiffs for six months commencing on 30th September. On 22nd September the plaintiffs' clerk without their authority told the defendants that their offer was accepted. On 24th September the defendants withdrew their offer as they realised that they had made a mistake as to the price of the eggs. On 6th October the plaintiffs resolved to hold the defendants to the contract and on 8th October affixed their seal to the contract. The defendants contended that the contract was not binding on them.
>
> *Held*, by the Queen's Bench Division, that the contract was not binding on the defendants. Although the defendants were not entitled to withdraw their offer (as decided in *Bolton & Partners Ltd.* v. *Lambert*), the purported ratification by the plaintiffs was too late because it had not been made by the date at which performance under the contract was to commence.

FRY, J. (at page 217)

In the beginning of September, 1888, the plaintiffs advertised for the supply of various kinds of food, and on 18th September the defendants sent in a tender for the supply of eggs on the form issued by the plaintiffs, and to which I will more particularly refer hereafter. On 22nd September the Board held a meeting, at which they passed a resolution that the defendants' tender should be accepted, and that the common seal of the corporation should be affixed. On the same day the plaintiffs' clerk wrote to the defendants informing them that their tender had

---

[12] *Supra*.

been accepted. On 24th September the defendants wrote that they had made a mistake in drawing up the tender, having inserted a wrong price for the goods to be supplied. It was admitted that this letter amounted to a withdrawal of the defendants' tender. On 6th October a meeting of the managers (the plaintiffs) was held, at which it was resolved that the defendants should be held to their contract. The seal was not in fact affixed until after 6th October. The defendants contended that the contract was not binding on them, and refused to supply any eggs. Now the question is whether the defendants did effectually withdraw by their letter of 24th September. The case of *Bolton & Partners Ltd.* v. *Lambert*[13] has been pressed upon me. In that case an offer by the defendant was accepted by an unauthorised agent on the part of the plaintiffs. The defendant withdrew his offer, and after the withdrawal the plaintiffs ratified the acceptance of the offer by the unauthorised agent. The Court of Appeal held there that the ratification by the plaintiffs related back to the acceptance by the unauthorised agent, and therefore the withdrawal by the defendant was inoperative. I am bound by that decision. It seems to establish that an offer accepted by an unauthorised person can be ratified by letter or by action brought. If ratification is to bind, it must be made within a reasonable time after acceptance by an unauthorised person. That reasonable time can never extend after the time at which the contract is to commence. I have to consider the terms of this offer in the form supplied by the plaintiffs. It says that contractors may learn the result by 24th September. The operative part is that the defendants contract and agree to supply eggs from 30th September, 1888, until 30th March, 1889. Upon any breach on the part of the contractors the contract may be determined. As to the form of acceptance, it appears to me that the course of business was that tenders must be delivered by 14th September. Meeting of the Board on 22nd September. Resolution that common seal should be put to the contract. Two days are allowed the clerk to put the common seal to the contract. The fair meaning is that defendants contracted to supply after seal affixed; then, and then only, they will deliver. Each party has contracted as if the common seal was to be the acceptance of the contract. I do not think that the doctrine in *Bolton & Partners Ltd.* v. *Lambert*[14] applies in this case. The ratification on 8th October was too late. The contract came into force on 1st October, a whole week before the ratification. The defendants could not know whether they were to supply the eggs then or not. I think the ratification was too late, and I dismiss this action with costs.

Grover and Grover Ltd. *v.* Mathews

(1910) 102 L.T. 650

Where an agent acting without authority has effected a fire insurance policy for his principal, the principal cannot ratify it after and with knowledge of the loss.

---

[13] (1889) 60 L.T. 687, C.A. See p. 76, *ante.*
[14] *Supra.*

On 4th March, 1909, an agent without authority from the plaintiffs insured their factory under a fire policy issued by the defendant. The factory was destroyed by fire in the afternoon of 27th March. In the evening with knowledge of the loss the plaintiffs purported to ratify the contract made by the agent, and claimed from the defendant the sum insured under the policy.

Held, by the King's Bench Division, that the action failed, for the ratification was ineffective.

HAMILTON, J. (at page 653)

The ratification of 27th March, whether you take it to be by the instructions given by Messrs Grover to Mr Brows on the Saturday night, or whether you take it to be by the letter written on their behalf by Mr Brows, is after a loss, and knowledge of the loss by the assured; and it appears to me that the authority of *Williams* v. *North China Insurance Company*[15] in the Court of Appeal binds me to say, if it be necessary to say so, that it is too late for ratification in this case; because, as it appears to me, the Court there recognised that a rule which would permit a principal to ratify an insurance even after the loss was known to him was an anomalous rule which it was not, for business reasons, desirable to extend, and which according to the authorities, had existed only in connection with marine insurance.[16] No case has been cited to me to suggest that this anomalous rule ought to be extended to fire insurance. I think the expressions used by the Lords Justices in that case show that they did not consider it should be extended beyond the existing cases.

Forman & Co. Pty. Ltd. *v.* The Ship "Liddesdale"

(1900) 82 L.T. 331

An unauthorised act of the agent may be ratified by the conduct of the principal. What amounts to ratification by conduct depends on the circumstances of each case.

A shipowner instructed Captain Clark, who was the master of a vessel damaged by stranding, to arrange for the damage to be repaired. Clark entered into a contract with ship repairers to do the equivalent of the stipulated repairs and also to do repairs due to deterioration. The repairers did both sets of repairs and tendered the vessel to the shipowner. The shipowner then sold her. The repairers now brought an action against the shipowner for the price of all the repairs on the ground that by receiving the vessel from them and selling her he had ratified the contract made by Clark.

Held, by the Judicial Committee of the Privy Council, that the action failed, for the shipowner's conduct did not amount to ratification.

---

[15] (1876) 1 C.P.D. 757. For a discussion of this case see Ivamy, *General Principles of Insurance Law* (5th edn., 1986) p. 538, footnote 4.

[16] Section 86 of the Marine Insurance Act 1906 sets out the present rule in these words:—"Where a contract of marine insurance is in good faith effected by one person on behalf of another, the person on whose behalf it is effected may ratify the contract even after he is aware of the loss".

LORD HOBHOUSE (at page 336)

Then the plaintiffs rely on the fact that the defendant took the ship and sold it; this being, as they contend, an acquiescence by the defendant, and a ratification of all that the plaintiffs had done. The mere fact that the defendant took the ship, which was his own property, and made the most he could of it, cannot give the plaintiffs any additional right. It is not like the case of an acceptance of goods which were not previously the property of the acceptor. But the plaintiffs connect the possession and sale of the ship with communications which, as they say, showed that the defendant had knowledge of the true state of the case. The messages passing on 4th and 5th January have just been cited for another purpose. On the 6th, Clark cabled as follows: "Contract provides renewals schedule prices. Girders, plates, under boilers more badly damaged than first anticipated; much deteriorated. Could not have remained in their present condition. Surveyors order renewal. Will make what repairs are absolutely necessary only through stranding". On the 28th the defendant wrote, being then under the impression that the cost of repairs was £11,000, which he treats as falling upon the underwriters. That, however, would not be the case with the cost of repairing deterioration. Up to that time nothing had been said to warn the defendant that he would be charged for repair of deterioration, and [the defendant] says that he had no suspicion of it. After he had written his letter of the 28th January he received a message bearing same date from Clark, which informed him that the expense would be £16,000, and some particulars were added which showed that it was for other than stranding damage. Upon that the defendant took legal advice, and resolved to dispute the claim. Ever since that time the parties have been hostile. There is nothing in these communications to show acquiescence and ratification. When the defendant wrote under the impression that £11,000 would be charged, he believed that it was all for stranding damage. He never in any way accepted the charge of £16,000. It was only in the course of the action that he learned that the plaintiffs had failed to perform their contract. The plaintiffs have not been led by the defendant's conduct to do anything prejudicial to themselves, and their Lordships cannot see in what respect the defendant has precluded himself from disputing his legal liability.

(3) Apparent authority of agent[17]

Farquharson Brothers & Co. v. King & Co.

(1902) 86 L.T. 810

Where a principal holds out his agent as having authority to sell the principal's

---

[17] See further, *Blades* v. *Free* (1829) 9 B. & C. 167, which is set out at p. 118, *post*; *Drew* v. *Nunn* (1879) 40 L.T. 671, which is set out at p. 119, *post*; and *Willis Faber & Co. Ltd.* v. *Joyce* (1911) 104 L.T. 576, which is set out at p. 121, *post*. Since the question of whether there is apparent authority is a matter of fact, only a few cases on this subject are included in this casebook.

property, and the agent sells it to a bona fide *purchaser, the principal is estopped from denying the purchaser's title. Whether there is such a holding out will depend on the facts.*

The plaintiffs, who were timber merchants, employed a Mr Capon as a confidential clerk. They informed the Surrey Commercial Dock Co. that he had authority to sign delivery orders in respect of any of their timber stored at the docks. Capon opened an account in the dock company's books in the name of Brown (who was a fictitious person). He transferred some of the plaintiffs' timber into Brown's name, and then in Brown's name sold it to the defendants, who bought it in good faith. The plaintiffs claimed the return of the timber, but the defendants contended that the plaintiffs had held out Capon as having authority to sell the timber, and were, therefore, estopped from denying the defendants' title to it.

Held, by the House of Lords, that the action succeeded, for, on the facts, the plaintiffs had not held out Capon as having authority to sell the timber.

LORD LINDLEY (at page 814)

The fact that the [defendants] bought the timber honestly did not confer on them a good title as against the real owners, who had done nothing which precluded them from denying, as against the [defendants], Capon's right to sell it. What have the [plaintiffs] done to mislead the [defendants] or to induce them to trust Capon? Absolutely nothing. There is nothing connecting the Surrey Commercial Dock Company with the [plaintiffs] in this transaction. The [defendants] were misled, not by what the [plaintiffs] did, or by any authority they gave to the dock company, but by the fraud of Capon. It is true in one sense that the [plaintiffs] enabled Capon to occasion this loss by placing him in the position which he occupied; but this is an instance of the unsoundness of the doctrine that where one or two innocent persons must suffer by the acts of a third, he who has enabled such third person to occasion the loss must sustain it. This *dictum* has never, to my knowledge, been applied where nothing has been done by one of the innocent parties which has, in fact, misled the other.

Waugh *v.* H. B. Clifford & Sons Ltd.

[1982] 1 All E.R. 1095

A solicitor's ostensible authority vis-à-vis *an opposing litigant to compromise an action is wider than his implied authority* vis-à-vis *his own client to do so.*

Waugh bought a house from Clifford & Sons Ltd., who were builders. He alleged that the walls were defective, and brought an action against them claiming damages for negligence. Negotiations between the parties' solicitors took place with a view to the compromise of the action whereby Cliffords would buy the house at an agreed valuation. Subsequently they withdrew their instructions to their solicitor and said that they no longer wished to buy the house. Waugh now brought an action for specific performance of a contract to buy the house which he contended arose out of the correspondence between the parties' solicitors. Cliffords denied liability on the ground that their solicitor had no authority to compromise the first action by making an agreement on their behalf to buy the house.

Held, by the Court of Appeal, that a decree of specific performance would be ordered, for Cliffords' solicitor had ostensible authority, even though he had no implied authority, to compromise the action. Such an authority did not extend to matters collateral to the suit. The agreement to buy the house did not involve matters collateral to the action, but went to the very heart of the action.

BRIGHTMAN, L.J. (at page 1105)

In none of the cases cited to us has there been any debate on the question whether the implied authority of the advocate or solicitor as between himself and his client is necessarily as extensive as the ostensible authority of the advocate or solicitor *vis-à-vis* the opposing litigant. The possibility of a difference seems to have been adverted to by BYLES, J. in *Prestwich* v. *Poley*.[18] In my judgment there is every reason to draw a distinction.

Suppose that a defamation action is on foot; that terms of compromise are discussed; and that the defendant's solicitor writes to the plaintiff's solicitor offering to compromise at a figure of £100,000, which the plaintiff desires to accept. It would in my view be officious on the part of the plaintiff's solicitor to demand to be satisfied as to the authority of the defendant's solicitor to make the offer. It is perfectly clear that the defendant's solicitor has *ostensible* authority to compromise on behalf of his client, notwithstanding the large sum involved. It is not incumbent on the plaintiff to seek the signature of the defendant, if an individual, or the seal of the defendant if a corporation, or the signature of a director.

But it does not follow that the defendant's solicitor would have *implied* authority to agree damages on that scale without the agreement of his client. In the light of the solicitor's knowledge of his client's cash position it might be quite unreasonable and indeed grossly negligent for the solicitor to commit his client to such a burden without first inquiring if it were acceptable. But that does not affect the *ostensible* authority of the solicitor to compromise, so as to place the plaintiff at risk if he fails to satisfy himself that the defendant's solicitor has sought the agreement of his client. Such a limitation on the ostensible authority of the solicitor would be unworkable. How is the opposing litigant to estimate on which side of the line a particular case falls?

It follows in my view that a solicitor (or counsel) may in a particular case have ostensible authority *vis-à-vis* the opposing litigant where he has no implied authority *vis-à-vis* his client. I see no objection to that. All that the opposing litigant need ask himself when testing the ostensible authority of the solicitor or counsel, is the question whether the compromise contains matter "collateral to the suit". The magnitude of the compromise, or the burden which its terms impose on the other party, is irrelevant. But much more than that question may need to be asked by a solicitor when deciding whether he can safely compromise without reference to his client.

If I am right so far, all that has to be considered in the present appeal, which

---

[18] (1865) 18 C.B.N.S. 806 at p. 809; 144 E.R. 662 at p. 664.

concerns *ostensible* and not *implied* authority, is whether the repurchase of the allegedly defective dwelling houses is properly to be described as matter collateral to the action. For the buyers and their solicitors had no notice of any limitation imposed by the builders on the *ostensible* authority of the builders' solicitors.

In the instant case the subject matter of the dispute was the performance of the agreements made on 13 and 18 July 1977. We have not seen these agreements but it was accepted before us that the builders agreed to sell and convey the sites, and to erect the dwelling houses thereon. The action which was compromised sought damages for breach of contract and for distress and inconvenience. In the pleadings in the action before us it was alleged that the properties were unsaleable in their present condition. The purpose of the 1977 agreements between the builders and the buyers was that each pair of buyers should receive for the stated price a properly built house in which they could live, and which they could place on the market when they wished to live elsewhere. They received nothing of the sort, if the plaintiffs are able to prove their case as pleaded.

I think it would be regrettable if this Court were to place too restrictive a limitation on the *ostensible* authority of solicitors and counsel to bind their clients to a compromise. I do not think we should decide that matter is "collateral" to the action unless it really involves extraneous subject matter, as in *Aspin* v. *Wilkinson*[19] and *Re a debtor (No. 1 of 1914)*.[20] So many compromises are made in Court, or in counsel's chambers, the solicitor but not the client being present. This is inevitably so where a corporation is involved. It is highly undesirable that the Court should place any unnecessary impediments in the way of that convenient procedure. A party on one side of the record and his solicitor ought usually to be able to rely without question on the existence of the authority of the solicitor on the other side of the record, without demanding that the seal of the corporation be affixed; or that a director should sign who can show that the articles confer the requisite power on him; or that the solicitor's correspondence with his client be produced to prove the authority of the solicitor. Only in the exceptional case, where the compromise introduces extraneous subject matter, should the solicitor or counsel retained in the action be put to proof of his authority. Of course it is incumbent on the solicitor to make certain that he is in fact authorised by his corporate or individual client to bind his client to a compromise. In a proper case he can agree without specific reference to his client. But in the great majority of cases, and certainly in all cases of magnitude, he will in practice take great care to consult his client, and I think that his client would be much aggrieved if in an important case involving large sums of money he relied on his implied authority. But that does not affect his *ostensible* authority *vis-à-vis* the opposing litigant.

I can see no difference, except in degree and in the importance of the subject

---

[19] (1879) 23 S.J. 388.
[20] [1914] 2 K.B. 758.

matter, between this case and the case of the sale of an imperfect chattel. In an action for damages by the purchaser of a defective chattel, it would be within the *ostensible* authority of the vendor's solicitor to agree terms of compromise involving the handing back of the defective chattel in exchange for the price paid. So it was within the *ostensible* authority of the solicitor in the present case to agree terms of compromise which involved the handing back of the defective houses in return for a price reflecting their current value in proper condition. I do not regard that as a compromise which trespasses on collateral matters. On the contrary, it is a compromise which goes to the very heart of the bargain which the plaintiffs made.

I wish to emphasise that I am not saying that the terms of compromise in the present case would have been within the *implied* authority of the builders' solicitors. That point does not arise, and cannot arise, since it is common ground that the builders had instructed their solicitors not to compromise on the proposed terms. I doubt whether it would have been within their *implied* authority to agree to a compromise which could lead to an immediate liability to pay £58,500, without asking first.

(4) Dispositions under the Factors Act 1889

Lowther *v.* Harris

[1926] All E.R. Rep. 352

By s. 1(1) of the Factors Act 1889: ". . . The expression 'mercantile agent' shall mean a mercantile agent having in the customary course of his business as such agent either authority to sell goods, or to consign goods for the purpose of sale, or to buy goods, or to raise money on the security of goods." A person can be a "mercantile agent" even though he acts for one principal only.

> Lowther, the owner of some tapestry, left it with Prior to dispose of for him. Prior had his own shop, and gave receipts and took cheques in his own registered business name. He had no general occupation as an agent, and acted only for one principal, i.e. Lowther. Although he had no authority to complete a sale without Lowther's authority, he sold the tapestry to Harris. Lowther then claimed damages for conversion from Harris.
>
> *Held*, by the King's Bench Division, that the claim failed. Harris had obtained a good title under the Factors Act 1889, for Prior was a mercantile agent within the meaning of s. 1(1), and the other conditions necessary under the Act in order to pass a good title had all been fulfilled.

WRIGHT, J. (at page 354)

The first question is whether Prior was a mercantile agent—that is, an agent doing a business in buying or selling, or both, having in the customary course of his business as such authority to sell goods. I hold that he was. Various objections have been raised. It was contended that Prior was a mere servant or shopman and had no independent status such as is essential to constitute a mercantile agent. It was held under the earlier Acts that the agent must not be a mere servant or shopman: *Cole* v. *North Western Bank*,[21] *Lamb* v. *Attenborough*,[22] *Hayman* v. *Flewker*.[23] I think this is still law under the present Act. In my opinion, Prior, who had his own shops and who gave receipts and took cheques in his own registered business name and earned commissions, was not a mere servant, but an agent, even though his discretionary authority was limited. It is also contended that even if he were an agent, he was acting as such for one principal only, the plaintiff, and that the Factors Act requires a general occupation as agent. This, I think, is erroneous. The contrary was decided under the old Acts in *Hayman* v. *Flewker*,[24] and I think the same is the law under the present Act. In *Weiner* v. *Harris*[25] it appears the agent was not acting for any other principal than the plaintiff, and this was the case also in *Hastings Ltd.* v. *Pearson*,[26] in respect of which case the Court of Appeal, in *Weiner* v. *Harris*[27] held that the agent was a mercantile agent.

Staffs Motor Guarantee Ltd. *v.* British Wagon Co. Ltd.[28]

[1934] All E.R. Rep. 322

Even though a buyer buys goods from a "mercantile agent", he will not get a good title to them where the agent was not in possession of them in his capacity as a "mercantile agent". Possession in any other capacity is not enough.

Heap, a car dealer, owned a lorry. He sold it to the British Wagon Co. Ltd., which thereupon let it out to him under a hire-purchase agreement. He then sold it to the Staffs Motor Guarantee Ltd., which now claimed that it had a good title to the lorry under the Factors Act 1889, for the company had bought it from Heap, who was a mercantile agent, in good faith, without knowledge of his lack of authority.

Held, by the King's Bench Division, that the claim had failed, for Heap, although he was a mercantile agent, was not in possession of the vehicle in that capacity, but only in the capacity of hire-purchaser.

MACKINNON, J. (at page 323)

Assuming that the transaction between Heap and the defendants was valid and

---

[21] (1875) L.R. 10 C.P. 354.

[22] (1862) 31 L.J.Q.B. 41.

[23] (1863) 32 L.J.C.P. 132.

[24] *Supra.*

[25] [1910] 1 K.B. 285.

[26] [1893] 1 Q.B. 62.

[27] *Supra.*

[28] This case was held in *Pacific Motor Auctions Pty., Ltd.* v. *Motor Credits (Hire Finance) Ltd.* [1965] 2 All E.R. 105, P.C., to have been wrongly decided, in so far as it concerned a point on the correct interpretation of s. 25(1) of the Sale of Goods Act 1893. There is nothing to suggest that the decision concerning s. 2(1) of the Factors Act 1889 set out above in the text is in any way affected. See generally, *Astley Industrial Trust Ltd.* v. *Miller (Oakes, Third Party)* [1968] 2 All E.R. 36, at p. 42 (*per* CHAPMAN, J.). The facts of that case were particularly involved, so, although it is an older authority, it seems preferable to include *Staffs Motor Guarantee Ltd.* v. *British Wagon Co. Ltd.* [1934] All E.R. Rep. 322 in this casebook, because the facts are less complicated. Section 25(1) of the Sale of Goods Act 1893 is now s. 24 of the Sale of Goods Act 1979.

that they purchased the lorry from him, the plaintiffs put their claim on one or other of two alternative grounds. The first of these alternative grounds is that this case falls within the Factors Act 1889, s. 2(1):

"Where a mercantile agent is, with the consent of the owner, in possession of goods or of the documents of title to goods, any sale, pledge, or other disposition of the goods, made by him when acting in the ordinary course of business of a mercantile agent, shall, subject to the provisions of this Act, be as valid as if he were expressly authorised by the owner of the goods to make the same; provided that the person taking under the disposition acts in good faith, and has not at the time of the disposition notice that the person making the disposition has not authority to make the same."

The plaintiffs say that the defendants entrusted the possession of the lorry to Heap, who was a mercantile agent for the sale of second-hand lorries, and that they, the plaintiffs, in good faith and without any notice of his want of authority, entered into a contract with him for the purchase of the lorry, and, therefore, they claim that they have a good title to the lorry as against the defendants pursuant to the provisions of that section. There was no doubt some evidence that Heap did deal in second-hand motor vehicles as an ordinary seller of them. I will suppose that, if the owner of a motor car had brought his car to Heap and asked him to sell it for him, and Heap had sold it to someone at a lower price than that authorised by the true owner or otherwise not in accordance with his instructions, the purchaser from Heap would be entitled under the section which I have quoted to claim as against the true owner. I think, however, that it has rightly been pointed out on behalf of the defendants that there would be this difficulty in the way of the plaintiffs' assertion of that claim—that, if the transaction between the defendants and Heap was a genuine transaction—and the plaintiffs' claim in this respect arises on that basis—the lorry had been sold by Heap to the defendants and had been entrusted by the defendants to Heap, not as a mercantile agent dealing in or selling motor vehicles, but as a hirer of the car, and, therefore, as its bailee. In these circumstances I do not think that it is open to the plaintiffs to say that the defendants entrusted the car to Heap as a mercantile agent. In *Oppenheimer* v. *Frazer and Wyatt*[29] CHANNELL, J., in examining the meaning of the Act of 1889, said:

"It seems to me that where there is a consent of the owner of the goods to the possession of the goods by the mercantile agent as a mercantile agent—and that is the important part of the matter—that then the statute applies, provided the other conditions are fulfilled."

I observe that Sir Mackenzie Chalmers, the learned draftsman of the Sale of Goods Act 1893, in his comment on this section, makes the same suggestion and illustrates it by what seems to be a very forcible example:

"Suppose a house were let furnished to a man who happened to be an auctioneer. Could he sell the furniture by auction and give a good title to the buyers? Surely not."

---

[29] [1907] 1 K.B. 519, at p. 527.

(*Chalmers' Sale of Goods Act 1893* (11th edn.), p. 176[30]). That, of course, is an extreme case, but, I think, the same principle applies here. Because one happens to entrust his goods to a man who is in other respects a mercantile agent, but with whom he is dealing, not as a mercantile agent, but in a different capacity, I do not think that it is open to a third party who buys the goods from that man to say that they were in his possession as a mercantile agent and that, therefore, he had power to sell them to a purchaser and so give him a good title to them. The claimant must be able to assert not only that the goods were in the man's possession as a mercantile agent, but also that they were entrusted by the owner to him as a mercantile agent. As CHANNELL, J., said, it is the consent of the owner of the goods to the possession of them by the mercantile agent as a mercantile agent that is the important part of the matter. I, therefore, think that this ground of the plaintiffs' claim fails.

Oppenheimer *v.* Attenborough & Son

[1904–7] All E.R. Rep. 1016

A buyer of goods from a "mercantile agent" will not get a good title to them under s. 2(1) of the Factors Act 1889 unless the sale takes place when the agent is "acting in the ordinary course of business of a mercantile agent".

> Oppenheimer, a diamond merchant, was induced by Schwabacher, a diamond broker, to let him have some diamonds so that he could show them to potential purchasers. Instead of selling them, Schwabacher pledged them with Attenborough & Son (a firm of pawnbrokers), as security for an advance to himself. The pawnbrokers did not know of a custom in the diamond trade that a broker had no authority to pledge diamonds, and they took the diamonds in good faith.
>
> *Held*, by the Court of Appeal, that the pledge was valid under the Factors Act 1889, s. 2(1), for the disposition had been made by a mercantile agent acting in the ordinary course of business, even though he had no authority to pledge by the custom of the trade.

LORD ALVERSTONE, C.J. (at page 1017)

It has been strenuously contended before us that the insertion of the words "when acting in the ordinary course of business as a mercantile agent" in sub-s. (1) of s. 2 was intended to impose some limit upon the generality of the previous Act. I think, after carefully considering the argument of counsel for the defendants, who pointed out the change from the expression in sub-s. (1) of s. 1, "course of his business" to the expression in sub-s. (1) of s. 2, "course of business of a mercantile agent", that there is a good deal to be said in favour of the view which he presented, that we ought not, at any rate unless we see clearly the argument in favour of such a view, to hold that the words "the ordinary course of business of a mercantile agent" were meant to deprive the pledgee of the protection given by former legislation, solely on the ground that the

---

[30] See now 18th edn. (1981), p. 296.

mercantile agent has acted in a way contrary to the custom of the particular trade and contrary to the way in which his principal in the particular case intended he should act.

In this case evidence was tendered before CHANNELL, J.,[31] and, I understand, not seriously disputed, that it was very unusual indeed, if not without exception, for diamond merchants ever to get advances on diamonds through agents. It was said that they always did this business themselves. For the purpose of this case, therefore, I will assume that counsel for the plaintiff has satisfied us, on evidence that was practically uncontradicted, that diamond merchants, as a matter of the custom of the trade, did not employ agents to obtain advances on diamonds. It seems to be conceded by the plaintiff's argument that an express prohibition by a principal to his agent would not be sufficient to prevent a pledge made by the agent in the course of business being protected in favour cᶠ the pledgee. I think my brother CHANNELL has taken a right view in this case, and that the protection given by the Act to a pledgee cannot be cut down by evidence of a custom of a particular trade that merchants in that trade always themselves conduct their business of obtaining advances on goods which were the subject of that trade. However, I think my brother CHANNELL has taken the right view, that evidence of this custom was not admissible for the purpose of defeating the protection which otherwise would be given to the pledgee.

It is quite plain when you are dealing with a person who is a mercantile agent, you have got to find out whether in the ordinary and customary course of his business as such agent he has authority to sell goods or consign them for sale or buy or raise money on them. I think one can clearly see, therefore, why the words "the customary course of his business as such agent" were inserted in sub-s. (1) of s. 1. There are many agents, such as carriers of goods, who receive goods, and yet it is not part of the customary course of the business of such agents to sell or consign them for the purpose of sale or to buy or raise money on them. Therefore, when you are dealing with an agent in possession of goods you have, no doubt, to consider what the condition of the agent is, and what his habits and customs would be when he is acting in the capacity of agent. Undoubtedly the case of an auctioneer entrusted with goods for sale, which counsel for the plaintiff pressed us with, is one of difficulty. He suggested that under sub-s. (1) of s. 2, if that subsection is not construed in the way he maintains it should be, an auctioneer would have power to pledge. But it seems to me that there may be particular agents, such for instance as auctioneers, by whom a pledge would be such a departure from the ordinary course of their business as to put the pledgee upon notice. No question of that kind arises here. Having therefore got the class of mercantile agent whose transactions are to be protected in the interest of the pledgee, you now get to sub-s. (1) of s. 2 as to the circumstances under which the transaction must be carried out. [His Lordship read the sub-section.] I think the expression in question means "acting in the transaction as a mercantile agent". There is no doubt that includes the limits

---

[31] In the Court below.

suggested, such as that the sale must not take place outside business hours, or under circumstances under which no agent in the trade would transact business.

In my opinion, these words "acting in the ordinary course of business of a mercantile agent" means that he shall be acting in the transaction as a mercantile agent would act who was carrying out a transaction which his master authorised him to carry out.

BUCKLEY, L.J. (at page 1020)

There is a difference between the expression in s. 1(1) and that used in s. 2(1), one being "in the course of his business", and the other "course of business of a mercantile agent", and I think I see the reason. Section 1(1) says:

> "A mercantile agent having, in the customary course of his business as such agent, authority either to sell",

and so on. That is speaking of the arrangement made between the true owner of the goods and the mercantile agent. It contemplates that the principal has given possession of the goods to the agent in the customary course of the business which the principal knows, or believes, the mercantile agent carries on as such. That has to do with the circumstances under which the agent gets possession of the goods, and to satisfy the definition he must get them in the customary course of his business as a mercantile agent. Section 2(1) deals with another matter. It deals with the stage at which the agent is going to deal with the goods in his possession with reference to some other person, and then the form of expression is altered thus: "when acting in the ordinary course of business of a mercantile agent".

The plaintiff's argument involves that we should read that as "of such mercantile agent", or, "of a mercantile agent in such trade as that in which he carries on business". I do not think it means that. I think it means "acting in such a way as a mercantile agent in the ordinary course of business as a mercantile agent would act"; that is to say, within business hours, at a proper place of business, and in other respects in the ordinary way in which a mercantile agent would act, so that there is nothing to lead the pledgee to suppose that anything is being done wrong, or to give him notice that the disposition is one which the mercantile agent had not authority for. Dealing with it in that way, it seems to me there is no great difficulty in the Act of Parliament.

KENNEDY, L.J. (at page 1021)

I do not feel quite sure as to the exact effect of the words in s. 2(1) "when acting in the ordinary course of business of a mercantile agent", and I reserve to myself the right to consider further what these words mean. But I am sure of this, that CHANNELL, J., was right in saying that they ought not to be taken to exclude a case in which a mercantile agent would not, as agent, have authority according to the custom of a particular trade to pledge goods which are the subject of that trade, on the ground that the pledging of such goods is a transaction which, in accordance with the custom of the particular trade, merchants prefer to do for

themselves. I think that what has been already said by my Lord and by
BUCKLEY, L.J., affords admirable reasons for that view, and the learned Judge
himself has pointed out that it would be a very strange thing if the members of
any particular trade could take themselves out of the operation of the Factors
Act by saying that they only authorised their agents to sell, and never gave them
authority to pledge. If, as it has been said, it is notorious in any business that the
person who is in the position of an agent does not have authority in the ordinary
course of business to pledge, then the proviso at the conclusion of the subsection protects the real owner of the goods whose property has been
improperly dealt with by the agent. What is exactly meant by the words, "made
by him when acting in the ordinary course of business of a mercantile agent", I
am not quite sure. I am inclined to think that it is meant to apply to a person
who, being a mercantile agent, is acting in time, and manner, and other
circumstances when he pledges as a mercantile agent, as if he had authority to
do it, and might reasonably do it.

Pearson *v.* Rose & Young Ltd.

[1950] 2 All E.R. 1027

*For the purposes of s. 2(1) of the Factors Act 1889 a mercantile agent is in
possession of the goods "with the consent of the owner" even though he may have
obtained possession of them by a trick.*[32]

> Pearson left his car with Hunt, a mercantile agent, to see what offers for it were made.
> He had not authorised Hunt to conclude a sale, nor did he intend to pass the property
> in the car. Hunt had the *animus furandi* when he obtained it. Shortly after obtaining
> the car he sold it to a third party. One of the contentions in the case was that a good
> title could not be passed under the Factors Act 1889 because Pearson had not
> "consented" to Hunt having possession of the car.
>
> *Held*, by the Court of Appeal, that even though possession of the car had been
> obtained by a trick, this was sufficient "consent" for the purpose of the Act.

DENNING, L.J. (at page 1031)

If the goods are stolen from the true owner by the mercantile agent, does that
mean that the owner does not consent to the mercantile agent having possession
of them? At first sight the answer seems to be obvious. No man ever consents to
the theft of his goods, but therein lurks a fallacy. There are many cases of

---

[32] A considerable part of the case was concerned with the difference between obtaining by false
pretences and larceny by a trick. These offences have been abolished by the Theft Act 1968, s. 33(3).
Section 15(1) of that Act creates the new offence of obtaining property by deception, and this covers
both obtaining by false pretences and larceny by trick. Accordingly, those parts of the extract of the
judgment concerning obtaining by false pretences and larceny by a trick are omitted as they are no
longer relevant.

larceny where the true owner consents to the thief having possession of the goods, but not to his stealing them. For instance, if the true owner allows the agent to have the goods on hire or for repair, and the agent later on makes up his mind to steal them and does so, either by breaking bulk . . . or by converting them to his own use . . . the true owner undoubtedly consented to his having possession of them. Take the same instance where the owner lets the agent have the goods on hire or for repair, but, with this difference, that the agent from the very beginning intended to steal the goods, . . . the owner undoubtedly consented to his having possession of them. His state of mind is the same in both instances. He consented to possession, but not to the theft of the goods. . . .

If the true owner was induced to part with the goods by some fraud on the part of the mercantile agent, does that mean that he did not consent to the mercantile agent having possession of them? Again the answer at first sight seems obvious. A consent obtained by fraud is no consent at all, because fraud negatives consent. The effect of fraud, however, in this, as in other parts of the law, is as a rule only to make the transaction voidable and not void, and if, therefore, an innocent purchaser has bought the goods before the transaction is avoided, the true owner cannot claim them back. For instance, if a mercantile agent should induce the owner to pass the property to him by some false pretence, as by giving him for display purposes, by falsely pretending that he was in a large way of business when he was not, then the owner cannot claim the goods back from an innocent purchaser who has bought them in good faith from the mercantile agent. . . . Whether the owner intended to pass the property or not, at any rate he consented to the agent having possession. The consent may have been obtained by fraud but, until avoided, it is a consent which enables the Factors Act to operate: see *per* SCRUTTON, L.J., in *Folkes* v. *King*.[33]

Newtons of Wembley Ltd. *v.* Williams

[1964] 2 All E.R. 532

By s. 9 of the Factors Act 1889: "Where a person having bought or agreed to buy goods, obtains with the consent of the seller possession of the goods . . . the delivery . . . of the goods . . . under any sale . . . to any person receiving the same in good faith and without notice of any lien or other right of the original seller in respect of the goods shall have the same effect as if the person making the delivery were a mercantile agent in possession of the goods . . ."

On 15th June 1962, the plaintiffs sold a car to a Mr Andrew, who gave them a cheque in payment. On 18th June they learnt that the cheque would not be met and disaffirmed the contract, but could not find the car. In July 1962, Andrew sold the car to a Mr Biss in Warren Street, London, which was an established street market for selling used cars. Biss bought in good faith and sold the car to the defendant. The plaintiffs claimed the car from him. The defendant claimed that he had a good title because Biss had a good title under s. 9 of the Factors Act 1889, for Andrew had acted

---

[33] [1923] 1 K.B. 282, at pp. 301 to 302, C.A.

in the way in which he would have been expected to act if he had been a mercantile agent, and must be regarded as having done so in view of the fact that the sale had taken place in a recognised street market.

Held, by the Court of Appeal, that this contention succeeded, and that the action failed.[34]

SELLERS, L.J. (at page 535)

Andrew had bought the goods and obtained them with the consent of the plaintiffs. He had subsequently delivered them on a sale to Biss and, if Biss was a person receiving them in good faith and without notice of any lien or other right of the original seller, then this section provides that the transaction shall have the same effect as if the person making the delivery (that is Andrew) were a mercantile agent in possession of the goods or documents of title with the consent of the owner. So the first part of s. 9 is complied with on the facts of this case, and the question arises whether the second part, the receiving of the goods in good faith (and it was not suggested that Biss had notice of any lien or other right of the original seller), had been complied with, and whether, in treating Andrew as a mercantile agent, the requirement had been complied with.

That requires a consideration in the first place of the question what is a mercantile agent. In s. 1(1) of the Factors Act 1889:

> "The expression 'mercantile agent' shall mean a mercantile agent having in the customary course of his business as such agent authority either to sell goods, or to consign goods for the purpose of sale, or to buy goods, or to raise money on the security of goods."

That description is to be applied to Andrew on the facts of this case. Section 2(1) deals with the powers of a mercantile agent with respect to the disposition of goods; it provides:

> "Where a mercantile agent is, with the consent of the owner, in possession of goods . . . any sale . . . made by him when acting in the ordinary course of business of a mercantile agent, shall, subject to the provisions of this Act, be as valid as if he were expressly authorised by the owner of the goods to make the same: provided that the person taking under the disposition acts in good faith, and has not at the time of the disposition notice that the person making the disposition has not authority to make the same."

One of the points taken on behalf of the plaintiffs was that although at the outset Andrew was a person who obtained, with the consent of the seller, possession of

---

[34] In April 1966 the Law Reform Committee in their 12th Report (Transfer of Title to Chattels) (Cmnd. 2958), in commenting on the decision in the above case, said in para. 33: "We do not think it is satisfactory that a person who obtains goods under a voidable contract which is avoided should nevertheless be treated for the purpose of s. 25(2) of the Sale of Goods Act as a person 'who having bought or agreed to buy goods obtains, with the consent of the seller, possession of the goods' and thus enabled to pass a good title to a third party. This is the result of the reference in s. 25(2) to a mercantile agent. . . . We accordingly think that where a contract of sale has been effectively rescinded by the owner notifying the person in possession of the goods it should not be possible for the latter to pass a good title, and it should be made clear that for this purpose s. 23 of the Sale of Goods Act prevails over s. 25(2)". Section 23 of the Sale of Goods Act 1893 is now s. 23 of the Sale of Goods Act 1979. Section 25(2) of the Act of 1893 is now s. 25(1) of the Act of 1979.

the goods, at the time when this transaction took place that consent no longer operated: it had been withdrawn by the rescission of the contract; but Andrew was in possession of the goods of the plaintiffs, a possession which he had obtained at the outset with their consent. Sub-section (2) of s. 2 provides that

> "Where a mercantile agent has, with the consent of the owner, been in the possession of goods . . . any sale . . . which would have been valid if the consent had continued, shall be valid notwithstanding the determination of the consent . . ."

That is an express provision which altered the law as it had been laid down in an earlier case[35] some time in 1868. Notwithstanding that which the plaintiffs had done to terminate their contract and withdraw their consent, they had in fact—true, through inability to do otherwise—left the possession of their car with Andrew.

The only other question which arises is how far, on the construction of this section, that takes the buyer (the defendant in this case), relying on what happened between Andrew and Biss. It had been treated by the learned Judge[36] applying s. 9, as placing Andrew in the position of a mercantile agent but with the obligation on the defendant of establishing not only that Biss took in good faith (I leave out the other position: nothing arose on that) but also that the transaction between Andrew and Biss (Andrew being treated as a mercantile agent in accordance with s. 9) was an "acting in the ordinary course of business of a mercantile agent". There is a possible construction which was urged on us that he would be so acting under s. 9 as a mercantile agent—that it would be assumed or deemed that he was acting in the ordinary course of business; and investigations were made in other parts of the Act of 1889, and in particular s. 8, to see whether any support could be got for that view. . . .

Before one takes too favourable a view for the buyer and too harsh a view against the true owner of the goods where s. 9 can be invoked, one must remember that it is taking away the right which would have existed at Common Law, and for myself I should not be prepared to enlarge it more than the words clearly permitted and required. It seems to me that all that s. 9 can be said clearly to do is to place the seller on this second sale, the sub-sale to the buyer, in the position of a mercantile agent when he has in fact in his possession the goods of somebody else and does no more than clothe him with that fictitious or notional position in this transaction. Then when one comes to look at s. 2(1), a mercantile agent to whom that section applies has, in order that the buyer may get the full advantage of this section, to establish that he, the mercantile agent, was acting in the ordinary course of business. It is said that that is a somewhat vague phrase, and we have referred to some authorities with regard to that. It may be that in some cases precisely what is in "the ordinary course of business" of a mercantile agent may call for some special investigation, but on the face of it it seems to me that it envisages a transaction by a mercantile agent and is to be

---

[35] *Fuentes* v. *Montis* (1868) L.R. 3 C.P. 268, *affd.* Ex. Ch. (1868) L.R. 4 C.P. 93.
[36] [1964] 2 All E.R. 135, at p. 139.

derived from such evidence as is either known to the Court or established by evidence as to what would be the ordinary course of business.

The question arises here on the evidence whether this transaction is to be said to have been in the ordinary course of business of a mercantile agent. Learned counsel for the plaintiffs sought to establish that a transaction taking place in this somewhat unusual market, the street kerb in Warren Street, was on the face of it something which was not an ordinary business transaction in any way, by a mercantile agent or anybody else, but was to some extent suspect; but the learned Judge had evidence about this and he said[37] (and I think it is within the knowledge of the Court) that there had been an established market in secondhand cars in this area on this very site for a long time. Although the learned Judge said[38] that he had some doubt at one time about this being in the ordinary course of business—as he pointed out, there were no business premises, the sale was in the street, and the sale was for cash—on the other hand, he comes to the conclusion, which I think cannot be challenged, that there was in Warren Street and its neighbourhood an established street market for cash dealing in cars. When one looks at what took place, and finds the prospective buyer coming up and getting into contact with the prospective seller in regard to a car in that area, with an offer and an acceptance, with the trial of the car and a looking over it and some questions asked and a delivery—I do not find anything to indicate that it was not in the ordinary course of business of a mercantile agent. It seems to me that the defendant has established that essential fact.

That leaves only the other matter which has to be proved, likewise by the defendant, whether Biss acted in good faith. If he did, then the requirements of s. 9 are complete, and the result follows that he got a good title, as if the goods had been sold to him with the consent of the owner.

Now on good faith we had a submission made to us stressing very largely the price that was paid. I do not propose to go into all the evidence about that. This was apparently a secondhand car. It may have been in fact a 1960 model. It had not the advantage of being licensed in 1960. It was in fact licensed in November, 1959. Neither had it an overdrive. When all the evidence is gone into, it does reveal that Andrew gave a cheque for £745 for the car, but that in no way is an indication of its value or the price that any honest buyer would have paid for it. Andrew never intended to pay a penny for it. The evidence goes further and makes reference to figures £600 or more appearing in Glass's Guide, which is some indication of its value but it is by no means conclusive, and one has in fact at the other end a sale which has not been attacked as not being a *bona fide* one, no later than 12th July, 1962, when all that the buyer, Mr Biss, could get for it from the defendant was £505. Those matters have all to be looked at in the light of the Judge's finding on the evidence. He appreciated the point that was being made of a low price, of a receipt held by Andrew and not, as would have been

---

[37] *Ibid.*, at p. 139.
[38] *Ibid.*, at p. 139.

appropriate, by Biss, and the whole of the circumstances in which the transaction took place—and the fact that there was a £45 loss on the sale. On the matter of good faith he said:[39]

> "One can follow these and other criticisms of the Andrew/Biss deal, but the fundamental answer to counsel for the plaintiffs' submission is that I saw and heard Mr Biss and I entirely accept his evidence. I am completely satisfied, and find, that he acted throughout in complete good faith and without the slightest idea of any defect in Andrew's title."

In those circumstances I find nothing to complain about in the learned Judge's judgment. He applied the facts to s. 9. He interpreted the section in the way in which the plaintiffs submitted it ought to be interpreted. The learned Lord Justice said:[40]

> "It follows, therefore, that the sale by Andrew to Biss was covered by s. 9 and s. 2 of the Factors Act 1889. It had the same effect as though Andrew were a mercantile agent in possession of the car with the consent of the plaintiffs; that is to say, that, if the sale was in ordinary course of business of a mercantile agent, it was effective to transfer title provided that Biss acted in good faith without notice of any rights of the plaintiffs in respect of the car and without notice that Andrew had no authority to sell."

I think that that was established.

(5) Effect of judgment against agent

Kendall v. Hamilton

(1879) 41 L.T. 418

A third party may sue either the principal or the agent. But if a third party obtains judgment against the agent, he cannot then sue the principal.

LORD CAIRNS, L.C. (at page 419)

Now, I take it to be clear that where an agent contracts, in his own name, for an undisclosed principal, the person with whom he contracts may sue the agent, or he may sue the principal, but if he sues the agent and recovers judgment, he cannot afterwards sue the principal, even though the judgment does not result in satisfaction of the debt. But the reasons why this must be the case are, I think, obvious. It would be clearly contrary to every principle of justice that the creditor who had seen and known, and dealt with, and given credit to the agent, should be driven to sue the principal if he does not wish to sue him, and, on the

---

[39] [1964] 2 All E.R. 135, at p. 139.
[40] *Ibid.*, at p. 139.

other hand, it would be equally contrary to justice that the creditor, on discovering the principal, who really has had the benefit of the loan, should be prevented from suing him if he wishes to do so. But it would be no less contrary to justice that the creditor should be able to sue first the agent and then the principal, when there was no contract, and when it was never the intention of any of the parties that he should do so. Again, if an action were brought and judgment recovered against the agent, he, the agent, would have a right of action for indemnity against his principal, while, if the principal were liable to be also sued, he would be vexed with a double action. Further than this, if actions could be brought, and judgments recovered, first against the agent and afterwards against the principal, you would have two judgments in existence for the same debt or cause of action; they might not necessarily be for the same amounts, and there might be recoveries had, or liens and charges created, by means of both, and there would be no mode upon the face of the judgments, or by any means short of a fresh proceeding, of showing that the two judgments were really for the same debt or cause of action, and that satisfaction of one was, or would be, satisfaction of both.

(6) Third party's right of set-off

Cooke & Sons v. Eshelby

(1886) 56 L.T. 673

A third party cannot set-off against an undisclosed principal a debt due to him from the agent, where he has no belief one way or the other whether the person with whom he is dealing in the transaction is acting for himself or on behalf of another person.

> Livesey & Co., a firm of brokers, acting in fact on behalf of an undisclosed principal, sold some cotton to Cooke. The price was not paid, so Eshelby (who had been appointed trustee in bankruptcy when the undisclosed principal went bankrupt) claimed it from Cooke. Cooke contended that he was entitled to set-off against the price a debt owed to him by the brokers. At the time of the sale Cooke did not know whether the brokers were acting for a principal or on their own account.
>
> *Held*, by the House of Lords, that Cooke was not entitled to set-off the debt, for, at the time of the making the contract, he did not in fact believe that the brokers were selling on their own account.

LORD WATSON (at page 675)

According to the practice of the Liverpool Cotton Market, with which [Cooke was] familiar, brokers in the position of Livesey, Sons, and Co., buy and sell both for themselves and for principals, and in the latter case they transact sometimes in their own name without disclosing their agency, and at other times in the name of their principal. In their answer to an interrogatory by [Eshelby] touching [his] belief that Livesey, Sons, and Co. were acting on behalf of principals in the two transactions in question [Cooke says]: "We had no belief upon the subject. We dealt with Livesey and Co. as principals, not knowing whether they were acting as brokers on behalf of principals, or on their own account as principals". That is a very candid statement, but I do not think any other answer could have been honestly made by persons who at the time of the transactions were cognisant of the practice followed by members of the Liverpool Cotton Association. A sale by a broker in his own name to persons having that knowledge does not convey to them an assurance that he is selling on his own account; on the contrary, it is equivalent to an express intimation that the cotton is either his own property or the property of a principal who has employed him as an agent to sell. A purchaser who is content to buy on these terms cannot, when the real principal comes forward, allege that the broker sold the cotton as his own. If the intending purchaser desires to deal with the broker as a principal, and not as an agent, in order to secure a right of set-off, he is put upon his inquiry. Should the broker refuse to state whether he is acting for himself or for a principal, the buyer may decline to enter into the transaction. If he chooses to purchase without inquiry, or, notwithstanding the broker's refusal to give information, he does so with notice that there may be a principal for whom the broker is acting as agent, and should that ultimately prove to be the fact, he has, in my opinion, no right to set-off his indebtedness to the principal against debts owing to him by the agent.

Greer v. Downs Supply Co.

(1927) 137 L.T. 174

Constructive notice to the third party that the person he is dealing with is only an agent does not disentitle the third party from setting-off against the principal a debt due to the third party from the agent.

The defendant carried on business as the Downs Supply Co. He had sold goods to the value of £17 to a Mr Godwin, but had not been paid for them. Godwin offered to sell him some timber. The defendant, hoping to get payment by means of a set-off, agreed to buy it on the terms that he should only pay the difference between the price of the timber and the £17. He honestly believed that he was making a contract with Godwin alone. An invoice was sent to him bearing on it the name "W. MacGregor Greer", which was the plaintiff's name. When the defendant next met Godwin, he asked him who MacGregor Greer was, and Godwin said that he himself was MacGregor Greer. The defendant believed what he was told. In fact, Godwin was the plaintiff's agent to sell timber on commission. The timber was not paid for, so the plaintiff claimed the price from the defendant. The defendant contended that he was entitled to set-off the £17. The plaintiff, however, maintained that no set-off was possible because the defendant on receipt of the invoice had notice which would have put him on inquiry, and he would have found out that Godwin was only an agent.

Held, by the Court of Appeal, that the defendant was entitled to set-off the amount of £17. The doctrine of constructive notice did not apply in commercial transactions.

LAWRENCE, L.J. (at page 177)

The appellant based his claim upon a contract which was in fact made between the respondent and Godwin and of which one of the terms was that the respondent should be allowed to set-off £17 against the contract price. The appellant suing upon that contract is, of course, bound by the terms of the set-off unless he can show that the respondent is estopped from relying upon it, or has so conducted himself that a contract of sale and purchase arose between himself and the appellant free from any right of the purchaser to set-off. The appellant contends that the respondent is so estopped because he had constructive notice that Godwin was not the real vendor of the goods. But that contention cannot prevail in view of the judgment of LINDLEY, L.J., in *Manchester Trust* v. *Furness*,[41] that it is most undesirable that the doctrine of constructive notice should be extended to ordinary commercial transactions. The result is that the respondent, who *bona fide* believed that he was contracting with Godwin, is not to be treated as having contracted with the appellant merely because further inquiries might have disclosed the appellant as the real vendor.

(7) Effect of principal settling with agent

Armstrong v. Stokes and others

(1872) 26 L.T. 872[42]

Where an undisclosed principal has settled with the agent for the price of goods bought from a third party and the agent does not pay the third party, the third party cannot claim payment from the principal.

> On 5th June, 1871, the plaintiff sold some pieces of unbleached shirtings to Ryder & Co., who bought the goods in their own name. They were, however, acting as agents for the defendants, but did not inform the plaintiff of this. On 11th August the defendants paid the price of the goods to Ryder & Co. On 30th August Ryder & Co. were in financial difficulties, and could not pay the plaintiff for the shirts. The plaintiff discovered the existence of the defendants, and brought an action against them to recover the price.
>
> *Held*, by the Court of Queen's Bench, that the action failed.

BLACKBURN, J. (at page 877)

PARKE, B., lays down generally that[43] "if a person orders an agent to make a purchase for him, he is bound to see that the agent pays the debt, and the giving the agent money for that purpose does not amount to payment unless the agent pays it accordingly". After commenting on several of the cases already referred to he concludes,[44] "I think that there is no authority for saying that a payment made to the agent precludes the seller from recovering from the principal unless

---

[41] [1895] 2 Q.B. 539.
[42] This decision must be read in the light of *Irvine & Co.* v. *Watson and Sons* (1880) 42 L.T. 800. See p. 101, *post.*
[43] In *Heald* v. *Kenworthy* (1855) 10 Ex. 739, at p. 745.
[44] *Ibid.*, at p. 747.

it appears that he has induced the principal to believe that a settlement has been made with the agent". He states this as generally true wherever a principal has allowed himself to be made a party to a contract; and makes no exception as to the case where the other side made the contract with the agent, believing him to be the principal, and continued in such belief till after the payment was made. He certainly does not in terms say that there is no qualification of the principle he lays down, when applicable to such a case; but, recollecting how careful PARKE, B., always was to lay down what he thought to be the law fully with accuracy, we think the counsel for the plaintiffs were justified in arguing that PARKE, B., thought that the exception did not exist. It is also to be observed that POLLOCK, C.B., concurred in the opinion expressed by PARKE, B., and this is, in our opinion, a weighty authority in favour of the plaintiff's contention, more especially as POLLOCK, C.B., assents in his judgment to the remark thrown out by PARKE, B., during the argument, and afterwards more elaborately stated by him in his judgment. And ALDERSON, B., in his judgment, appears entirely to assent to the judgment of PARKE, B. We think that we could not, without straining the evidence, hold in this case that the plaintiff had induced the defendants to believe that he (the plaintiff) had settled with J. and O. Ryder at the time when the defendants paid them. This makes it necessary to determine whether we agree in what we think was the opinion of PARKE, B., acquiesced in by POLLOCK, C.B., and ALDERSON, B. We think that if the rigid rule thus laid down were to be applied to those who were only discovered to be principals after they had fairly paid the price to those whom the vendors believed to be the principals, and to whom alone the vendors gave credit, it would produce intolerable hardship. It may be said, perhaps truly, that this is the consequence of that which might originally have been a mistake in allowing the vendor to have recourse at all against one to whom he never gave credit, and that we ought not to establish an illogical exception in order to cure a fault in a rule. But we find an exception (more or less extensively expressed) always mentioned in the very cases that lay down the rule; and without deciding anything as to the case of a broker who avowedly acts for a principal (though not necessarily named), and confining ourselves to the present case, which is one in which, to borrow Lord TENTERDEN's phrase in *Thomson* v. *Davenport*,[45] the plaintiff sold the goods to Ryder and Co., supposing at the time of the contract he was dealing with a principal, we think such exception is established. We wish to be understood as expressing no opinion as to what would have been the effect of the state of the accounts between the parties if J. and O. Ryder had been indebted to the defendants on a separate account, so as to give rise to a set-off, or mutual credit between them. We confine our decision to the case before us, where the defendants after the contract was made, and in consequence of it, *bona fide*, and without moral blame, paid J. and O. Ryder at a time when the plaintiff still gave sole credit to J. and O. Ryder, and knew of no one else. We think that after that it was too late for the plaintiff to come upon the defendants.

---

[45] (1829) 2 Sm. L.C. 300.

Irvine & Co. *v.* Watson and Sons

(1880) 42 L.T. 800

Where a third party sells goods to an agent acting for an unnamed principal, and the principal pays the price to the agent, but the agent does not hand the money to the third party, the third party is entitled to claim payment from the principal unless he has led the principal to infer that the agent has paid over the money, or that he will look to the agent alone for payment.

On 10th March, 1879, the defendants instructed Conning & Co. to buy a quantity of oil for them. On 12th March Conning & Co. bought the oil from the plaintiffs, who knew that they were not buying for themselves, but were acting for unnamed principals. The oil was delivered to Conning & Co. on 15th March, and on that date the defendants paid the price to Conning & Co. The plaintiffs were unable to get payment from Conning & Co. On 28th March the plaintiffs claimed payment from the defendants, who they had discovered were the unnamed principals in the transaction. The defendants denied liability on the ground that they had already paid the price to Conning & Co., and were under no liability to see that it was paid over to the plaintiffs.

Held, by the Court of Appeal, that the action succeeded. The plaintiffs had not led the defendants to infer that the price had been paid to them by Conning & Co., nor that they would look to Conning & Co. alone for payment.

BRAMWELL, L.J. (at page 800)

The defendants gave Conning and Co. an order to buy certain goods for them, and Conning and Co., in pursuance of this order, bought from the plaintiffs. The plaintiffs sold the goods by a written contract, on the face of which Conning and Co. were the purchasers; but the plaintiffs knew that Conning and Co., were agents. The plaintiffs therefore knew that they had a remedy against two distinct persons, that is, against Conning and Co., and against some other person, the principal, who was then unknown to them. The defendants knew that Conning and Co., bought as brokers; therefore they knew that the seller had a remedy against themselves alone, if their names had been given by the brokers, or that, as the fact was, the seller had a remedy against them and against the brokers also. Then acceptances were given by the defendants to the brokers in anticipation of a debt which the brokers would have to discharge when the goods were delivered. In my opinion, it is impossible to say that the defendants were discharged. The only way in which they could be said to be discharged would be by the plaintiffs misleading the defendants. But the plaintiffs did not mislead the defendants. The stipulation as to payment was for the benefit of the plaintiffs, and they could waive it. If there were a practice always to enforce such a stipulation, perhaps the defendants might be fairly entitled to complain of the plaintiffs not having done so. But this is not so in this case, for there is no such practice. It is enough to state this to show that the defendants' contention cannot be maintained. Then as to the authorities. I cannot take the language used by Lord TENTERDEN and BAYLEY, J., in *Thomson* v. *Davenport*[46] literally; but I

---

[46] (1829) 9 B. & C. 78.

think it must be taken, not as having been overruled or qualified, but as having been uttered with an intention the same at that of PARKE, B., in delivering judgment in *Heald* v. *Kenworthy*.[47] Taking the words literally, I think the view of PARKE, B., is preferable, where he says:[48]

> "If the conduct of the seller would make it unjust for him to call upon the buyer for the money; as, for example, where the principal is induced by the conduct of the seller to pay his agent the money on the faith that the agent and seller have come to a settlement on the matter, or if any representation to that effect is made by the seller either by words or conduct, the seller cannot afterwards throw off the mask and sue the principal. It would be unjust for him to do so. But I think that there is no case of this kind where the plaintiff has been precluded from recovering, unless he has in some way contributed either to deceive the defendant or to induce him to alter his position."

One word as to *Armstrong* v. *Stokes*.[49] That was a very remarkable case. It seems as if the Court there were not obliged to hold that J. and O. Ryder had authority to bind the defendants, and on the facts it must be taken that J. and O. Ryder there were not mere agents of the defendants, but a sort of intermediate parties, and in that way there is a difference between that case and the present. BLACKBURN, J., in delivering judgment in that case says:[50]

> "We find an exception (more or less extensively expressed) always mentioned in the very cases that lay down the rule; and without deciding anything as to the case of a broker who avowedly acts for a principal (though not necessarily named), and confining ourselves to the present case, which is one in which, to borrow Lord TENTERDEN's phrase in *Thomson* v. *Davenport*,[51] the plaintiff sold the goods to J. and O. Ryder and Co., 'supposing at the time of the contract he was dealing with a principal', we think such an exception is established. . . . We confine our decision to the case before us, where the defendants, after the contract was made, and in consequence of it, *bona fide* and without moral blame, paid J. and O. Ryder at a time when the plaintiff still gave sole credit to J. and O. Ryder, and knew of no one else. We think that after that it was too late for the plaintiff to come upon the defendants".

That is not the case here, for when payment was made, although the plaintiffs did not know of these particular defendants, they knew that there was some one else on whose behalf Conning and Co. had bought. From reading the above passage from the judgment in *Armstrong* v. *Stokes*,[52] one would think that the rights and duties of a buyer depended upon what the vendor knew; but how can the buyer have different rights according to whether the seller knew that there was a principal or not? Here the defendants employed brokers to buy, and they knew that those brokers had pledged their credit to the sellers, whoever they might be, and that there would be a claim on them, the defendants, unless the brokers paid for the goods, and, knowing this, they gave the acceptances to the brokers at their own peril.

---

[47] (1855) 10 Exch., 739.
[48] *Ibid.*, at p. 746.
[49] (1872) L.R. 7 Q.B. 598. See p. 99, *ante*.
[50] *Ibid.*, at p. 610.
[51] *Supra*.
[52] *Supra*.

(8) Effect of third party settling with agent

Butwick *v.* Grant

[1924] All E.R. Rep. 274

There is no hard and fast rule that an agent, who has authority to sell, has also authority to receive payment.

> A principal appointed an agent to sell some coats for him. The purchaser of the coats paid the agent, but the agent did not pay the money to the principal. So the principal sued the purchaser for the price.
>
> *Held*, by the Divisional Court of the King's Bench Division, that the action succeeded because, on the facts, the agent had no authority to receive payment of the price.

SANKEY, J. (at page 276)

I found my decision on the judgment of LUSH, J., in *Drakeford* v. *Piercy*.[53] The learned Judge there said:[54]

> "that an agent authorised to sell has a necessary legal consequence authority to receive payment is a proposition utterly untenable and contrary to authority".

It may be open to the purchaser, who has paid the purchase price to the agent, to show that the latter in fact had authority to receive payment, or that he had ostensible authority to receive payment, or it may be shown that the payment to the agent was a payment made in the ordinary course of such agencies. In the present case, however, the learned County Court Judge has held that none of these things was here shown.

Bradford & Sons Ltd. *v.* Price Brothers

(1923) 129 L.T. 408

Where an agent is authorised to receive payment in cash, a third party who gives him a cheque is discharged from liability to the principal if the cheque is duly honoured on presentation.

> The plaintiffs sold some coal to the defendants. The plaintiffs' agent was authorised by them to receive payment in cash. The defendants paid him by means of a cheque made payable to him. The cheque was duly honoured, but the proceeds were not paid over by the agent, and the plaintiffs now claimed the price of the coal from the defendants.
>
> *Held*, by the King's Bench Division, that the action failed. The defendants were discharged from liability for which the cheque was cashed, the agent had the money, and it was his duty to hand it to the plaintiffs.

---

[53] (1866) 7 B. & S. 515.
[54] *Ibid.*, at p. 522.

McCARDIE, J. (at page 412)

If Walley could take cash, he could take a bearer cheque, provided it was duly cashed. So too of an open cheque payable to his order, inasmuch as a cheque is crossed merely for safety. So too, I think, if the cheque is crossed "a/c payee" or "a/c payee only", for this also is a mere precaution. A cheque crossed "a/c payee" may be paid with substantially the same certainty as an open cheque to order. The main points seem to be that the cheque must in fact be cashed and that mere machinery is not vital. When cashed, the agent has the money, and it is his duty to hand it to his principal.

If the plaintiffs desired to be safe, they should have given a plain and unambiguous direction to the defendants that payment could only be made by cheques in a specific form, and not by cash at all. The creditor who desires to limit the *prima facie* authority of his agent or servant as to payment, must tell the debtor plainly of that limitation of authority. It follows from what I have said that, in my opinion, the defendants are entitled to judgment on the ground that the cash, expressly the proceeds of their cheques, was in fact received by Walley, who had authority to receive payment in cash on behalf of the plaintiffs.

Sorrell v. Finch

[1976] 2 All E.R. 371

An estate agent generally has no authority to receive a pre-contract deposit.

> The plaintiff paid a pre-contract deposit to an estate agent in relation to the purchase of the defendant's house. The agent disappeared and the plaintiff brought an action against the defendant claiming the return of the deposit.
> *Held*, by the House of Lords, that the claim failed for the agent had no authority to receive the deposit.

LORD RUSSELL OF KILLOWEN (at page 383)

Accordingly we have a situation in which (i) the vendor did not expressly authorise the estate agent to receive as agent for the vendor pre-contract deposits from possible purchasers; (ii) the estate agent did not purport to receive any deposit as agent for whoever might be the vendor of the property.

An estate agent, despite the style, is an independent person, engaged, ordinarily on a commission basis, to find and introduce a willing purchaser; he is not the agent of the vendor to contract on his behalf; his actions are attributable to the vendor only in a strictly limited sense, as for example the making of representations as to the condition of the property. In my opinion an estate agent has neither actual (implied) nor ostensible (apparent) authority to ask for or receive a pre-contract deposit as agent for the vendor. It is true that it has become quite common for estate agents to receive pre-contract deposits, and that in one sense this earnest of genuine interest is beneficial to the vendor; but it is also beneficial to the purchaser who hopes thereby to get his foot in the door; indeed in time of acute housing shortage it is I believe not unknown for a would-be purchaser to press a deposit on the estate agent for that very reason. . . .

The subject-matter of these decisions is of course at large in this House. In my opinion (i) in cases such as the present it is wrong to say that by the engagement of an estate agent there is conferred on the estate agent either implied or ostensible authority to receive a deposit from a would-be purchaser as agent for the vendor; (ii) if the estate agent receives a deposit either without other definition of his character or in terms "as stakeholder" and the estate agent goes bankrupt or otherwise defaults, the vendor is not liable to the purchaser. (As to "stakeholder", I adhere to the view expressed by me *obiter* in *Maloney* v. *Hardy and Moorshead*.[55])

The crucial point in my opinion is that at all times until contract the purchaser is the only person with any claim or right to the return of the deposit moneys, and his right is a right on demand: whereas the vendor has no such claim or right and no control over the deposit moneys. It has been said that "in justice" the one of two innocent people to suffer should be the vendor who chose the estate agent. But this seems to me too loose an approach to the problem, which should be solved by analysis of legal rights and relationships. A would-be purchaser is not obliged to pay a pre-contract deposit, and can in any event require that it be paid into joint names. The vendor on the other hand, if the line of cases mentioned is upheld, may (as here) find himself liable to repay a whole string of deposits—worth perhaps more than the house—without being able to avoid or control the situations; for the suggestion that he might insist that the cyclostyled particulars should bear, in bold lettering, the warning that any pre-contract deposits be not paid to the estate agent's sole name is hardly practical. My opinion is not, of course, intended to cast any doubt on the liability of the vendor for the default of a stakeholder auctioneer; in such cases the deposit is paid to the auctioneer on contract, and the purchaser is required by the vendor to make the payment; he has no option.

(9) *Bribery of agent*[56]

Shipway *v.* Broadwood

(1899) 80 L.T. 11

Where his agent has received a bribe, the principal is entitled to avoid the contract which the agent has made with a third party.

Broadwood wished to buy some horses, so he asked Pinkett, a veterinary surgeon, to keep a look out for some for him. Pinkett introduced him to Shipway, and it was

---

[55] (1970) 216 E.G. 1582.
[56] For the effect of bribery on the relation between principal and agent, see p. 12, *ante*.

agreed that, if Pinkett certified as sound some horses to be supplied by Shipway, he would buy them. Pinkett certified them as sound, and Broadwood bought them. Later he found that they were not sound, and refused to pay on discovering that Shipway had given a bribe to Pinkett.

Held, by the Court of Appeal, that Broadwood was not liable on the contract in view of the bribe being given. What effect the bribe had on Pinkett was quite immaterial.

SMITH, L.J. (at page 12)

Now, Pinkett was retained by the defendant to examine the horses on his behalf, and to report as to their soundness. He took a bribe from the seller of the horses, and then gave his certificate that they were sound. Now that it has come out at the trial that the person who was to certify as to the soundness of the horses had been bribed by the seller, can the transaction be sustained in a Court of law? In my opinion, the true effect of the evidence is that Pinkett was bribed before he gave his certificate. It is clear that Shipway offered to Pinkett a commission by way of bribe to pass the horses as sound. That, I think, is clearly the effect of the evidence. That is, in my opinion, amply sufficient to upset a sale of this kind, which was to be effected upon such a certificate. When this fact was elicited, there was an obvious defence to the action.

CHITTY, L.J. (at page 12)

The agreement between the vendor and the purchaser was that there was not to be a sale unless Pinkett passed the horses as sound. Under those circumstances it is quite immaterial to go any further, and to embark upon any further inquiry as to whether Pinkett was influenced. As soon as a case of bribery is established, it is quite immaterial to inquire what effect the bribe, whether promised or actually given, has had upon the mind of the person bribed. Now, in this case, Pinkett occupied something in the nature of a judicial position towards the parties, when he was instructed to examine the horses for the purpose of certifying whether they were sound. He was placed in a position where his duty conflicted with his interest, and he was placed in that position by Shipway. The rule, which is a rule of Common Law as well as of equity, was thus stated by ELLENBOROUGH, J. in *Thompson* v. *Havelock*:[57] "no man should be allowed to have an interest against his duty". That is the great principle which has been applied in innumerable cases. It is never proper to inquire what influence a bribe has had upon an agent to whom it has been given. I agree that, if that which has been promised or given is so small as to come within the rule *de minimis non curat lex*, then it may be disregarded. That is not, however, the case here, for it is quite clear that the onus is upon the plaintiff to show that what he offered to the agent was something very small.

---

[57] (1808) 1 Camp. 527.

Mahesan *v*. Malaysia Government Officers' Co-operative Housing Society Ltd.

[1978] 2 All E.R. 405

Where an agent has been bribed by a third party, the principal must elect whether to claim the amount of the bribe from the agent or to claim damages from the third party. The remedies are alternative and not cumulative.

M. was an employee of a housing society which wished to purchase land. He helped a third party in connection with the purchase by the society of land belonging to the third party, and received payment for his services. The society sought to recover the amount of the bribe from M. and damages from the third party.

Held, by the Judicial Committee of the Privy Council, that the society must elect between the two remedies and could not claim both.

LORD DIPLOCK (at page 409)

In *Bagnall* v. *Carlton*[58] the principal brought an action against the briber for rescission of the contract in respect of which the bribe had been given and against the agent for recovery of the bribe. He compromised the action against the briber on terms that he was paid a sum of money by the briber and the contract remained afoot. It was held that this did not affect the principal's right to recover the bribe from the agent. There is nothing in the report to indicate how the amount paid under the compromise was arrived at. So far as the agent was concerned it was *res inter alios acta*. No question of double recovery against him was involved.

Bagnall v. *Carlton*[59] was, however, followed by *Salford Corpn.* v. *Lever*.[60] Again it was an action brought by the principal against the briber, but not in this case for rescission of the contracts for sale in respect of which the bribes were given but for damages for fraud. Rescission was not available as the goods which were the subject of the sales had been consumed. It was established by the evidence that the briber had sold the goods at prices which exceeded the market prices by the amount of the bribes; so the amount of the bribes was also the measure of the damage caused to the principal by the briber's fraud. The principal had previously brought an action in the Chancery Division against the agent for recovery of the bribe and had compromised this on terms that the agent should co-operate with him for the purpose of suing the bribers and would put up security in the sum of £10,000 which would be released progressively by the amounts received by the principal by way of damages from the bribers.

In the action against the briber the latter relied on the compromise with the agent as amounting to the release of a joint tortfeasor. The Court of Appeal (Lord ESHER, M.R., LINDLEY and LOPES, L.JJ.) held that it was not, on the ground, among others, that the principal's cause of action for recovery of the

---

[58] (1877) 6 Ch.D. 371, C.A.
[59] *Supra.*
[60] [1891] 1 Q.B. 168, C.A.

bribe from the agent was a separate and different cause of action from his cause of action against the briber for damages for fraud. *Bagnall* v. *Carlton*[61] was cited as authority for this proposition. The terms of the compromise of the action against the agent were such that no question of double recovery of any of the bribes could arise, nor was the agent a party to the action against the briber. Nevertheless all three members of the Court expressed the opinion accurately summarised in the headnote as follows:[62]

> "Where an agent, who has been bribed so to do, induces his principal to enter into a contract with the person who has paid the bribe, and the contract is disadvantageous to the principal, the principal has two distinct and cumulative remedies: he may recover from the agent the amount of the bribe which he has received, and he may also recover from the agent and the person who has paid the bribe, jointly or severally, damages for any loss which he has sustained by reason of his having entered into the contract, *without allowing any deduction in respect of what he has recovered from the agent under the former head*, and it is immaterial whether the principal sues the agent or the third person first."

The liability of the briber to the principal for damages for the loss sustained by him in consequence of entering into the contract in respect of which the bribe was given is a rational development from his former right in equity to rescission of the contract. The cause of action against the briber was stated by Lord ESHER, M.R., and LOPES, L.J., to be fraud, and, since the agent was necessarily party to the bribery, it follows that the tort was a joint tort of briber and agent for which either or both could be sued. But fraud is a tort for which the damages are limited to the actual loss sustained; and if the principal has recovered the bribe from the bribed agent, the actual loss he has sustained in consequence of entering into the contract is reduced by that amount. The words that their Lordships have caused to be italicised in the citation from the headnote were unnecessary to the actual decision of the case and appear to be in conflict with established principles of the law of tort.

Although as a matter of decision the *Salford* case[63] was concerned only with the liability of the briber, the dicta summarised in the headnote deal also with the liability of the agent. It was accurate to say that the principal had two distinct remedies against the agent, one for money had and received and the other for the tort of fraud; but it was flying in the face of a long line of authority to say that these two remedies were not alternative but cumulative. The authorities to this effect are discussed at length in the speeches in *United Australia Ltd.* v. *Barclays Bank Ltd.*,[64] a case in which the House of Lords confirmed the principle that where the same facts gave rise in law to two causes of action against a single defendant, one (formerly lying in *assumpsit*) for money had and received and

---

[61] (1877) 6 Ch.D. 371, C.A.
[62] *Supra.*
[63] [1891] 1 Q.B. 168, C.A.
[64] [1941] A.C. 1; [1940] 4 All E.R. 20, H.L.

the other for damages for tort, the plaintiff must elect between the remedies. It held, however, that such election was not irrevocable until judgment was recovered on one cause of action or the other. The House of Lords also held that where the same facts gave rise in law to a cause of action against one defendant for money had and received and to a separate cause of action for damages in tort against another defendant, judgment recovered against the first defendant did not prevent the plaintiff from suing the other defendant in a separate action; but that to the extent that the judgment was actually satisfied this constituted satisfaction *pro tanto* of the claim for damages in the cause of action against the second defendant.

Insofar as what was said in the *Salford* case[65] conflicts with this, in their Lordships' opinion it can no longer be regarded as good law and the words that are italicised in the citation of the headnote are wrong.

Industries & General Mortgage Co. Ltd. *v.* Lewis

[1949] 2 All E.R. 573

Where a third party has paid a secret commission to the agent, the principal can recover the amount of the commission without having to show that it was paid with a corrupt motive.

> The defendant wished to buy some property and employed a Mr Vermont to arrange for the plaintiffs to find a person to lend him £45,000 for a short period to finance the purchase. The plaintiffs arranged the loan, and agreed to pay Vermont half the procuration fee which they would charge the defendant. At no time did the plaintiffs or Vermont tell the defendant of this payment. The plaintiffs had no intention of causing Vermont to persuade the defendant to accept the procuration fee which was charged or to act to his disadvantage. The plaintiffs claimed commission, and the defendant counterclaimed for the amount paid to Vermont on the ground that it was a bribe, alleging that proof of corruption or of a corrupt motive was unnecessary in a civil action.
>
> *Held*, by the King's Bench Division, that the claim failed and the counterclaim succeeded. Proof of corruption or of a corrupt motive was unnecessary. The mere fact that the bribe had been given was sufficient to entitle the defendant to claim the amount of the bribe.

SLADE, J. (at page 575)

For the purposes of the civil law a bribe means the payment of a secret commission, which only means (i) that the person making the payment makes it to the agent of the other person with whom he is dealing; (ii) that he makes it to that person knowing that that person is acting as the agent of the other person with whom he is dealing; and (iii) that he fails to disclose to the other person with whom he is dealing that he has made that payment to the person whom he knows to be the other person's agent. Those three are the only elements

---

[65] *Supra.*

necessary to constitute the payment of a secret commission or bribe for civil purposes. I emphasise "civil purposes" because the Prevention of Corruption Act 1906, s. 1(1), introduces the adverb "corruptly", and, except in the cases provided for in s. 2 of the amending Act of 1916, the onus is put on the prosecution of showing that the payment has been made corruptly. I hold that proof of corruptness or corrupt motive is unnecessary in a civil action.

Where you have two parties to a contract introduced by an agent of one of them, once it is established that one of the parties to a contract makes a secret payment to the person whom he knows to be the agent of the other, the law will presume against him that he has acted corruptly, that the agent has been influenced by the payment to the detriment of his principal, and that the principal, the defendant in this case, has suffered damage to at least the amount of the bribe.

(10) Knowledge of agent

Newsholme Brothers *v.* Road Transport and General Insurance Co. Ltd.

[1929] All E.R. Rep. 442

The agent's knowledge of a fact will not be imputed to his principal where the agent is acting as the agent of the third party and not on behalf of the principal.[66]

A proposer for a motor insurance policy orally gave correct answers to the questions in a proposal form to the agent of an insurance company. The answers were written down incorrectly by the agent. The proposer then signed the form, which stated that it was to be the "basis" of the contract, and that he warranted the truth of the statements contained in it. He claimed an indemnity for a loss arising under the policy, but the insurance company repudiated liability on the ground that some of the answers in the proposal form were untrue. The proposer, on the other hand, maintained that the knowledge of the agent that the answers as filled in by him were incorrect was notice to the company, and that the company was accordingly liable.

Held, by the Court of Appeal, that the action failed. The agent's knowledge that the answers as filled in by him were incorrect could not be imputed to the company because when he filled in the form, he was acting as the agent of the proposer and not of the company.

SCRUTTON, L.J. (at page 451)

If the answers are untrue and he knows it, he is committing a fraud which prevents his knowledge being the knowledge of the insurance company. If the answers are untrue, but he does not know it, I do not understand how he has any

---

[66] See further, Ivamy, *General Principles of Insurance Law* (5th edn. 1986), pp. 548–553.

knowledge which can be imputed to the insurance company. In any case, I have great difficulty in understanding how a man who has signed, without reading it, a document which he knows to be a proposal for insurance, and which contains statements in fact untrue, and a promise that they are true and the basis of the contract, can escape from the consequences of his negligence by saying that the person he asked to fill it up for him is the agent of the person to whom the proposal is addressed.

GREER, L.J. (at page 454)

I also take the view that notice to the agent whose duty was to obtain a signed proposal form and send it to the company, was not notice to the company of anything inconsistent with the signed proposal form, and that in filling up the form, whether he mistook the instructions of the insured, or whether he intentionally filled in something different from what he was told, he was not acting as the agent of the company, but as the agent of the insured.

Vacuum Oil Co. *v.* Union Insurance Society of Canton Ltd.

(1926) 25 Ll.L.Rep. 546

Notice to an agent will only bind the principal if the agent had authority to receive it.

Some tins of petroleum had been insured and were a constructive total loss.[67] The assured did not give the insurers notice of abandonment[68] in accordance with s. 61 of the Marine Insurance Act 1906. One of the issues which arose was whether the notice of abandonment, if it had been given to a Lloyd's Agent, would have bound the insurers.
Held, by the Court of Appeal, that such a notice would have been ineffective, for a Lloyd's Agent had no authority to receive such notice on behalf of the insurers.

ATKIN, L.J. (at page 554)

The question arises whether a notice of abandonment in those circumstances can be given to Lloyd's Agent as an agent of the underwriter to receive notice of abandonment. Now it seems to me plain that inasmuch as notice has to be given to the underwriter, any person who is relying upon notice being given to some person other than the underwriter or an official of the underwriting company, has got to prove the authority, and I am bound to say that I am not satisfied that there was any authority in Mr Fakher to receive notice of abandonment. It seems to me quite outside the usual authority of Lloyd's Agents, and outside the usual course of business, because I am satisfied that the usual course of business is for the assured (when they remember to give notice of abandonment, which

---

[67] As to "constructive total loss", see Ivamy, *Marine Insurance* (4th edn. 1985), pp. 362–377.
[68] As to "notice of abandonment", see Ivamy, *ibid.*, pp. 381–382.

they constantly do not) to communicate with the underwriter in London, or wherever he may be, through the insurance broker, and it is the duty of the broker to pass on the notice at once to the underwriter; and inasmuch as rapid means of communication now exist I am satisfied that in the ordinary course of business the assured ought to communicate direct in the way I have mentioned, and give notice in that way directly to the underwriter, and I do not think that Lloyd's Agents in different parts of the world are persons who, in ordinary circumstances, have authority to receive notice of abandonment. One point of importance about it, I think, is this: the person who receives notice of abandonment receives it for the purpose of determining whether he shall accept or not, and it is quite plain that Lloyd's Agent has no authority to accept the notice so that the property shall pass there and then to his principals; I think it is intended that the principals shall decide, and I think that the notice must be given to the principals, or, of course, to an agent whom they have expressly or impliedly authorised to receive it. In this case it appears to me that there is no evidence that Lloyd's Agents, as such, or by reason of any definite authority which they received, had authority to receive this notice.

Wilkinson *v*. General Accident Fire and Life Assurance Corporation Ltd.

[1967] 2 Lloyd's Rep. 182

Knowledge acquired by an agent otherwise than in the course of his employment on the principal's behalf is not imputed to the principal.

The plaintiff insured a Morris Minor reg. no. LFV 730 with the defendant insurance company through a Mr Middleton, who was the company's agent. Middleton was also a garage owner. The policy expired on 2nd December, 1961. On 9th October, 1961, the plaintiff sold the Morris Minor and Middleton witnessed the contract of sale. On 2nd December, 1961, Middleton asked the plaintiff for a renewal premium, and the plaintiff paid it. Middleton told him that he would be covered against third party risks when driving a car not belonging to him, provided he had the consent of its owner. On 27th September, 1962, the plaintiff was driving a Morris Oxford reg. no. PVR 150 with the consent of its owner, and was involved in an accident. The plaintiff now claimed an indemnity from the defendant company. The company denied liability on the ground that the policy had lapsed because the Morris Minor had been sold.[69] But the plaintiff maintained that the policy had been renewed, and that Middleton with knowledge of the sale had told him that he would be covered against third party risks when driving a car not belonging to him with the owner's consent, and that the company was estopped from disputing liability.

Held, at Manchester Assizes, that the company was not estopped, for Middleton's knowledge that the Morris Minor had been sold had been acquired in his capacity of car dealer. Accordingly, such knowledge could not be imputed to the company, for he was not acting as the company's agent in that transaction.

---

[69] As decided in *Rogerson* v. *Scottish Automobile and General Insurance Co. Ltd.* (1931) 41 Ll.L.Rep. 1, H.L., and *Tattersall* v. *Drysdale* (1935) 52 Ll.L.Rep. 21, K.B. As to this point, see Ivamy, *Fire and Motor Insurance* (4th edn. 1984), pp. 244–246.

Miss Commissioner Heilbron (at page 191)

It is, of course, true that Mr Middleton was a party to the sale and certainly had knowledge of the sale of the car LFV 730 in October, 1961. I am satisfied, however, that when he obtained knowledge of the sale of that car, he in fact acquired such knowledge as a car dealer and not as agent of the defendants. Middleton was employed, as I have held, not as general agent but for a limited purpose, namely, to submit proposal forms and to issue short-term notes.

In *The "Hayle"*[70] it is stated that knowledge acquired by an agent otherwise than in the course of his employment on the principal's behalf is not imputed to the principal. I do not think that the knowledge acquired by Middleton in October can or ought to be imputed to the defendant company.

(11) Principal's liability for agent's misrepresentation

Armstrong v. Strain and others

[1952] 1 All E.R. 139

A principal who does not purposely employ an agent in the hope that he will make a misrepresentation to a third party, but knows that the innocent misrepresentation on the agent's part is false, cannot himself be made liable for fraudulent misrepresentation since his knowledge and the agent's statement cannot be combined so as to form dishonesty.

> Mr Strain employed a firm of estate agents, in which a Mr Skinner was a partner, to sell a bungalow. Skinner made an innocent misrepresentation to the plaintiff that any building society would lend £1,200 on it. Strain knew that such a statement was untrue. Cracks appeared in the bungalow and it began to settle. The plaintiff claimed damages for fraudulent misrepresentation against both Strain and Skinner.
>
> *Held*, by the Court of Appeal, that both actions failed. Strain had not purposely employed Skinner in the hope that he would make the representation, and he himself was not guilty of fraud. There was no way of combining the knowledge of the principal and the innocent misrepresentation by the agent to produce liability for fraud.

Singleton, L.J. (at page 141)

"Guilty knowledge" means knowledge of fraud or dishonesty on the part of someone, and without it there can be no finding of fraudulent misrepresentation. Again, as Lord Herschell said in *Derry* v. *Peek*:[71]

> "First, in order to sustain an action of deceit, there must be proof of fraud, and nothing short of that will suffice."

I maintain that, at least since the year 1889, it has not been open to any Court to

---

[70] [1929] P. 275.
[71] (1889) 14 App.Cas. 337, at p. 374.

find for the plaintiff in an action of fraudulent misrepresentation unless there is proof of fraud or dishonesty.

In *Anglo-Scottish Beet Sugar Corpn. Ltd.* v. *Spalding Urban District Council*,[72] ATKINSON, J., was called on to consider the *London County Properties* case,[73] and in the course of a masterly analysis of it and of the authorities on the subject, he said:[74]

> "I cannot myself see how a principal can be held liable for fraud when there has been no fraud, no element of fraud, either on the part of himself or on the part of anyone for whose acts he is responsible."

Later[75] he said it was decided in that case

> ". . . that a principal is liable for fraud where the fraudulent information supplied by one agent is handed on to a third party through an innocent agent".

I agree with the reasoning of ATKINSON, J., and, with all respect, I think that DEVLIN, J., took a wrong view of the decision of the Court of Appeal in the *London County Properties* case.[76] That may well have arisen from the somewhat nebulous way in which the judgments in the case are expressed.

Difficulties may arise in a claim against a company which can only speak or act through its agents or officers, but if an officer of a company writes and represents that which is untrue when many other officers of the company know the true facts, it may well be found that he made the representation without belief in its truth, or that he made it recklessly, careless whether it was true or false. That must depend on the evidence. In the case before us the principal is an individual; it was the agent who made the representation which was false. The Judge[77] negatived fraud on the part of both. In those circumstances an action for fraudulent misrepresentation cannot succeed against either.

Ludgater *v.* Love

(1881) 4 L.T. 694

Where an undisclosed principal knowingly allows an innocent agent to make a false representation which induces a third party to enter into a contract, the third party can hold the principal liable in damages.

> Love knowingly allowed his son, who was unaware that some sheep had rot, falsely to represent to Ludgater that they were in sound condition. Ludgater bought them and later found out the true facts. He sued Love for damages for fraudulent misrepresentation.

---

[72] [1937] 3 All E.R. 335.
[73] I.e. *London County Freehold and Leasehold Properties Ltd.* v. *Berkeley Property and Investment Co. Ltd.* [1936] 2 All E.R. 1039.
[74] [1937] 3 All E.R. at p. 346.
[75] *Ibid.*, at p. 347.
[76] *Supra.*
[77] I.e. DEVLIN, J., in the Court below: [1952] 1 T.L.R. 856.

Held, by the Court of Appeal, that the action succeeded. Love was liable for the fraudulent misrepresentation even though he did not make it himself.

BRETT, L.J. (at page 696)

We were on the hearing clearly of opinion that there was ample evidence to justify a finding of fraudulent intention in the defendant; and that the admitted truthfulness of the plaintiff justified the jury in finding, as we think they did, that the plaintiff was induced to purchase by the representation that the sheep were all right. We took time to consider the questions which were discussed as to whether there was such authority from the defendant to his son as was sufficient to bind him by reason of his son's representations to a liability to pay damages in an action for deceit. These questions were to be determined, as it seemed to us, upon the finding of fraud in the father without a finding of fraud in the son. If the son was authorised to make the representations, whether such authority was express or implied, we are of the opinion that the defendant was, by reason of his own fraudulent mind, liable, notwithstanding want of fraud in the son.

Armagas Ltd. *v.* Mundogas S.A.: The "Ocean Frost"

[1986] 2 Lloyd's Rep. 385, H.L.

The principal is not vicariously liable for a fraudulent misrepresentation by his agent that he was acting in the course of the principal's business if (i) the agent is not authorised to do what he purported to do, (ii) if what he purported to do is not within a class of acts that an agent in his position is usually authorised to do, and (iii) if the principal has done nothing to represent that the agent was so authorised.

Armagas bought the vessel *Ocean Frost* from Mundogas and the parties then entered into an agreement whereby Armagas chartered her to Mundogas for 36 months, the charter-party being signed by Mr Magelssen, who was the chartering manager of Mundogas, and who had told Armagas that he had authority to sign such a charter-party. In fact, he had no such authority. Mundogas repudiated the charter-party. Armagas brought an action against Mundogas, claiming damages on the ground that they were vicariously liable for the fraudulent misrepresentation by Mr Magelssen.

Held, by the House of Lords, that Mundogas were not liable for (i) Mr Magelssen was not authorised to enter into such a charter-party; (ii) to do so was not within the usual authority of a chartering manager; and (iii) Mundogas had done nothing to represent that he was so authorised.

LORD KEITH OF KINKEL (at page 394)

In the end of the day the question is whether the circumstances under which a servant has made the fraudulent misrepresentation which has caused loss to an innocent party contracting with him are such as to make it just for the employer to bear the loss. Such circumstances exist where the employer by words or conduct has induced the injured party to believe that the servant was acting in the lawful course of the employer's business. They do not exist where such belief, although it is present, has been brought about through misguided reliance on the servant himself, when the servant is not authorised to do what he is purporting to do, when what he is purporting to do is not within the class of acts that an employee in his position is usually authorised to do and when the employer has done nothing to represent that he is authorised to do it. In the present case Mr Magelssen was not authorised to enter into the three-year charter-party, to do so was not within the usual authority of an employee holding his position, and Armagas knew it, and Mundogas had done nothing to represent that he was authorised to do so. It was contended for Armagas that concluding the contract for the sale of the vessel was within Mr Magelssen's actual authority, and that inducing the sale by falsely representing that he had authority to enter into the charter-party amounted to no more than an improper method of performing what he was employed to do, such as in other contexts was sufficient to attract vicarious liability. But the sale of a ship backed by a three-year charter-party is a transaction of a wholly different character from a straightforward sale, even if the charter-party is not to be regarded as a transaction separate and distinct from the sale, and [Armagas] knew that Mr Magelssen had no authority to enter into a transaction of that character on his own responsibility.

I conclude that the Court of Appeal rightly held that Mundogas was not vicariously liable in English law for Mr Magelssen's deceit.

Overbrooke Estates Ltd. *v.* Glencombe Properties Ltd.

[1974] 3 All E.R. 511

Where the principal limits the authority of an agent to make representations on his behalf, such a limitation is not rendered void by the Misrepresentation Act 1967, s. 3.

> Condition R(b) in an auctioneers' catalogue stated: "The vendors do not make or give and neither the auctioneers nor any person in the employment of the auctioneers has any authority to make or give any representation or warranty in relation to [the property]". The auctioneers told intending purchasers that the Greater London Council had no schemes for the property. The prospective purchasers bought the property, but then discovered that the auctioneers' statement was inaccurate so they stopped payment of the cheque which they had given to the vendor. The vendor claimed summary judgment for specific performance of the contract. One of the defences pleaded by the purchasers was that Condition R(b) was rendered void by the Misrepresentation Act 1967, s. 3.
>
> *Held*, by the Chancery Division, that summary judgment in favour of the vendor would be given for s. 3 did not in any way qualify the right of a principal publicly to limit the authority of his agent.

BRIGHTMAN, J. (at page 516)

Counsel for the defendant company's second argument is based on s. 3 of the Misrepresentation Act 1967. This reads:

> "If any agreement (whether made before or after the commencement of this Act) contains a provision which would exclude or restrict—(*a*) any liability to which a party to a contract may be subject by reason of any misrepresentation made by him before

the contract was made; or (*b*) any remedy available to another party to the contract by reason of such a misrepresentation; that provision shall be of no effect except to the extent (if any) that, in any proceedings arising out of the contract, the Court or arbitrator may allow reliance on it as being fair and reasonable in the circumstances of the case."

The argument of counsel is as follows. The words in s. 3(a), "misrepresentation made by him before the contract was made" must include a misrepresentation made by the contracting party's agent. The authority of the contracting party's agent in such a case is a necessary ingredient of any liability sought to be imposed on such contracting party. Therefore a provision restricting the ostensible authority of the agent is a provision which restricts the liability of the contracting party for the misrepresentation. Therefore, if such a provision is relied on to negative the principal's liability for the misrepresentation, the Court has to consider what is fair and reasonable in the circumstances of the case and that can only be done in the course of the trial of the action. To put the matter more shortly, condition R(b) excludes, or restricts, liability because it excludes, or restricts, an essential ingredient of liability, namely, the ostensible authority of [the auctioneers].

In my judgment, s. 3 of the 1967 Act will not bear the load which counsel for the defendant company seeks to place on it. In my view the section only applies to a provision which would exclude or restrict liability for a misrepresentation made by a party or his duly authorised agent, including, of course, an agent with ostensible authority. The section does not, in my judgment, in any way qualify the right of a principal publicly to limit the otherwise ostensible authority of his agent. The second argument of the defendant company fails.

<h2 style="text-align:center">UBAF Ltd. v. European American Banking Corp.</h2>

[1984] 2 All E.R. 226, C.A.

A representation signed on behalf of a limited company by a properly authorised officer acting in the course of his duties constitutes the company's signature for the purpose of the Statute of Frauds Amendment Act 1828, s. 6.

The plaintiffs, an English bank brought an action against the defendants, an American bank, claiming damages for deceit on the ground that a fraudulent misrepresentation made by the defendants' assistant secretary had induced them to lend money to a shipping group and that they had suffered a loss in consequence. The defendants contended that they were not liable on the ground that the assistant secretary's signature was not the company's signature for the purposes of the Statute of Frauds Amendment Act 1828, s. 6.[78]

Held, by the Court of Appeal, that the defendants were not entitled to rely on s. 6 of the Act for the assistant secretary's signature was the company's signature.

---

[78] Which states: "No action shall be brought whereby to charge any person upon or by reason of any representation or assurance made or given concerning or relating to the character, conduct, credit, ability, trade or dealings of any other person, to the intent or purpose that such other person may obtain credit, money, or goods upon, unless such representation or assurance be made in writing, signed by the party to be charged therewith."

ACKNER, L.J. (at page 234)

In any event, even if 80 years ago or so it was assumed that the signature of a duly authorised officer or employee, acting in the course of his duties in the business of the company, was not the signature of the company, then it must also be recalled that it was not until *Barwick's*[79] case in 1867 that it was finally decided that the doctrine of vicarious liability extended to the fraudulent act of the agent of the company committed in the course of its business and for its benefit. The law relative to corporate activities has developed considerably over the years and cannot be taken to have stood still all this time. Parliament is continually placing the obligation on corporate bodies to serve notices in writing of one kind or another and, in the case of local authorities, has expressly provided for such documents to be signed by the proper officer (see s. 234(2) of the Local Government Act 1972). Since a company, not being a physical entity, can only act in relation to the outside world by its agents, no one nowadays would question that the signature of the duly authorised agent of the company, acting in the course of the company's business, is the signature of the company. Take as a simple, yet frequent, example the statutory notice of termination of a tenancy given by a company landlord under s. 25 of the Landlord and Tenant Act 1954. While there may always be questions as to the authority of the agent who purported to sign the notice, given that he had the company's authority to give such notices and was doing so in the course of his duties in the business of the company, no one would nowadays question that his signature is to be taken as the signature of the company.

We do not, therefore, find any impediment in authority against deciding, and we think that it should now be decided, that the signature on behalf of a company of its duly authorised agent acting within the scope of his authority is, for the purpose of s. 6 of the 1828 Act, the signature of the company.

(12) Effect of termination of agency

Blades v. Free

(1829) 9 B. & C. 167

Where a principal has held out an agent as having authority to act for him, the principal's personal representatives will not be liable to a third party who dealt with the agent after the principal's death, even though this was unknown to the third party.

From 1822 onwards the plaintiff supplied goods on credit to a Mr Clark on the orders of a Mrs Steers with whom Clark was living. Clark held out Mrs Steers as having authority to act for him. On 31st December, 1824, Clark died. The plaintiff continued

---

[79] I.e. *Barwick* v. *English Joint Stock Bank* (1867) L.R. 2 Exch. 259; [1861–73] All E.R. Rep. 194, Ex. Ch.

to supply goods on the orders of Mrs Steers until August, 1825, when he discovered that Clark had died. The plaintiff now brought an action for the price of the goods against Clark's personal representative.

Held, by the Court of King's Bench, that the action failed, for the authority which Clark had given Mrs Steers was revoked by his death, and his estate could not be made liable to the plaintiff.

BAYLEY, J. (at page 170)

There is no doubt that a man may make an express contract for goods to be supplied to his wife or mistress after his death, for which his estate would be liable. But here there was no express contract. What then is the inference of law? That the woman had the same authority to bind the deceased by her contracts, as if she had been his wife, and such an authority would be revoked by his death? It is said that this is hard upon the tradesman. But he trusts, at his peril, whether the credit is given upon the order of a married woman or mistress. If he is unwilling to run the risk, he should require an express contract, if he does not do so, and sustains a loss, that is by reason of his own carelessness. It seems to me that the woman in this case had the authority of a wife, and that she could not make any contract to bind the estate after the death of the testator.

LITTLEDALE, J. (at page 171)

In this case there was no express contract, and none can be implied from which the plaintiff can derive a right to recover. There was no continuing implied contract made by the deceased, but an authority to the woman with whom he cohabited to make contracts for him from time to time, and at his death that authority ceased. The tradesman cannot be better off than if this had been a question upon the contract of a wife, and her contracts cannot bind the husband's estate if made after his death.

Drew *v.* Nunn

(1879) 40 L.T. 671

Where a principal has held out an agent as having authority to act for him, the principal will be bound by the agent's acts even though the principal later becomes insane, unless the third party with whom the agent has dealt knew of the principal's insanity.

From 1872 onwards the defendant held out his wife as having authority to act for him. The plaintiff, acting on the wife's order, supplied goods to the defendant. In 1873 the defendant, unknown to the plaintiff, became insane. Between April, 1876, and June, 1877, the plaintiff supplied further goods to the defendant on the wife's order, and now sought to make the defendant liable for the price. The defendant contended that his wife had no authority because it had been revoked by his insanity.

Held, by the Court of Appeal, that the action succeeded. The authority given to the wife continued *vis-à-vis* the third party, even though the principal had become insane.

BRETT, L.J. (at page 673)

Who is liable where the authority of the agent has been held out to a person dealt with who had no notice of the principal's lunacy? An agent may be held out as having authority in one of two ways. Where some instrument such as a power of attorney asserts that he has the authority, then the fact of the power of attorney having been previously given is an assertion that the person holding it may act for the principal, and if the agent is acting within that authority, the principal is bound. The other way in which an agent may be held out as having authority is where something has been done as in the present case, where the principal whilst sane has held out that his agent had authority to act for him in particular cases, and then the principal having become insane, and the agent knowing of the lunacy, nevertheless acts with a third person as though the authority continued. What is the consequence? It seems to me that a person who deals with the agent without knowledge of the principal's lunacy has a right so to deal, and that the lunatic is bound by having held out the authority of the agent. It is difficult to state what are the grounds upon which this principle rests. It is sometimes said that the right depends on contract. I cannot see it. It is also put on the ground of estoppel. It is somewhat difficult to see how in strictness there can be an estoppel. It is also said that the right depends upon representations made by the principal upon which a person with no notice to the contrary is entitled to act. There is an elaborate note in *Story on Agency* by the editors of the 7th edition in which they say the principle is to be defended on the ground of public policy. It is said by others to be in aid of rendering effectual business transactions. To my mind the better way of stating the ground is, that it is because of a representation, made by the principal when he was sane and could make it, to an innocent party upon which the latter has a right to act until he knows of the lunacy. Supposing there is no lunacy, but a principal holds out a person to be his agent, and then of his own accord withdraws the agency. As between the principal and the agent the right to bind the principal has ceased, and then the agent does a wrongful act by acting with a third person as though the authority continued; nevertheless if the agent has been held out as having authority to the third person, and the latter acts with the agent before he has received any notice of the authority having ceased, the principal is still bound upon the ground that he made representations upon which the third person had a right to act, and cannot retract from the consequences of those representations. It is true that if the principal becomes lunatic, he cannot himself give notice to the third person of the agency having ceased, and he may be an innocent sufferer from the wrongful act of the agent. But so is the other; and it is a principle of law that where it is a question which of two innocent parties shall suffer, that one must suffer who caused the state of things upon which the other has acted. Therefore, in my opinion, although the lunatic recovers his reason, he cannot, after his recovery, any more than if he had never been a lunatic, say that an innocent person who acted on representations made before lunacy had not a right to do so.

Willis Faber & Co. Ltd. *v.* Joyce

(1911) 104 L.T. 576

Where the principal has represented to a third party that an agent has authority to act for him, he will be bound by the agent's act even though he has revoked the agent's authority, unless such revocation is known to the third party.

Since 1907 the plaintiffs, who were insurance brokers, had effected many insurance policies which had been subscribed by the defendant underwriter through a Mr Angove, who was the defendant's agent. Angove was appointed for two years terminating on 31st December, 1909, but continued to subscribe policies after that date. The plaintiffs claimed against the defendant for losses arising under the policies signed by Angove after the termination of his appointment. They did not know that he had ceased to be the defendant's agent.

Held, by the King's Bench Division, that the action succeeded. The defendant had held out Angove as having authority to subscribe policies and had not notified the plaintiffs of the termination of such authority, and was accordingly liable to them.

SCRUTTON, J. (at page 576)

The point which I have to decide at present, and which is enough to decide the case, is this: Mr Joyce's written authority to Angove terminated on 31st December, 1909. After 31st December, 1909 Angove put Mr Joyce's name on policies which would have been within the terms of the authority if they had been before 31st December, 1909. Assuming Mr Joyce to have revoked his authority, or to have terminated his authority by this agreement, he gave no notice of that termination at Lloyd's, and the plaintiffs dealt with Angove, and took Mr Joyce's name on the policy, without any knowledge that Mr Joyce's written authority to Angove had ceased some two months before. Now is it permissible for Mr Joyce to say to people who sue on these policies: "Angove had no authority to write in my name; my authority had terminated two months before"? It appears to me that I, sitting as a Judge of first instance, am bound by the present state of the authorities to hold that it is no answer for Mr Joyce to say that the authority was determined in writing unless he proves that he gave notice of it. I find that Lord SELBORNE stated in *Scarf* v. *Jardine*,[80] in the House of Lords, when dealing with the question of partnership:[81]

"The principle of law, which is stated in *Lindley on Partnership*, is incontrovertible— namely, that 'when an ostensible partner retires, or when a partnership between several known partners is dissolved, those who dealt with the firm before a change took place are entitled to assume, until they have notice to the contrary, that no change has occurred'; and the principle on which they are entitled to assume it is that of the estoppel of a person who has accredited another as his known agent from denying that agency at a subsequent time as against the persons to whom he has accredited him, by reason of any secret revocation."

[80] (1882) 7 App.Cas. 345, H.L.
[81] *Ibid.*, at p. 349.

The principle puts the reason of the partnership rule not on anything peculiar to partnership, but on the general principle of agency. The passage in the earlier part of Lord LINDLEY's book, to which I will not refer, but which I have looked at, is dealing not with anything in the Partnership Act because it is made part of the law of the land by statute (s. 36 of the Partnership Act is expressly embodied), but is dealing with the Common Law of partnership; and Lord LINDLEY also, as Lord SELBORNE did, bases it upon the application of the ordinary law of agency. I find the Court of Appeal in the case of *Drew* v. *Nunn*[82] laying down the same principle. There the wife had authority to bind her husband with tradesmen. The husband became insane, and the Court held that the wife's authority to bind her husband ceased; but they held that as she had been the husband's agent, and no notice had been given to the tradesmen that her agency was determined, the husband was bound; and the two members of the Court, perhaps the three, who decided that, put it upon a general principle of agency, that an agent's authority once held out cannot be withdrawn to third persons without giving them notice of withdrawal. It appears to me that Lord SELBORNE's statement and the Court of Appeal's decision in *Drew* v. *Nunn* bind me, and if they are to be reversed, they must be reversed by a higher tribunal than mine. The case that Mr Bailhache handed to me of *Trueman* v. *Loder*[83] appears to me to decide the same thing. There the defendant was acting through an agent. He had been dealing with him for some years and he withdrew the agent's authority. The agent made a contract in his own name, and because it was known on the market that he was always acting for the defendant, the defendant was held bound, although he had withdrawn his authority, because he had not given good notice of the withdrawal.

---

[82] (1879) 40 L.T. 671. See p. 119, *ante*.
[83] (1840) 11 Ad. & El. 589.

PART III

RELATION BETWEEN AGENT AND THIRD PARTY

(1) Personal liability of agent in respect of contract

Universal Steam Navigation Co. Ltd. *v.* James McKelvie

(1923) 129 L.T. 395

Where an agent indicates that he is contracting as such, he cannot be made liable on the contract.

A charter-party was entered into between T. H. Seed & Co., as agents for the owners of a vessel and "James McKelvie & Co., charterers". It was signed by J. A. McKelvie "for and on behalf of James McKelvie, & Co. (as agents)". When sued for breach of the charter-party, McKelvie & Co. pleaded that they had acted as agents for an Italian company, and were not personally liable.

Held, by the House of Lords, that they had incurred no personal liability. Their signature "as agents" indicated clearly that they were acting only in that capacity.

LORD SHAW (at page 399)

I agree that for many years past it has, I believe, been generally understood in business that to add "as agents" to the signature is all that is necessary to save a party, signing for a principal, from personal liability on the contract, and I agree also that, even as a matter of construction, when a signature so qualified is attached to a general printed form with blanks filled in *ad hoc*, preponderant importance attaches to the qualification in comparison with printed clauses or even with manuscript insertions in the form. It still, however, remains true that the qualifying words "as agents" are a part of the contract and must be construed with the rest of it. They might have been expressed as a separate clause—e.g., "it is further agreed that the party signing this charter as charterer does so as agent for an undisclosed principal", and that clause would obviously have to be construed. They are a form of words and not a mere part of the act of signifying assent and closing a negotiation by duly attaching a name. They purport to limit and explain a liability, and not merely to identify the person signing or to justify the inscription of a name by the hand of a person other than the owner of it. They are more than the addition of "junior" or "(Revd.)" to the signature, which serves to identify the signatory by distinguishing him from others. They are more than a mere "per procuration", which only alleges authority to write another's name. If Mr J. A. McKelvie had written in his own handwriting

"Brandt Pagnini and Co." and no more, then, on proof of due authority, Brandt Pagnini and Co. would have been bound by the charter, and (subject to the effect of the words at the beginning of the charter "and James McKelvie and Co., Newcastle-upon-Tyne, charterers") McKelvie and Co. would not. . . .

They are more, too, than words of description of the signatory's business. It has sometimes been said that when "agents" is the word added to the signature, it is a mere word of description, and so does not qualify the liability, which the act of signing imports. I question this explanation. One's signature is not the place in which to advertise one's calling, nor is "agent" ordinarily used to describe a trade, as "tailor" or "butcher" would be. I have no doubt that when people add "agent" to a signature to a contract, they are trying to escape personal liability, but are unaware that the attempt will fail. The result, however, is the same. When words added to a signature in themselves qualify liability, it is because, as words, they can be so construed in conjunction with the contract as a whole.

Gadd v. Houghton & Co.

(1876) 35 L.T. 222

Where an agent indicates that he is contracting as such, he cannot be made liable on the contract.

> Houghton & Co. sold 2,000 cases of oranges to Gadd, the "sold note" stating:—"We have this day sold to you on account of James Morand & Co. . . ." and being signed "Houghton & Co." The goods were not delivered, so Gadd sued Houghton & Co. for damages for non-delivery.
> *Held*, by the Court of Appeal, that the action failed, for Houghton & Co. by the words of the "sold note" had clearly indicated that they were not to be personally liable on the contract.

MELLISH, L.J. (at page 223)

The question is whether, upon the true construction of this contract, Houghton and Co., who sold the goods, are themselves liable, or whether they have entered into a contract on behalf of James Morand and Co. This question is to be decided by interpreting the language which has been used according to the plain natural interpretation of the words. I agree with what was said by Lord CAMPBELL in *Parker* v. *Winlow*[1] and in the note to *Thomson* v. *Davenport*[2] in *Smith's Leading Cases*, (6th edn., vol. 2, 343), that *prima facie* where a man signs a contract in his own name, he is a contracting party, and there must be something very strong on the face of the instrument to prevent that liability attaching to him. But I cannot understand why, under the circumstances of this case, where there are plain words to that effect in the contract, we are not to say

---

[1] (1857) 7 E. & B. 942.
[2] (1829) 9 B. & C. 78.

that he is contracting on behalf of somebody else. I am of opinion that there is no difference between a person saying "I, as agent for C. D., have sold to you", and saying "I have sold to you", and signing that in his own name "for C. D.". Where you find a person in the body of the instrument treating himself as the seller or charterer, no doubt it is different, and you can say that he intended to bind himself; but where there is nothing of that kind, and all that appears is that he has been making a contract on behalf of somebody else, it seems to necessarily follow that that somebody else is the person liable. Here they say, "We have this day sold to you on account of J. Morand and Co.". How can the words "on account of" be inserted merely as a description? They do not describe who Houghton and Co. were at all, but they say on whose account the contract has been entered into. It is "Houghton and Co. on account of J. Morand and Co.". Meaning that J. Morand and Co. are really the people who have sold. It follows that the persons who signed the contract were merely the brokers, and were not liable.

Benton *v.* Campbell, Parker & Co. Ltd.

[1925] All E.R. Rep. 187

Where an auctioneer sells specific goods for an unnamed principal, he cannot normally be held liable if the principal has no title to them.

An auctioneer sold a car at an auction on behalf of an unnamed principal. The buyer discovered that it was already subject to a hire-purchase agreement, so he sought to hold the auctioneer personally liable on the contract of sale.

Held, by the King's Bench Division, that the action failed, for the auctioneer had not warranted the principal's title to sell.

SALTER, J. (at page 188)

When an agent purports to make a contract for a principal, disclosing the fact that he is acting as an agent but not naming his principal, the rule is that, unless a contrary intention appears, he makes himself personally liable on the authorised contract. It is presumed that the other party is unwilling to contract solely with an unknown man. He is willing to contract with an unknown man and does so, but only if the agent will make himself personally liable, if called on, to perform the contract which he arranges for his principal. The agent is presumed to agree. The liability of the agent is not joint, nor is it contingent on default by the principal. Two contracts are made in identical terms, one with the principal and the other with the agent, and the opposite party, unless prevented by some election, can enforce either, but not both.

The first question is whether this general rule applies in this case, or the circumstances are such as to rebut the presumption. Where the agency is to buy goods, whether ascertained or not, so that the liability imposed on the principal by the contract is a liability to accept and pay, there is nothing in the circumstances inconsistent with a presumption that the seller requires that the agent shall make himself personally liable to take and pay for the goods in accordance with the contract of sale, if called on, or with a presumption that the agent agrees to do so. So, again, if the agency is to sell unascertained goods, there is nothing inconsistent with a presumption that the buyer stipulates, and the agent agrees, that the agent will himself deliver goods in accordance with the contract of sale if called on. If he has not the necessary goods, he can procure them and make delivery. But when the agency, as in this case, is an agency for the sale of a specific chattel, which the buyer knows is not the property of the agent, it seems to me impossible to presume that the buyer, who contracts to buy that chattel from the principal, would stipulate that the agent, if called on, shall himself sell the chattel to the buyer, and shall warrant his own title to a thing which the buyer knows is not his. It is impossible to presume that the agent would agree to undertake such a liability. The only way in which he could discharge it would be by acquiring the chattel from his principal, a thing he has no right to demand and a thing inconsistent with the contract he has been instructed to make, by which the principal sells that chattel to the buyer. For this reason, I think that the presumption above mentioned is rebutted in the case of a sale of a specific chattel by a known agent for an undisclosed principal.

This applies to an auctioneer as to any other selling agent. An auctioneer has a special property in the chattel delivered to him for sale. He has a lien on it and on the price of it; he has rights against the buyer, and liabilities to him which do not accrue to other selling agents. These rights and liabilities do not arise from the contract of sale, which binds only the buyer and the principal; they arise from the contract which the auctioneer makes on his own account with the buyer. Every agent to contract, when he makes the authorised contract between his principal and the other party, makes also a contract on his own account with the other party—he warrants his authority. If he is an agent for sale, he also warrants that he knows of no defect in his principal's title. If he is an auctioneer to whom a chattel has been delivered for sale, he gives both these warranties, he undertakes to give possession against the price paid into his hands, and he undertakes that such possession will not be disturbed by his principal or himself. There may, of course, be other terms in this contract, arising on the facts of the case. The warranties are implied terms; the duty to deliver and the right to receive the price are usually expressed in the conditions of sale. But whatever its terms may be, the contract is entirely independent of the contract of sale. To that contract the auctioneer who sells a specific chattel as an agent is, in my opinion, no party; he has no right to enforce it and is not bound by it.

N. & J. Vlassopulos Ltd. *v*. Ney Shipping Ltd.: The "Santa Carina"

[1977] 1 Lloyd's Rep. 478

Although the third party knows that the person with whom he is dealing is an agent acting for an unnamed principal, the facts may indicate that the third party is content to look to the credit of the principal whoever he may be.

The defendants, who were brokers on the Baltic Exchange, telephoned the plaintiffs, who were also brokers there, and asked them to supply bunkers to the vessel *Santa Carina*. The plaintiffs did not know the defendants' principals. The invoice for the bunkers remained unpaid, so the plaintiffs claimed the price from the defendants.

Held, by the Court of Appeal, that there would be judgment for the defendants, for the plaintiffs had not proved that the defendants were personally liable to them.

LORD DENNING, M.R. (at page 481)

On the facts I have stated, it is clear that Vlassopulos, the brokers for the suppliers, knew that Ney, the brokers for the time charterers, were ordering the fuel simply as agents. They were agents either for the owners or the time charterers of the vessels. The brokers for the suppliers knew they were agents. They received a telephone message saying: "Please supply this fuel oil to the vessel". But they knew it was from the agents as agents.

The [trial] Judge held that the brokers who ordered the fuel were personally liable. He was much influenced by the cases where a person gives a written order for goods or signs a written contract when he is known to be acting as an agent. Nevertheless, although he is known to be acting as an agent, he will be liable on that order or liable on that contract if he signs in his own personal name without qualification. That is settled by cases both in this Court and in the House of Lords: see *H. O. Brandt & Co.* v. *H. N. Morris & Co. Ltd.*,[3] and *Hichens Harrison, Woolston & Co.* v. *Jackson*.[4] In order to exclude his liability he has to append to his signature some such words as "as agent only" or "for and on behalf of " or such exclusion must be apparent elsewhere in the document. That is clear from *Universal Steam Navigation Co.* v. *James McKelvie & Co.*[5]

The Judge thought that those cases on written orders and written contracts should be applied to the present case of an oral contract. He felt that if there is an oral conversation on the telephone, as in this case ordering bunkers, the broker is liable unless he uses some express words so as to show that he is acting as agent only and is not to be held personally liable. He said:[6]

"Thus, some words must be used to indicate that the agent is not himself undertaking any financial obligation or liability."

I have no doubt that those cases on written orders and written contracts arose out of the old rule of evidence whereby it was not permissible to admit oral evidence to alter or contradict a written contract. Those cases still apply today to written orders and written contracts. But they do not apply to oral orders or oral contracts. At any rate not so rigidly. In many cases if a man, who is an agent for another, orders goods or makes a contract by word of mouth, but does not disclose the name or standing of his principal (so that his credit is unknown to the other contracting party) the agent himself is liable to pay for the goods or to

---

[3] [1917] 2 K.B. 784, C.A., at p. 796 (*per* SCRUTTON, L.J.).
[4] [1943] A.C. 266, H.L., at p. 273 (*per* Lord ATKIN).
[5] [1923] A.C. 492, H.L. See p. 123, *ante*.
[6] [1976] 2 Lloyd's Rep., at p. 226.

fulfil the contract. It may be that the other contracting party knows that the man is only an agent, but, as he does not know who the principal is, it is to be inferred that he does not rely on the credit of the principal but looks to the agent. That, I think, is the thought underlying the dictum of SALTER, J., in *Benton* v. *Campbell, Parker & Co. Ltd.*,[7] and the American Restatement on Agency in the comment to par. 321. But in other cases that may not be the proper inference. There are cases where, although the man who supplied the goods knows that the other is an agent and does not know his principal, nevertheless he is content to look to the credit of that principal whoever he may be. This is something which DIPLOCK, L.J., contemplated in the case of *Teheran-Europe Co. Ltd.* v. *S. T. Belton (Tractors) Ltd.*[8] He said[9] that

> ". . . he is willing to treat as a party to the contract anyone on whose behalf the agent may have been authorised to contract . . ."

This applies particularly to the case of a broker. As BLACKBURN, J. said in *Fleet* v. *Murton*:[10]

> ". . . I take it that there is no doubt at all, in principle, that a broker, as such, merely dealing as broker and not as purchaser of the article, makes a contrat from the very nature of things between the buyer and the seller and he is not himself either buyer or seller".

It seems to me that the present case falls into that second category. It was known to both sides that the agents, Ney Shipping Ltd., were only brokers. They were brokers ordering bunkers for a vessel. It was obvious that they were only agents, and they were ordering bunkers for the time charterers or the owners of a vessel. They had often done it before. The accounts for the fuel had always been paid by the principals either directly or through the brokers. It cannot be supposed that the brokers were ever intended to be personally liable. The suppliers would look to the time charterers or the owners, whoever they might be, they being the people to be relied upon. Although they were not named or specified or disclosed, they would be the people to whom the suppliers would look for payment of the oil.

It is just the same, it seems to me, as if the brokers had given a written order for the bunkers and added to their signatures "as agents only". In that case they would not have been personally liable. Nor should they be liable in this case when it was done by word of mouth, and when the inference from the conduct and the whole of the circumstances was that they were ordering the fuel as agents only.

It can be tested by taking the converse case. Suppose the fuel had been of bad quality and the engines of the ship had been damaged, or the ship delayed, could

---

[7] [1925] 2 K.B. 410, at p. 414. See p. 125, *ante.*
[8] [1968] 2 Lloyd's Rep. 37, C.A.
[9] *Ibid.*, at p. 41.
[10] (1871) L.R. 7 Q.B. 126, at p. 131.

the brokers Ney Shipping have sued for damages? Or the brokers Vlassopulos have been made liable in damages? Clearly not. It would be for the principals on either side to have sued. So here the brokers Vlassopulos could not sue for the price, nor the brokers Ney be liable for it.

I know that in many trades there is a custom by which the broker is liable. Those cases rest on a custom of the trade. There was no such custom alleged or proved in respect of the brokers on the Baltic Exchange. It seems to me that, in the circumstances of this case, the proper inference is that the agents here were, when they gave the telephone message, giving it as agents only. By their conduct it is to be inferred that it was just the same as if they had given a written order excluding their personal liability and the suppliers looked to the owners or time charterers of the vessel who were the people really liable. It is the unfortunate fact that they have proved insolvent or unable to pay, but it seems to me that that is not a sufficient ground for now making the brokers liable.

J. S. Holt & Moseley (London) Ltd. *v.* Sir Charles Cunningham & Partners

(1950) 83 Ll.L.Rep. 141

There is no longer any presumption that an agent acting for a foreign principal (i.e., one outside the jurisdiction) is personally liable. In each case it is a question as to what the parties intended.

> The plaintiffs were shipping agents, who carried on business in England. They were instructed by the defendants, who also carried on business in England, to ship a quantity of cut glass to their principals, Kaisar Ahmad & Co., in Bombay. The plaintiffs did so, and incurred freight and insurance charges which they now claimed from the defendants on the ground that there was a presumption that an agent acting for a foreign principal was personally liable.
>
> *Held*, by the King's Bench Division, that there was no such presumption at the present time and the action failed. The evidence showed that it was never contemplated by the parties that the defendants should be personally liable. The whereabouts of the principal was only one of the factors to be taken into account by the Court.

PRITCHARD, J. (at page 145)

The plaintiffs and the defendants never contemplated that the defendants should become liable to the plaintiffs for freight and insurance except in so far as they might become liable to distribute the Indian company's credits in part to the plaintiffs.

In these circumstances, there is no room for the presumption for which the plaintiffs contend, namely, the presumption that the defendants contracted personally because they were home agents contracting for a foreign principal. Since the decision of the Court of Appeal in *Miller, Gibb & Co.* v. *Smith & Tyrer Ltd.*,[11] the so-called presumption or trade usage to this effect cannot, I

---

[11] [1917] 2 K.B. 141.

think, be regarded as existing as part of the law governing commercial contracts, and the true view seems to be merely this—that when a question is raised as to the legal position of an agent contracting for a foreign principal, it is in each case a question as to what the parties intended. The intention of the parties can only be ascertained from the facts as proved in evidence, and the nationality and whereabouts of the principal is no more and no less than one of the facts to which such weight will be given as in any particular case the Court thinks proper.

Hersom *v.* Bernett

[1954] 3 All E.R. 370

Where an agent acting for an unnamed principal later gives the principal's name to the third party in answer to an inquiry, he is bound by that representation and is not entitled to state that he was really acting for another person. If the representation is untrue, he himself will be personally liable as principal.

> The plaintiff purchased some cases of peppermint oil from the defendant, who told him that he was contracting on behalf of a principal, but did not state his principal's name. The goods were found to have been stolen, and the plaintiff had to return them to their true owner. The plaintiff sued the defendant for the price, but the defendant contended that he was acting for an unnamed principal, and therefore was not liable. In answer to the plaintiff's inquiries he said that his principal's name was "Williams". Williams was not, in fact, his principal. On the faith of the statement the plaintiff prepared his case and demolished the representation. The defendant then sought to show that someone else was his principal.
> *Held*, by the Queen's Bench Division, that the defendant was not entitled to show that someone else was his principal, and must himself be treated as principal, and liable to the plaintiff accordingly.

ROXBURGH, J. (at page 373)

It seems to me that a fundamental principle of justice requires that a defendant, who has given false evidence that his principal was X, should not be heard to say through his counsel in argument that his principal may have been somebody else, but he must thereafter be treated as having no principal, or, in other words, as being himself the principal. I need only add that this sort of estoppel, if that is a correct description of this fundamental principle (and I am by no means sure that it is), could not by reason of its very nature, be pleaded, because it only arises during the course of the trial in consequence of the finding of the Judge that the evidence of the defendant that X was the principal was false.

(2) Personal liability of agent on bill of exchange

Elliott v. Bax-Ironside and another

(1925) 133 L.T. 624

By s. 26(1) of the Bills of Exchange Act 1882: "Where a person signs a bill as drawer, indorser, or acceptor, and adds words to his signature, indicating that he signs for or on behalf of a principal, or in a representative character, he is not personally liable thereon; but the mere addition to his signature of words describing him as an agent, or as filling a representative character, does not exempt him from personal liability."

The plaintiff drew a bill of exchange on Fashions Fair Exhibitions Ltd. The defendants were directors of that company and accepted the bill in these words: "Accepted . . . H. O. Bax-Ironside, Ronald A. Mason, directors Fashions Fair Exhibitions Ltd.". They also indorsed the bill in a similar way. The plaintiff sued the defendants, but they denied liability.

Held, by the Court of Appeal, that the defendants were personally liable under s. 26 of the Act.

SCRUTTON, L.J. (at page 627)

When a person puts his name on a bill with an addition, there are two classes of cases into which the addition may fall. The addition may be such as to show that he is contracting as agent for another, putting his name on the bill as agent for another, excluding any personal liability of his own. When a man signs "For and on behalf of Jones as agent", he is clearly not undertaking any personal liability of his own as a principal, but is purporting to makes Jones liable.

On the other hand, there is a class of case where the man puts after his signature a description for the purpose of showing who he is and how he comes to sign: "So and so, Churchwarden". It was in one of the cases where there was a question about a parish, and where it was held that the fact that the person who put his name upon the document described himself as churchwarden, did not mean that he was signing as agent for the parish, and had no personal liability, but merely was an explanation of how he came to put his name on the document.

In the early history of the cases Lord ELLENBOROUGH, in a picturesque passage in *Leadbitter* v. *Farrow*,[12] gave his judgment in this way:[13]

"Is it not a universal rule that a man who puts his name to a bill of exchange thereby makes himself personally liable, unless he states upon the face of the bill that he subscribes it *for* another, or by procuration of another, which are words of exclusion? Unless he says plainly, 'I am the mere scribe', he becomes liable."

---

[12] (1816) 5 M. & S. 345.
[13] *Ibid.*, at p. 349.

That is put in a less picturesque way, perhaps, by COCKBURN, C.J., in the case of *Dutton* v. *Marsh and Others*[14] to which my Lord has referred:[15]

> "The effect of the authorities is clearly this, that where parties in making a promissory note or accepting a bill describe themselves as directors, or by any similar form of description but do not state on the face of the document that it is on account or on behalf of those whom they might otherwise be considered as representing—if they merely describe themselves as directors, but do not state that they are acting on behalf of the company—they are individually liable. But, on the other hand, if they state they are signing the note or the acceptance on account of or on behalf of some company or body of whom they are the directors and the representatives, in that case, as the case of *Lindus* v. *Melrose and Others*[16] fully establishes, they do not make themselves liable when they sign their names, but are taken to have been acting for the company, as the statement on the face of the document represented".

Those were pre-codification cases, and when Parliament came to codify and to some extent alter the law, they codified it in this way in s. 26 of the Bills of Exchange Act 1882:

> "(1) Where a person signs a bill as drawer, indorser, or acceptor, and adds words to his signature, indicating that he signs for or on behalf of a principal, or in a representative character, he is not personally liable thereon; but the mere addition to his signature of words describing him as an agent, or as filling a representative character, does not exempt him from personal liability. (2) In determining whether a signature on a bill is that of the principal or that of the agent by whose hand it is written, the construction most favourable to the validity of the instrument shall be adopted".

I look at this document. It is accepted by two directors, with the name of the company, and I find on the back an indorsement of the names of the same two directors describing themselves as directors, with a stamp of the name of the company above. If both these indorsements are to be read in the same way, the second indorsement is valueless. You add nothing whatever to the bill by its being indorsed by a man who is already an acceptor. He is adding no value to the bill at all. He has already accepted, and adds no additional value to the bill by putting an indorsement on. If, on the other hand, the company having accepted a bill, two directors put their names on as indorsers in order to give their personal security, you do add to the bill, you give an additional commercial value to the bill, and in one's experience it is a very frequent commercial document that you do find—a bill accepted by a company and indorsed by directors. Therefore, working out s. 26 of the Bills of Exchange Act 1882 I find a document with a signature on it which may mean either, and I construe it in the way most favourable to the validity of the instrument.

I find a document signed by one of the defendants answering a letter from Mr Elliott: "I enclose herewith two drafts for £1,000 each, payable on the 4th and 14th March" (which fits in with the document I have under consideration) "duly signed by two directors of the company as requested by you". Turning to see

---

[14] (1871) L.R. 6 Q.B. 361.
[15] *Ibid.*, at p. 364.
[16] (1858) 3 H. & N. 177.

what that "as requested by you" is in the letter which is answered, I find "These drafts are to be indorsed by your company's directors on the back", and I think I am entitled to take that into account as confirming the view I have arrived at, that the company's directors were undertaking personal liability when they put those two signatures on the back. And if it is allowable to go farther (I do not know whether it is or not), it is eminently satisfactory to find that Sir H. Bax-Ironside himself thought he was incurring a liability by putting his signature on the back because he thought he was guaranteeing the bill.

(3) Effect of judgment against principal

London General Omnibus Co. *v*. Pope

(1922) 38 T.L.R. 270

Where a third party has sued the principal to judgment, he has no right of action against the agent even though the judgment remains unsatisfied.

> The plaintiffs brought an action against Macdonald and Turner, who were boxing promoters, in respect of the cost of some advertisements of the boxing match between Joe Becket and "Boy" McCormick. The contract for the advertisements had been entered into between the plaintiffs and the defendant acting as agent for Macdonald and Turner. The plaintiffs recovered judgment against Macdonald and Turner, which remained unsatisfied. They now brought an action against the defendant.
>
> *Held*, by the King's Bench Division, that the action failed, for the plaintiffs were not entitled to sue the defendant after they had obtained judgment against his principal even though it remained unsatisfied.

ROCHE, J. (at page 270)

Macdonald and Montagu were the principals. In his opinion, as the plaintiffs had got judgment against Macdonald and Montagu, they could not get it against Pope. He was satisfied that Mr Pope was a mere agent and had no personal interest in the contest. He was also satisfied that Turner knew it. That was not of itself sufficient to absolve Pope from liability. He made these contracts personally without disclosing who were the persons responsible for this exhibition, but, the plaintiffs, having discovered it, could elect between the principal and the agent. Their remedy was an alternative, not a joint remedy.

It could make no difference that the principal was sued first instead of the agent, and he gave judgment for the defendant, without costs.

(4) Third party's right of election

Clarkson, Booker Ltd. v. Andjel

[1964] 3 All E.R. 260

Where a third party has contracted with an agent acting for an undisclosed principal, and after discovering the existence of the undisclosed principal, "elects" to sue him, he cannot then hold the agent liable on the contract. What constitutes an "election" is a matter of fact in each case.

> The plaintiffs booked flights for 12 persons from Athens to London at the request of the defendant, who was acting for undisclosed principals, Peters & Milner Ltd. The defendant did not pay for the cost of the flights. In the meanwhile the plaintiffs discovered the existence of Peters & Milner Ltd. and on 26th July, 1962, the plaintiffs' solicitors wrote letters both to the defendant and to the company stating that if payment was not made, proceedings would be brought against both of them. On 3rd August the plaintiffs' solicitors wrote to Peters & Milner Ltd. stating that they had instructions to obtain judgment against them. On 13th December they issued and served a writ on Peters and Milner Ltd., but did not proceed further because the company was insolvent and going into voluntary liquidation. The plaintiffs now sued the defendant, but he contended that he was under no liability to them, because the institution of proceedings against Peters & Milner Ltd. constituted an "election" by them to hold the company alone liable.
>
> *Held*, by the Court of Appeal, that in the circumstances of the case the institution of proceedings against Peters and Milner Ltd. was not an "election", and the defendant was liable to pay for the cost of the flights.

WILLMER, L.J. (at page 266)

In order to constitute an election which will bar the present proceedings against the defendant the decision to sue Peters & Milner Ltd., must, in the first place, be shown to have been taken with full knowledge of all the relevant facts. In the circumstances of this case I feel no difficulty on that point, for it cannot be suggested that when the plaintiffs made their decision to sue Peters & Milner, Ltd., they were in any way ignorant of their rights against the defendant. Secondly, it must be shown that the decision to institute proceedings against Peters & Milner, Ltd., was a truly unequivocal act, if it is to preclude the plaintiffs from subsequently suing the defendant. This, I think, involves looking closely at the context in which the decision was taken, for any conclusion must be based on a review of all the relevant circumstances. One highly relevant circumstance is the fact that it was the defendant to whom the plaintiffs gave credit, as they had done over previous transactions. The correspondence shows that down to the letters of 26th July, 1962, the plaintiffs throughout were looking to the defendant for payment of their debt, i.e., to the person to whom they had given credit, although they also adumbrated a possible claim against Peters & Milner, Ltd. On 26 July, as I have already stated, they caused letters to be written to both the defendant and Peters & Milner, Ltd., threatening proceedings against both. Clearly up to that time there was no election to proceed only against the latter.

The whole case for the defendant rests on the fact that on 3rd August, having taken instructions, the plaintiffs' solicitors wrote to Peters & Milner, Ltd., announcing their intention "to obtain judgment" against them. It is true that they did not at that time write any similar letter to the defendant, but they did not then or at any other time ever withdraw their threat to take proceedings against him. There is not (and could not be) any suggestion that the defendant was in any way prejudiced by the course which the plaintiffs took, or that he was in any sense lulled into a false sense of security. Had the plaintiffs carried out their threat to obtain judgment against Peters & Milner, Ltd., they would, of course, have been precluded from subsequently taking proceedings against the defendant, for their cause of action would then have been merged in the judgment obtained against Peters & Milner, Ltd., but in fact the plaintiffs took no step against Peters & Milner, Ltd., beyond the issue and service of the writ. On being informed of the proposal to put the company into liquidation, they took no further action whatsoever against that company. They did not, for instance (as in *Scarf* v. *Jardine*[17] and other cases cited), seek to prove in the liquidation; instead they proceeded to give effect forthwith to their already announced, and never withdrawn, threat to sue the defendant.

On the whole, though I regard the case as being very near the borderline, I find myself unable to disagree with the conclusion arrived at by the Judge.[17a] I do not think that the plaintiffs, by the mere institution of proceedings against Peters & Milner, Ltd., made such an unequivocal election as to debar them from taking the present proceedings against the defendant.

(5) Breach of warranty of authority

Yonge *v.* Toynbee

[1908–10] All E.R. Rep. 204

An agent can be sued for damages for breach of warranty of authority, even though he did not know he had no authority to act for his principal.

On 21st August a client instructed a firm of solicitors to institute proceedings against a third party in respect of a libel. On 8th October the client, unknown to the solicitors, was certified insane. On 30th September they started proceedings against the third party. On 5th April they found out about the client's insanity. The third party sued them for damages for breach of warranty of authority claiming that he was entitled to be paid by them the costs defending the action.

Held, by the Court of Appeal, that the action succeeded. The fact that the solicitors did not know of their client's insanity was immaterial.

---

[17] [1881–85] All E.R. Rep. 651.
[17a] Judge BLOCK.

BUCKLEY, L.J. (at page 207)

The liability of the person who professes to act as an agent arises (a) if he has been fraudulent; (b) if he has without fraud untruly represented that he had authority when he had not; and (c) also where he innocently misrepresents that he has authority where the fact is either (i) that he never had authority, or (ii) that his original authority has ceased by reason of facts of which he has not knowledge or means of knowledge. Such last-mentioned liability arises from the fact that by professing to act as agent he impliedly contracts that he has authority, and it is immaterial whether he knew of the defect in his authority or not. This implied contract may, of course, be excluded by the facts of the particular case. If, for instance, the agent proved that at the relevant time he told the party with whom he was contracting that he did not know whether the warrant of attorney under which he was acting was genuine or not, and would not warrant its validity, or that his principal was abroad and he did not know whether he was still living, there will have been no representation upon which the implied contract will arise.

SWINFEN EADY, J. (at page 210)

I wish to add that in the conduct of litigation the Court places much reliance upon solicitors, who are its officers; it issues writs at their instance, and accepts appearances for defendants which they enter, as a matter of course, and without questioning their authority: the other parties to the litigation also act upon the same footing, without questioning or investigating the authority of the solicitor on the opposite side; and much confusion and uncertainty would be introduced if a solicitor were not to be under any liability to the opposite party for continuing to act without authority in cases where he originally possessed one.

. . . The manner in which business is ordinarily conducted requires that each party should be able to rely upon the solicitor of the other party having obtained a proper authority before assuming to act. It is always open to a solicitor to communicate as best he can with his own client, and obtain from time to time such authority and instructions as may be necessary. But the solicitor on the other side does not communicate with his opponent's client, and speaking generally, it is not proper for him to do so. It is, in my opinion, essential to the proper conduct of legal business that a solicitor should be held to warrant the authority which he claims of representing the client; if it were not so, no one would be safe in assuming that his opponent's solicitor was duly authorised in what he said or did, and it would be impossible to conduct legal business upon the footing now existing; and, whatever the legal liability may be, the Court, in exercising the authority which it possesses over its own officers, ought to proceed upon the footing that a solicitor assuming to act, in an action, for one of the parties to the action warrants his authority.

Halbot *v*. Lens

(1901) 83 L.T. 702

A third party cannot successfully sue the agent for damages for breach of warranty of authority if he knew that the agent had no authority to act on behalf of the principal.

Halbot and Lens carried on business as merchants. They agreed to enter into an arrangement with their creditors, and entered into an agreement between themselves whereby Halbot was to take over the current business of the firm including the stock-in-trade and to meet any claims by customers. Lens agreed to take over the firm's remaining assets. Clause 3 of the agreement stated:—"All claims made or existing by Dr. Clarke or Mrs. Lens against Halbot to be released". Lens signed the agreement "for self and Dr. Clarke". Dr Clarke repudiated liability on the agreement, contending that he had given Lens no authority to sign on his behalf. Halbot now sued Lens for damages for breach of warranty of authority.

Held, by the Chancery Division, that the action failed, for it was proved that Halbot knew that Lens had no authority to sign the agreement.

KEKEWICH, J. (at page 703)

The result of the evidence is, I think, clearly to establish that both the plaintiff and the defendant Lens equally knew, not merely that the defendant Lens had no authority to bind Dr Clarke, but that Dr Clarke had positively declined to assent to the terms of the agreement so far as they affected him. Is it possible, under these circumstances, to say that the defendant Lens made a misrepresentation of fact? There is a passage in the judgment of MELLISH, L.J. in *Beattie* v. *Lord Ebury*[18] which, to my mind, throws much light on this question. He says:[19]

"Supposing when an agent comes and professes to make a contract on behalf of his principal, instead of trusting his representation that he has power to bind his principal, the person dealing with the agent were to ask to see his authority, and a power of attorney executed by the principal were shown to him, and he took the opinion of his lawyer as to whether the power of attorney was sufficient to bind the principal and was advised that it was sufficient to bind the principal, and then after that a contract was made, and it turned out when the point was raised in a Court of law that the power of attorney was insufficient—under such circumstances I am clearly of opinion that there would be no warranty on the part of the agent that the power of attorney was good in point of law".

The case put by MELLISH, L.J., is not on all fours with that I have to deal with here, but it strongly accentuates the position that in order to maintain such an action there must be a misrepresentation of fact trusted by the person to whom it is made, and I cannot see myself how a man can be properly said to have made such a misrepresentation where in truth and in substance he has said, "Although

---

[18] (1872) L.R. 7 Ch.App. 777.
[19] *Ibid.*, at p. 800.

I will, if you wish it, sign this on behalf of the alleged principal, I tell you plainly that I have no authority from him to do so and have every reason to believe that such authority will not be forthcoming". A man, of course, might say, "I have no authority and probably cannot obtain such authority, but yet I will contract to obtain it and run the risk of damages". Such a contract is conceivable, and would be good in law, but ought not I think, to be inferred except from facts leading directly to the conclusion; and I do not find those facts here. I think it far more likely that it was agreed between the parties that the defendant Lens should add his signature on behalf of Dr Clarke for what it was worth, each party recognising that in all probability it was worth nothing. In my judgment, therefore, the plaintiff has failed to establish misrepresentation of fact against the defendant Lens as regards his signature on behalf of Dr Clarke, and the action is not maintainable to that extent.

Lilly, Wilson & Co. *v.* Smales, Eeles & Co.

[1892] 1 Q.B. 456

The agent is not liable for damages for breach of warranty of authority if there is a term to that effect in the contract which he enters into with the third party.

The plaintiffs were the owners of a vessel which they chartered to Reischer at the rate of freight of 3s. 9d. per ton. The charter-party was signed by the defendants, who were shipbrokers, "by telegraphic authority of Sam Reischer, Smales, Eeles & Co., as agents". In fact, the rate of freight offered by Reischer was only 3s. 4½d., the mistake in the rate quoted by the defendants having occurred owing to a blunder by the telegraphic officials, who transmitted to the defendants the telegram instructing them to enter into the charter-party with the plaintiffs. Reischer repudiated the charter-party, and the plaintiffs claimed damages from the defendants for breach of warranty of authority on the ground that they had held themselves out as having an authority which they did not possess.

Held, by the Queen's Bench Division, that the action failed. The words "by telegraphic authority" merely warranted that the defendants had had a telegram which, if correct, authorised them to enter into the charter-party at the rate of freight stated.

DENMAN, J. (at page 457)

It was contended by the plaintiffs that the defendants were liable in the action as having warranted or held themselves out as having an authority which they did not possess. The defendants, on the other hand, relied upon the form in which they had signed as negativing the warranty of authority which would have been implied if they had merely signed "as agents", and as amounting to a representation that they took no such risk upon themselves, but merely warranted that they had such authority as a possible erroneous telegram might confer.

If the case depended merely upon the construction of such a signature as a matter of law, much is to be said on both sides. On the one hand, it is difficult to understand why such a mode of signing should be used if it left the agent signing under precisely the same liability as he would be under without it. On the other hand, there is force in the argument used by counsel for the plaintiffs, that, inasmuch as the shipowner is often half the globe away when charters are made, there would be great inconvenience if in every case it was necessary to verify the correctness of telegrams before a firm contract could be relied on. But I do not think it necessary to consider all the arguments which were used as to the possible meaning of the words here adopted, because I think that it was not a question wholly of legal construction, but that the words adopted were words the true meaning of which was to be ascertained by the evidence of persons engaged in the business of commerce of this nature; and if I am right in this, I have no hesitation in finding that the defendants' witnesses established that this form of signing is well understood in the trade as meaning to negative the implication of a warranty by the charterer's agent, at all events, to a greater extent than warranting that he has had a telegram which, if correct, authorises such a charter as that which he is signing.

It appeared from the evidence of trustworthy witnesses for the defendants that, whenever charters are entered into by brokers in accordance with telegraphic instructions, it is usual to sign in this form with the very object of avoiding the implication of an absolute warranty. I see no reason to doubt that this was the real object of the defendants in signing as they did; and, this being ·my opinion, I think that there can be no ground for fixing them with a warranty such as they never intended to give, and which would be wholly inconsistent with the general understanding of persons engaged in the business in which they were employed.

Starkey *v.* Governor and Co. of the Bank of England

(1903) 88 L.T. 244

A third party is entitled to sue an agent for damages for breach of warranty of authority where he has relied to his detriment on the agent's representation that he has the principal's authority. The remedy is not confined to cases where the third party has been induced by the representation to enter into a contract.

> Starkey, a stockbroker, produced to the Bank of England a power of attorney signed by two joint principals named Frederick Oliver and Edgar Oliver, and instructed it to sell some stock standing in their joint names, and pay the proceeds to Frederick Oliver alone. This the Bank did, but it was found that the signature of Edgar Oliver appearing in the power of attorney had been forged. So the Bank had to replace the stock which it had sold without his authority. The Bank then sued Starkey for damages for breach of warranty of authority, maintaining that he was liable for the loss it had sustained.
>
> *Held*, by the House of Lords, that the action succeeded. The remedy of damages for breach of warranty of authority was not confined to cases where the third party had been induced to enter into a contract.

LORD HALSBURY, L.C. (at page 245)

Here is a formal document, intended to be acted upon, which upon the face of it purports to be a representation of authority by the person whose signature is appended thereto. Upon the facts I should have thought it impossible to doubt that it was a representation of authority on the part of those two persons whose signatures purport to be to it, and that the person who produced the authority and demanded to act upon it was himself asserting the authority which he had to do the thing which he was doing. He had no such authority. The result is that the Bank have transferred a quantity of Consols standing in the names of two persons when only one person gave the authority . . .

. . . Under the circumstances of this document being presented to the Bank to be acted upon, and upon the representation that the agent had the authority of the principal, which he had not, that does import an obligation, the contract being for good consideration, on the part of the person that the thing which he represented to be genuine was genuine.

(6) Personal liability of agent under Misrepresentation Act 1967

Resolute Maritime Inc. and another v. Nippon Kaiji Kyokai and others: The "Skopas"

[1983] 2 All E.R. 1

An agent, acting under his express or ostensible authority, who makes a statement that is untrue in circumstances in which he did not have reasonable ground to believe that it was true, cannot be held liable under the Misrepresentation Act 1967, s. 2(1).

The plaintiffs purchased the vessel *Skopas* from the third defendants. They sought to make the thirteenth defendant, a broker, liable under the Misrepresentation Act 1967, s. 2(1) in respect of a misrepresentation which they alleged he had made.

Held, by the Queen's Bench Division (Commercial Court), as a preliminary point of law, that the broker was not liable under s. 2(1) for liability attached only to his principal as party to the contract.

MUSTILL, L.J. (at page 2)

The plaintiffs seek damages on the basis that representations were made (a) fraudulently or (b) negligently. In addition, the plaintiffs rely on s. 2(1) of the Misrepresentation Act 1967. It is this latter claim which raises the issue now for consideration, it being common ground that the kindred claims in fraud and negligence turn on matters of fact which will have to be tried. It has, however, been thought appropriate to decide in advance of the trial a question of law under the 1967 Act. It is this: if an agent, acting in his express or ostensible authority, makes a statement which is untrue in circumstances where he did not have reasonable ground to believe that it was true, can he be held liable under the 1967 Act?

It is sensible to approach the problem by looking at the words of s. 2(1) in isolation to see whether they point so clearly towards one conclusion that there is no need for consideration of the Act as a whole or of the purpose which it was intended to achieve. Counsel for the plaintiffs says that they do. The draftsman has, he points out, chosen the word "party" to describe the representee in the opening words of the subsection, and has then chosen "person" to describe the representor in the remainder of the subsection. This shift in language demonstrates, so it is contended, that the person intended to be liable is not the obligor under the contract, but the individual who actually makes the representation. To this, counsel . . . replies that the alteration in language was for the purpose of euphony. One could not speak of "another person thereto". This argument itself prompts the response that, if the intention had been to make the obligor liable to the exclusion of the agent, the draftsman would have continued to use "party" throughout the remainder of the subsection, instead of reverting to the word "person". Finally, the defendants can reply by pointing out that, since an agent who incurs no personal liability under a contract is not "a party thereto", the agent can only be brought within the description of the representor if the words "by another party thereto" are read as meaning "by or on behalf of another party thereto", which is not what they say.

In my judgment, none of these arguments is sufficiently clinching to provide an immediate answer to the problem, and one must look elsewhere for a solution. The key is, in my view, to be found by looking at the position of the principal, in a case where he has authorised his agent to make the representation, and had no reasonable grounds to believe that the representation was true. Common sense suggests that if anyone is liable under a statute concerned with representations inducing a contract it ought to be a principal as party to the contract. That this is, indeed, the case is shown by s. 2(3), which contemplates that credit will be given as between the recoveries under sub-ss. (1) and (2); and these relate to liabilities of the same person, as witness the words "he" and "his". The liabilities under s. 2(2) must attach to the principal, for they are conferred as an alternative to rescission, a remedy which is available only against a party to the contract. It follows, therefore, that the word "person" in s. 2(1) must be read as including the principal.

It may, however, be objected that even if this is so there is still room to read s. 2(1) as creating an additional liability in the agent. I do not agree. The 1967 Act is concerned with representations made in the particular context of a contract, and it seems to me that it was aimed at the position of the parties to the contract. It was therefore natural that there should be created under sub-ss. (1) and (2) rights which are *prima facie* absolute, and independent of any general duty of care, a concept which plays no part in the law of contract. The purpose of the 1967 Act was to fill a gap which existed, or was believed to exist, in the remedies of one contracting party for an innocent representation by the other. But there was no such gap in the case of the agent; he was already subject to the ordinary liabilities in fraud and negligence, the doctrine of *Hedley Byrne & Co. Ltd.* v. *Heller & Partners Ltd.*[20] having been recognised before the 1967 Act was

---

[20] [1963] 2 All E.R. 575; [1964] A.C. 465, H.L.

passed. What purpose would there be in creating an entirely new absolute liability, independent of proof that the representee fell within the scope of a duty of care, simply because the representor happened to be an agent, concerned in the making of a contract, but not himself a party to it? I can see none; and, since, as I have suggested, the words of s. 2(1) must be read as extending to the principal, I consider that their operation should be confined to him alone.

INDEX

AGENCY OF NECESSITY
  arisal thereof, 21
  original agency, from, 23
AUCTIONEER
  liability where specific goods sold for
    unnamed principal, 125
  party to sale of specific chattel, not, 126
  rights and liabilities, 126

BILLS OF EXCHANGE
  agent's liability, signing own name,
    131-133
BINDING CONTRACT
  meaning of, 38
BRIBE
  civil law, definition, 109-110

CHARTER-PARTY
  commission charterer as trustee thereof,
    34
  definition, 72
COMMISSION
  both parties, from, when entitled, 27
  breach of duty, where incidental, 28
  charger-parties, 34
  death of agent, after, 31
  "effective cause", 23
  estate agents. *See* ESTATE AGENTS.
  fixed term, agency terminated, 57-61
  secret commission received, 27
  termination of agency, after, 32
  waiver of breach of duty, where, 29

DEATH OF PRINCIPAL
  termination of agency, 54, 118
*DELEGATUS NON POTEST
  DELEGARE*, 7
DUTIES OF AGENT
  principal, to, 4
    ambiguous instructions, where, 4
    bribes, as to, consequent dismissal, 12
    care, of, 4
    delegation, as to, 7, 8

DUTIES OF AGENT — *cont.*
  disclosure, as to, 19
  estate agent, as. *See* ESTATE AGENTS.
  obedience, of, 1
  "public body", agent of, burden of
    proving bribe, 13-15
  reasonable care, professional advice, 5
  secret profit, as to, 11
  sub-agent's negligence, liability for, 9
    reasonable care in selection, 10
  third parties, to. *See* LIABILITY OF
    AGENT.
DUTIES OF PRINCIPAL
  indemnity to agent, 48
    breach of duty by agent, where, 49
    non-compliance by agent, on, 50
    termination of agency, effect of, 61-62
    third party, liability to, agency
      terminated, 62
  remuneration. *See* COMMISSION.

ELECTION
  third party's right to, 134
ESTATE AGENTS
  authority, 2, 104
  commission payable,
    contract voidable, 41
    damages for loss of, 46
    general rules, 35
    "in the event of business resulting", 37
    introduction of "able and willing"
      purchaser, on 39, 40, 41
    "on securing an offer", 38
    purchase price, from, 47
    purchase "subject to contract", 39
    uncertain terms of agency, 44
    "prospective purchaser", meaning of, 43
    "sole agent", position where, 36

FACTORS ACT 1889
  "consent of the owner", 91
  good faith, buyer in, 92-96
  "mercantile agent",

FACTORS ACT 1889 — *cont.*
  definition, 85
  possession as such, in, 86
  "ordinary course of business", 88-91
FOREIGN PRINCIPAL
  presumption of agent's liability, 129
FRAUD OF AGENT
  consent of owner negatived by, 91

HOLDING OUT
  general rule, 81

IMPLIED TERMS
  business efficacy, where, 57
  presumption of, 35
INDEMNITY
  right of, 48-49
INSANITY
  principal, of, effect, 119

JUDGMENT
  agent, against, effect of, 96
  principal, against. *See* LIABILITY OF
    AGENT.

KNOWLEDGE OF AGENT
  acquired not in course of employment,
    112
  imputed to principal, where, 110

LIABILITY OF AGENT
  contractual, agent contracting as such,
    123-130
  foreign principal, *See* FOREIGN
    PRINCIPAL.
  third parties, to,
    bills of exchange, on. *See* BILLS OF
      EXCHANGE.
    breach of warranty of authority, for,
      135-140
      misrepresentation, for, 140
      non-liability, term of, where, 138
      reliance by third party, 139
      third party not misled, 137
    capacity, principal without, 72
    election, in case of, 134
    judgment against principal, after, 133
    representation as to identity, where,
      130
    unnamed principal, specific goods, 125
LIABILITY OF PRINCIPAL
  agent, to. *See* DUTIES OF PRINCIPAL.
  fraudulent misrepresentation by agent,
    140
  innocent misrepresentation by agent,
    113

LIABILITY OF PRINCIPAL — *cont.*
  judgment against agent, after, 96
  misrepresentation, for, exclusion of, 114
  principal fraudulent, 114
  set-off, 98
  settlement with agent, effect, 99
    third party estopped, 101
  third persons, to,
    agent bribed, where, 105
  undisclosed principal, where. *See*
    UNDISCLOSED PRINCIPAL.
LIEN
  right of, 50

MERCANTILE AGENT. *See* FACTORS
  ACT 1889

NECESSITY, AGENCY OF. *See* AGENCY
  OF NECESSITY.
NORTH THAMES GAS BOARD
  "public body", a, 13
NOTICE
  agent, to, when imputed to principal,
    110

OFFER
  meaning of, 38

PAYMENT
  agent, to–
    authority to receive, 103, 104
    cheque, honoured, 103
PREVENTION OF CORRUPTION
  ACTS 1906-1916
  burden of proof of bribe, 13-15
  North Thames Gas Board, a "public
    body", 13

RATIFICATION
  capacity of principal, 72, 73
  conduct, by, 80
  fire insurance contract, 79
  time for, 78
  unauthorised acceptance, of, 76
    limitations, 77
  undisclosed principal, by, 74
REMEDIES OF PRINCIPAL
  against agent–
    account, 21
    damages, 21
    resistance of agent's claims, 21
  against third persons–
    secret commission, recovery of–
      corrupt motive, proof of, 109
      paid to principal, already, 107

RIGHTS OF AGENT
    commission. *See* COMMISSION.
    indemnity. *See* INDEMNITY.
    lien. *See* LIEN.

SET-OFF
    constructive notice of agency, where, 98
    principal undisclosed, where, 97
SOLICITORS
    warranty of authority, 135

TERMINATION OF AGENCY
    bribe, receival of, by agent, 12
    commission payable after termination, 32
    completion of transaction, by, 52
    death of principal, 54
        liability of estate, 118
    effect of, on commission. *See* COMMISSION.

TERMINATION OF AGENCY — *cont.*
    effect of, on right to indemnity. *See* DUTIES OF PRINCIPAL.
    frustration, by, 53
    insanity of principal, effect, 119
    irrevocable, where, 54
        authority coupled with interest defined, 56
    notice of revocation, 121
    notice of termination, period of, 63-66
        reasonable notice, 64-66
THIRD PERSONS. *See* LIABILITY OF PRINCIPAL *and* LIABILITY OF AGENT.

UNDISCLOSED PRINCIPAL
    authority, secret limitation on, 67
    enforceability of contract by principal, 69
    evidence, 71
    false representation by agent, 68
    personality material, 69
    set-off by third party, 97